10-1-73

Jacob and the Angel

Henri Desroche

Jacob and the Angel

An Essay in Sociologies

of Religion

Translated by John K. Savacool

The University of Massachusetts Press   Amherst

Contents

LENGYEL

Foreword

There are spiritual careers which, in their public intensity,
mirror an epoch. French culture has enriched the West with
a number of these: André Malraux or Jean Paul Sartre, Albert
Camus or Jean Genet. There are other pilgrimages, less remarked,
but no less significant. The work of Henri Desroche embodies
one of these. In it, the diverse and often contradictory currents
of the modern French spirit alternately conjoin, dissolve, and
re-combine. A conciliar and ecumenical Catholic theology confronts an open, yet powerful, Marxism. A rigorous structural-
ism of method encounters an insistence on the historicity of
societies. A pervasive, yet delicate, spirituality opposes a profound acknowledgment of the realities of power. The American
public already has Desroche's graceful book on the Shakers.[1]
Here, in brief compass, is a summary of his work on the sociology
of religion. The term often enough describes another academic
specialty in a fragmented universe of knowledge. In the text before us, it reclaims a meaning found in the classical sociological
tradition.[2] Desroche's book is a new account of human spirituality, an attempt to depict the structure of the religious component in history.

Born in 1914 of a working-class family, Desroche completed
his theological studies as a Dominican in 1942. He was involved
in those movements of renewal and *contestation* through which
French Catholicism attempted to come to terms with a world
which had transcended the simple antitheses of militant laicism
and intransigent integralism. The famous Mission de Paris, an
effort to reclaim the working class for Catholicism but also to
reclaim the Church for the workers; the worker priests, of course;

1. Henri Desroche, *Les Shakers américains* (Paris: Editions de Minuit,
1955). English translation by J. K. Savacool, *The American Shakers: From
Neo-Christianity to Pre-Socialism* (Amherst: University of Massachusetts
Press, 1971).

2. Norman Birnbaum and Gertrud Lenzer, *Sociology and Religion*
(Englewood Cliffs: Prentice-Hall, 1968).

finally, the Catholic sectors of the movement of political opposition to the incorporation of France in the Atlantic Alliance.
In the period (from 1942 to 1951) Desroche also found time to
write a book on Paul Claudel[3] and to participate in an experiment in a community of shared work and experience, la
Communauté Boimondau.[4] The most interesting literary testament of the period remains his *Signification du Marxisme*,[5] an
early contribution to the literature on Marxist humanism in its
concern with the theme of alienation, and a landmark in the
dialogue between, if not indeed the *rapprochement* of, Marxism
and a certain socially engaged Catholicism.

It is not easy to situate Desroche in his Catholic provenance.
The Catholicism in which he was educated derives in a major
part from the work of his teacher, Father M. D. Chenu.[6] A very
great scholar, Chenu must also be accounted one of the primal
fathers of the theology of the Second Vatican Council—and of
the Catholic *aggiornamento* generally. He has always sought to
de-absolutize theology, to make of it not an immutable doctrine
but a science, describing the interpenetration of the spiritual
and the concrete. His work on Thomism in its historical setting
refers it to the structure of medieval society, medieval technology,
the social role of the medieval church. Chenu's theology depicts
the spirit as working both within and against history and society.
It is at this point that Desroche (who has remained on terms of
friendship with Chenu and his other former associates in the
Church) seems to have renounced theology. It is unnecessary to
dwell on the details, but it cannot be said that all of Desroche's
ecclesiastical superiors were entirely enthusiastic about his
thought and activities. The incorporation, more properly the
incarnation, of the spirit in history is for the ex-Dominican

3. Henri Desroche, *Paul Claudel, poète de l'amour* (Paris: Editions du
Cerf, 1944).

4. L. J. Lebret and Henri Desroche, *La Communauté Boimondau*
(L'Arbrèsle, Rhône: Editions Economie et Humanisme, 1944, 2d ed., 1946).

5. Henri Desroche, *Signification du Marxisme* (Paris: Editions Ouvrières
Economie et Humanisme, 1949).

6. M. D. Chenu, O.P., *La Théologie au douzième siècle* (Paris: Librairie
Vrin, 1957). *La parole de Dieu; I, La foi dans l'intelligence, II, L'évangile
dans le temps* (Paris: Editions du Cerf, 1964).

Desroche not an assumption but a problem. The problem is so profound, however, that in his words, "I never worked as much on the phenomenon of religion as when I ceased, juridically, to be a monk."[7]

In 1952 Desroche joined that other great spiritual organization in France, the Ministry of National Education, and has remained there ever since. The ministry directs not only a school and university system, but a research foundation. Once the bearer of a world view entirely laicist (as well as Jacobin and radical), it has since become the patron of France's own version of pluralism—in which learned monks write on Marx and Marxists on Pascal. Sartre and de Beauvoir are, after all, lycée professors on leave; Merleau-Ponty was and Aron, Foucault, and Lévi-Strauss are at the Collège de France; Lefebvre is at Nanterre; Ellul is at Bordeaux. Amidst and through the conflict of world views, this creaking bureaucracy has a good deal of the intellectual avantgarde on its payroll. It is entirely characteristic of the French situation that Desroche should have been supported by both the late Gabriel Le Bras and Georges Friedmann. The one, a distinguished student of the canon law and the founder of an empirical-historical sociology of religion in modern France— and in addition to his deanship of the Sorbonne's Faculty of Law, the French Foreign Ministry's advisor on religious affairs (which is to say, an important influence on the naming of bishops).[8] The other, a noted sociologist of industry and of industrial society, a philosophical sceptic who struggled to retain some hope for human progress as ignorant armies clashed in western Europe's postwar ideological night.[9]

Desroche was an animator of the Groupe de Sociologie des Religions, a component of the Centre d'Etudes Sociologiques of the larger Centre National de la Recherche. With his colleagues (amongst them François Isambert, Jacques Maître, Emile Poulat, Jean Séguy, and—commuting occasionally from London and Oxford—myself), he mounted the review *Archives de sociologie des*

7. Henri Desroche, personal communication, 1972.

8. Gabriel Le Bras, *Etudes de sociologie religieuse,* 2 vols. (Paris: Presses Universitaires de France, 1955, 1956).

9. Georges Friedmann, *Où va le travail humain?* new ed. (Paris: Gallimard, 1963).

religions—which soon became an important medium of communication for an international sociology of religion. In this period, Desroche wrote on the Shakers, studied a variety of dissident religious groups, and was able to establish a systematic connection between his interest in religion and his communitarian researches. Communal and cooperative experiments were, after all, efforts to establish concrete utopias. The theme of incarnation, and of historical transcendence, did not readily go away. Primitive socialism, in Desroche's view, had connection with Christianity; it remained to investigate the structure of the relationship.[10]

In 1957 Desroche was named to a chair (technically termed a directorship of studies) at the most remarkable institution for the social sciences in the Western world—the sixth section of the Ecole Pratique des Hautes Etudes of the Sorbonne. The chair was designated one in cooperative studies. Desroche quickly founded a Center for Research on Cooperation and began another review, the *Archives internationales de sociologie de la coopération*. He undertook field work in Africa, the Maghreb, Latin America and Israel. From these journeys he returned not alone with materials on cooperation, but with a renewed sense of the complex texture of the religious elements in historical tradition and social action. The period was by no means exhausted in cooperative studies. Desroche also produced works on messianic and millennial movements,[11] and returned to the theme of Marxism and religions in a masterly little book which still awaits translation.[12]

Are there two Desroches, one immersed in the temporal order, one in the spiritual? How can we explain the paradox of a monk engaged in communal experiments, writing on Marxism, politically engaged, who then becomes a layman pro-

10. Henri Desroche, *Socialismes et sociologie religieuse* (Paris: Editions Cujas, 1955).

11. Henri Desroche, preface, *Dieux d'hommes: Dictionnaire des messianismes et millénarismes de l'ere chrétienne* (Paris-La Haye: Mouton, 1969); forthcoming work, tentatively titled *La Sociologie de l'espérance* (Paris: Calmann-Lévy).

12. Henri Desroche, *Marxisme et Religions* (Paris: Presses Universitaires de France, 1962).

foundly concerned with religion? The text before us provides
some of the elements of an answer. For Desroche, the forms
of spirituality are social. He alternates between historical and
structural modes of analysis, adumbrating now the recurrent
structural properties of history, now the historicity of all structures. (We may catch in this an application of the method developed by another of the older French sociologists who recognized Desroche's gifts, the late Georges Gurvitch.)[13] The im-
print of Desroche's communitarian interest is evident, and we
may also enjoy a new interpretation of Durkheim as an analyst
of both effervescence and order in socio-religious structures.
Perhaps the key to Desroche's thought lies approximately here.
Where social structures are relatively fixed, their spiritual content is regularized. Where history moves again, spirituality is
heightened, seeks new forms.

It is clear that Desroche's separation from the Dominicans
has not resulted in a typical journey from social and left
Catholicism to one or another variety of secularized ideology.
Desroche has said that from early on he found untenable the
Catholic project (common to both Left and Right of the Church)
of the incarnation of the Holy Spirit in a temporal structure.
He thinks of himself as Faustian, with two souls dwelling in
his breast—preoccupied with both religious systems and with
socio-economic structures. Yet his depiction of these phenomena
refuses to assume a complete parallelism, in which straight lines
never meet. His approach, rather, is ecumenical—and lends his
work an irenic cast. For Desroche, both social movements and
religions partake of humanity's struggle to meet its uncertain
destiny, to install itself in the temporal incertitude of history,
to confront the immeasurable abyss of eternity. The image with
which Desroche closes the text, and which lends it its title, is
of course from the Old Testament—from an early record of a
perpetual struggle of which this book is a contemporary and
extraordinary expression.

Norman Birnbaum

13. Georges Gurvitch, *La Vocation actuelle de la sociologie* (Paris: Presses
Universitaires de France, 1958).

Preface

The subtitle of this study was first announced in the singular: *Sociology of Religion.* As the subtitle now indicates I have treated the subject in the plural: *Sociologies of Religion.*

This does not mean that I have given up the hope that someday there will be a single discipline. Indeed, in another book,[1] I have already pleaded the case for this single discipline, and the pages that follow here will present Joachim Wach's argument for it. But, more and more, this ideal unity in sociology of religion has come to imply, even postulate, a polycentric configuration fed by a diversity of authors, approaches, and points of view, and by the fact that this ever increasing diversity among those concerned with the subject has been pluralizing the bases of reflective thought. It now seems almost certain that the sociology of religion will undergo the same proliferation that has already affected the history of religions. Over the past fifteen years the progress of this proliferation can be traced both in the East and in the West. At first the sociology of religion was treated as a single branch in the general field of sociology; now, within it, we can distinguish a variety of sociologies of religion which have appeared, one after the other, like plications, subsequent to the eruption of the "modern" world (this *New Moral World* whose godfather was Robert Owen) in the universe of theological traditions.

Whereas Henri Bergson spoke of the "two sources" of religion, I am tempted here to say that the following chapters constitute an essay on the two "end-points" (*destins*) of the sociology of religion. There are, indeed, at least two sociologies of religion which have been haggling and scrapping during its different phases of development, and they can be identified in the various important writings on the subject: these are the sociology studying the growth of a particular religion, and the sociology of religion studying a particular growth. In other words, there is a non-religious sociology of religion and a religious sociology of non-religion; or, more precisely, there is a sociology which treats the non-religious factors of the religious phenomenon, and a sociology which treats the religious factors of non-religious phenomena. By and large, the first of these has taken the lead, even (and perhaps above all) in those sociologies studying submission to ecclesiastic authority. Paradoxically, more often than not, the second of these has been favored by writers usually considered irreligious, such as Saint-Simon, Auguste Comte, Karl Marx and Emile Durkheim. In any event, there can be no significant sociology of religion without this internal debate which is similar (although located on another loop of the same spiral) to the dialectical tension instituted by the best theologians in the heart of their *intellectus fidei.* Without this dialectic of the two antagonistic ends, sociology would either slip back into a sociographic empiricism or dissipate into catch-all ideologies and pseudo-phenomenologies.

Some people wish that this thesis and antithesis could be resolved in a reassuring synthesis. A prolonged study of messianic doctrines has led me to prefer, if not outright failure, at least the example set by the Old Testament patriarch who wrestled until the break of day with an unknown adversary: the old man's victory was no victory at all, since when dawn broke his thigh was out of joint; but neither was his defeat really a defeat, since he had wrestled with the god, face to face, and, as the Bible tells us, his life had been preserved.[2]

Chapter 1

From Sociologies of Religion to a Sociology of Religions

> *. . . Just as some people treated sociology as an offensive weapon, so others, who were on the defensive, wanted it to be "religious," "Christian" or "Protestant."*—Joachim Wach

A science of religions was the hope of the nineteenth century.

> The present century will not end without seeing the establishment of a single science made up of elements that are still dispersed, a science unknown to preceding centuries, a science not yet even defined and which perhaps, for the first time, we will be able to call a science of religions.[1]

One finds a similar hope expressed at a more recent date, this time centered on sociology as an eventual keystone for the whole structure of scientific study of religion.

> Only in sociology, which has taken over the subject matter of comparative religion, will society completely define and explain the religious fact; and only through sociology will the science of religions be integrated into the main body of the social sciences.[2]

The fruit has not borne out the promise of the flowers that preceded it. And, after detecting a possible crisis in the oldest of the religious sciences (the history of religions),[3] we must point out the tensions incident to the development of sociology every time its methods have been applied to the religious phenomena of history or their confrontations. Most likely these are growing pains that appeared when a division of labor created new fields and even new disciplines in what was once a unified field, and pluralized the nature of research in a science which had always considered itself to be monolithic.

As a first step into the subject, we point out that there has been pluralization on three levels:

Pluralization of *writers* (Section One)
Pluralization of *fields* (Section Two)
Pluralization of *sectors* (Section Three)

At the end of our discussion, we shall attempt to indicate the various steps which, ever since theology first concerned itself with social facts (Section Four), have been leading us either to a single sociology or to multiple sociologies studying religious phenomena (Section Five).

1. The Pluralization of Writers

If only we had a *treatise* on the sociology of religions! And even *the* treatise on the subject![4] There are a few works, however, whose titles approximate this. Among the best known and more recent of these are:

The time-worn but still stimulating study by Roger Bastide, *Eléments de sociologie religieuse.*[5]
The fresco by Gustav Mensching, published in France under the title *Sociologie religieuse.*[6]
The classic study by Joachim Wach, *Sociology of Religion* (1947), published in French translation, 1955.[7]
The collection of *Etudes de sociologie religieuse* (1955, 1956) by Gabriel Le Bras to which could (and should) be added a third volume covering his writings of the past ten years.[8]
Religion, Society, and the Individual: An Introduction to the Sociology of Religion, edited by John Milton Yinger (1957).[9]
Thomas Ford Hoult's essay, *The Sociology of Religion* (1958), somewhat limited by restricting its discussion to problems and research done in English.[10]
Max Weber's anthology, *The Sociology of Religion* (1964), with an introduction by Talcott Parsons written for the English language edition, translated by E. Bischoff.[11]

Any such list of titles should also include the major works of these authors. Thus the aforementioned study by Bastide should certainly be supplemented by his *Religions africaines au Brésil*.[12] See also Wach's *Types of Religious Experience*,[13] Le Bras' monumental exploration of *Instituts chrétiens de l'occident*,[14] and Weber's definitive *The Protestant Ethic*.[15]

Futher, one should not overlook the considerable sociology of religion available in many basic works, even though terminologically they may not fit into this category. At the head of this list would be the Marxist classics, particularly studies by Friedrich Engels,[16] and, of more recent vintage, works reevaluating Marxism by writers like Ernst Bloch.[17] Then there is that other giant of the German tradition, Ernst Troelstch, with his inexhaustible *The Social Teaching of the Christian Churches*.[18] Also there are the French classics recognized in a recent symposium: *Sociologies et sociologues français de la religion*[19]; and, naturally, a prominent place on any such list should be given to the works of Comte,[20] Durkheim,[21] and Marcel Mauss,[22] all of which are extremely provocative.

This list of titles, of course, only approximates comprehensiveness. A more demanding inquiry would lead one to examine the extensive documentary survey done in Paris by the Groupe de Sociologie des Religions. This is the producing unit of the Comité International de Recherches en Sociologie des Religions, functioning within the framework of the Association Internationale de Sociologie. This group began its survey in 1956 with the publication of a specific *Trend-report*[23] and has continued for the past twelve years to edit, semester by semester, bibliographical bulletins for the *Archives de sociologie des religions*.[24]

2. The Pluralization of Fields

The survey will eventually include over six thousand titles. That this is a toilsome operation can be seen by our reflections after making a first selection for the *Trend-report*.[25] I can still remember the thousands of file cards piled high in front of F. Isambert and myself in the freshly repainted office on rue Saint-Guillaume where we laid the groundwork for what was to become the Groupe de sociologie des religions. There was endless discussion in the task of selecting 891 out of the three or four thousand titles we had collected. And then more discussion as we tried to impose some sociometric order onto our piles and packets of cards and tried to evaluate these as bases for useful classifications.[26] During subsequent editorial conferences we have continued these discussions in light of the countless catalogues with new material which came in. The questions were always the same: "Is it or is it not (is it no longer or not yet) sociology? Is it or is it not (is it no longer or not yet) religion?" From these empirical selections—which revealed as much about us as about them—there came, at the very least, the written matter, the "givens," of our discipline.

We knew that this discipline could appear suspect to certain already well-established fields of inquiry: theology, history, phenomenology, social philosophy. And yet, to our delight, in this in-between world which was the realm of our interest, we discovered connivances, complicities, alliances and groupings of fact that lead us to counter-facts.

At times we protected the old, stubbornly defended lines of demarcation: This is theology, this is history, philosophy, etc., this is not sociology. At other times we felt the urge to loosen up the rigid principles in the structure of this or that lurking dogma in order to favor a more general methodology which could live and let live. Some of these tensions will reappear later in this book when we attempt to set up a perspective for establishing distinctions between various fields of study. The result was a first pluralization in which figured all the mixed marriages between neighboring disciplines. These marriages had been made possible by widening the dimensions of our earlier totemic groupings to the point at which they coincided with the more general dimensions assumed by a science of religions similar to the one advocated a century ago by Emile Burnouf.[27]

This first sorting out resulted in oppositions which pointed up the uneven development in the sociology of religion (both all-inclusive and multi-disciplinary), in every case depending on the realm to which it was applied. Thus there is a sociology of Christianity that is probably more developed than its counterpart for Islam and the Indian religions.[28] Although within Christianity the sociology of

Catholicism has taken a form quite different from that of Protestantism, both the Catholic and the Protestant sociologists have already
begun openly to organize a common basis of investigation.[29] Alongside of them, the sociology of the Orthodox Church seems to have
remained largely undifferentiated from ecclesiology. On the other
hand, the sociology attributed to the various dissident Christian
sections has been particularly active. One could elaborate on this
indefinitely.[30]

It is as if sociological thought postulated the creation of a certain
distance between subject and object, or at least called for a type of
critical non-dogmatic reflection, a withdrawal permitting certain
basic questions to be asked, a minimum of living space in which un-
wonted queries could be formulated, an optimum of "modernism"
which could be infused into traditional attitudes.[31] The process of
adjusting the idea of socio-genesis to an ecclesiology or a theology
reminds us of the torments attending the first efforts to reconcile
cosmo-genesis or anthropo-genesis to the sacred cosmologies and
the theological humanisms. The classic taboo against counting heads
is just one example of what can stand in the way; there are others.
When analyzing a dissident group who lived and worked in common,
we found that our questionnaires remained unopened. "Why," they
said, "all this curiosity about our ages, the number of people in our
families, the social origin of our members, their motivations, their
aspirations, etc.? All that leads nowhere. That is not what will permit you to understand. Come with us. Join us. Get down on your
knees and you will understand everything, including why the curiosity that brought you here is futile." It is quite possible that this
density of the religious phenomenon makes it sociologically impenetrable: the believer is unable to observe, and the observer is unable to believe. So they close up the archives, refuse to answer our
questionnaires, and button up their lips. Perhaps the uneven development of sociology in the field of religious phenomena is due to the
intensity with which this field refuses to recognize any interpretation different from its own, fearing that any new view might, at the
very least, become a rival to its own self-interpretation.[32] This
threat is felt in all fields of sociology but it is particularly grave, or
supposed to be so, in the field of religious phenomena since the dis-
tortion it implies is judged to be a sin—the sin of vanity or the sin
of sacrilege.[33]

All studies of religion, including theology, have known these vicissitudes of fortune, but they are particularly intense in the case of sociology, and this aggravation should be examined. When dealing with religious phenomena, a sociology, even less than in any other field of study, has no right to proceed like the "sociology for cops" which Sartre has so justly denounced:

> The sociologist has no "situation," and even if he did have one a few concrete precautions would suffice to dismiss him; he may well try to integrate himself into the group, but this integration is provisional, since he knows that he will later disengage himself to record his observations on the level of objectivity; in short, like one of those model policemen we so often see in the movies, he gains the confidence of the gang in order to turn them all in. Even when the sociologist and the cop participate in a group activity, it goes without saying that this is a parenthetical action and that they are going through the gestures only because they have a "higher concern"....[34]

Since the field of religion is situated precisely on this level of "higher concerns," it follows that when its concerns and the concerns of those studying it are at variance there will be a sharp conflict of the kind described by Sartre. This is why the sociology of this field is, in a special way, torn between two poles: if it remains objectively removed from its subject and without authentic participation it becomes a "sociology for cops"; if it participates in the life of its subject, but without any real objective distance, it remains a "sociology for the gang."

3. The Pluralization of Sectors

If recognition of this alienated participation (or this alienation of the participator) is really one dimension of the sociology of religion, then one can expect success in the different sectors studied to vary according to the degree of resistance (hot and cold) which each offers to the investigator's initial pattern of behavior.

Wach has already indicated this:

So long as the subjects being investigated remain outside
the interests and immediate concerns of the researcher, the
difficulties do not seem so great. For example, there is no
reason why a Catholic, a Protestant or a Marxist scholar should
not agree on their studies of American Indian ceremonies, Babylonian mythology or Buddhist morality. But the difficulties become greater when the subject of investigation touches on the
causes of the Reformation or the structure of a sect.[35]

To this we add: these difficulties would be even greater if Buddhist morality became the subject for a simultaneous sociological
study by two sociologists, one Buddhist and the other non-Buddhist.
The fact is that sociological boldness always seems easier and often
expresses itself more radically when it is applied to someone else's
religion. In this respect Christopher Dawson displays an exemplary
boldness of thought in his study of the phenomena of religious
heterodoxy (schism or heresy):

But whatever view we may take of the causes of any particular
schism and the social significance of particular religious movements, there can, I think, be no question but that in the history
of Christendom from the Patristic period down to modern
times, heresy and schism have derived their main impulse from
sociological causes, so that a statesman who found a way to
satisfy the national aspirations of the Czechs in the fifteenth
century, or those of the Egyptians in the fifth, would have done
more to reduce the centrifugal force of the Hussite or the Mo-
nophysite movements than a theologian who made the most
brilliant and convincing defense of Communion in One Kind or
of the doctrine of the two natures of Christ. Whereas it is very
doubtful if the converse is true, for even if the Egyptians had
accepted the doctrine of Chalcedon, they would have found
some other ground of division so long as the sociological mo-
tive for division remained unaltered.[36]

One wonders whether this intrepidity would be the same if the
phenomena of orthodoxy were at stake, and if in the long run it is
pertinent to the argument since, by reversing Dawson's proposition,
one could just as well affirm that, if the Czechs of the fifteenth
century had obtained their national independence, they would not

only have clung to Calixtian demands (for "Communion in Two Kinds") but would also have reactivated their previous lay demand (for frequent communion of laymen, as postulated by Mathias de Ianov) or even have anticipated future lay demands (such as putting the liturgy into the vernacular). Had any of these occurred, the religious history of Christian laity in Europe would have been affected in unforeseeable ways and perhaps, in reaction to this, the history of European Christianity would have evolved differently. Why not? Such possibilities are no more gratuitous or arbitrary than those proposed by Dawson.

At the very least this logical skirmish reveals the variable character of the different branches in the sociology of religion. The sector concerned with dead religions allows a researcher to establish a certain distance between himself and the subject; it permits him to participate in the life of his subject only after crossing deserts of erudition and following paths of a minimal understanding which will never be more than comparative.[37] The sector concerned with living religion offers the researcher, provided he is an adherent, a chance for optimal participation; should he be an outsider, it assures him a measure of objectivity. But if he is an adherent he will have to keep an eye on the methodology assuring him an objective view, and if he is an outsider he will have to check the methodology governing his participation. Likewise, if he studies a "sect" without being a member, he should never forget the warnings issued by Emile G. Leonard objecting to research done on religious "sects." Leonard warned against the word itself when it is used as a label and becomes what he called an ecclesiastic security devise in the service of a dominant religion and, as such, is the product of a good conscience crossbred with "bad faith."

Finally, within the sociology of any given religion one will often find subdivisions disposed in layers: the sociology of comportment will be easier than the sociology studying symbolic representation of behavior; the sociology of societal norms (dogmatic or moral) will be easier than the sociology studying their origins in the society that decreed them:[38] the sociology of social ideologies will be easier than the sociology of a particular theology, and this latter will be easier than the sociology of a dogma. Indeed, even if sociology renounces—and it is evident that it is renouncing more and more—some of the reductionist postulates,[39] even if it renounces the process of reduction, it cannot, without denying its own right to exist, renounce the making of observations that are relative, which is to say, translating self-interpreted messages into a language based on a different interpretation. Moreover, in doing so, sociology is only continuing a movement which in other days called for the sacred books to be translated into the vernacular, or for divinely inspired texts to be transcribed into languages whose theological conceptions have been borrowed from philosophies quite foreign to the message held to be "revealed." Insofar as the collective or simply dominant religious consciousness believes that one tongue or language is an absolute identified with the absolute of the religious act itself, every attempt to translate it into another tongue or transcribe it into another language can only appear as a forbidden relativization—and, in fact, transcription has never appeared (and can never appear) to be anything more than this. Similarly, even when the transcriber limits himself to setting up reciprocal perspectives on religious and social phenomena, the simple act of transcription has already introduced a relativization that, most likely, denies the absolute quality of the original—a quality which the scholar, if he is a believer, is forbidden to question.

Thus the number and extent of subdivisions open to sociology tends to vary according to the sociologist's personal convictions. What to some may be an impenetrable mystery will, for others, be a penetrable myth. For some, what is mystery in one religion appears to be myth in another, and vice versa. For others, influenced by phenomenology, every myth is a penetrable mystery and carries within it its own means of understanding. For those who lean to radical thought, every mystery is a myth and can be deciphered when seen in a larger context. For others, who are more rare, everything is at once myth and mystery, dependent on a comprehensive explanation and an explanatory comprehension.[40]

4. Socio-Theology: Should the Theology of Society
Be Sociological or Sociologized?

"It is not surprising that in the beginning there prevailed a great confusion, due in part to difficulties of terminology and in part to disagreement on ends and methods. Just as some people treated sociology as an offensive weapon, others, who were on the defensive, wanted a sociology which would be 'religious,' 'Christian,' or 'Protestant.' . . ."[41] Today this quarrel of opposing camps is largely behind us.

Ludwig Feuerbach stated with animosity that "the spirit of this science" would be "completely opposed to the spirit of theology." And he spoke with irony of the multiple pseudo-sciences engendered by theology in its efforts to wall off and contain man's inquisitiveness about special phenomena.

> Soon there was left no natural sign which had not produced a special theology. There was an astro-theology, a litho-theology, an insecto-theology. In 1748 when swarms of locusts invaded the country, Rathlef, who was pastor in Diepholz, took advantage of the opportunity to invent, within a year, an akrido-theology or theology of locusts. . . . J. A. Fabricus wrote a hydro- and a pyro-theology; P. Ahlwardt composed a bronto-theology or "theology and rational considerations on thunder and lightning"; J. S. Preu offered a seismo-theology which was a physio-theological study of earthquakes. . . ."[42]

If such was the torment of theology when it tried to distinguish itself from the natural sciences, one should not be surprised to find similar woes attending its efforts to distinguish itself from the social sciences.

This problem of differentiation was particularly difficult when it came to the sociology of religion which, for a while, seems to have been assimilated into a special chapter of moral theology, the one dealing with social problems. In it the sociology of Christianity, since that is what it was called, appeared as a system of norms for an applied theology: "Social Christianity" or "Social Catholicism." The battle was fought on two fronts. As a "sociology" this system intended to keep its distance from any asocial Christianity in which social problems either seemed unimportant or were deemed amenable only to case by case therapy[43]; as "Christian" this sociology intended to remain distinct from the non-Christian sociologies which were generally suspected of socialistic or atheistic tendencies. Pushed to its limits, this "sociology of Christianity" became the theory or doctrine of "Christian Social Order" and its program was particularly characteristic of any Catholic movement which deems "not only the individual but also society" subservient to the laws of the Gospels, the Church, Christendom and the Realm of God.[44]

The title of Troeltsch's book, *The Social Teaching of the Christian Churches,* evokes this ambiguity, but only in order to examine it and go beyond it, for on this point the position of the author is clear; there is a tremendous gap between what *was already* Troeltsch's sociological conception of Christianity and its differentiations, and what *was still* in Christian sociology a system of Christian conceptions of society. Gradually, the gap will be bridged, but only after a complicated process of evolution.

During the Fourth Congress of Catholic Sociologists, Jacques Leclerc weighed heavily on the internal tensions underlying this evolution.

> The theological approach is essentially deductive and doctrinal. Its point of departure is not a collection of human facts; it begins with the teachings of Christ as a conceptual whole in which Greek philosophy has played a large role along with later speculations of human thought. Every time that a new problem is raised, the concern seems to be how to integrate this problem into the theological synthesis. This is known as "doing the theology" of the question. Thus the growth of historical studies called for a theology of history, and the appearance of sociology has given birth to a concern for "doing the theology" of sociology.

> This theology of sociology has only a distant relation to the positive science that I have been talking about. If I understand rightly, its goal is to determine the place of social life in the Christian conception of the world and of man. It raises the question of what God intended when he established social demands in human nature, and how the society of mankind can be reconciled with the fundamental theological values based on the Holy Trinity.

> The Catholic mind, formed to deal with traditional conceptions and methods, is much more at ease on this level than on the level of an objective study of religion as a social datum. This is why, as soon as one mentions the sociology of religion, a certain number of minds hastily turn to the theology of soci-

ology and do so, I dare say, with relief, since that is where they find themselves, once more in the atmosphere of their accustomed preoccupations. And since conceptual speculation opens the way for much, often subtle, discussion, it is possible for them to develop a theology of sociology which uses sociological vocabulary but remains alien to its real preoccupations.

By the very words I am using you can guess my lack of enthusiasm for this theology of sociology. I strongly believe that it is too soon to attempt this kind of synthesis. The sociology of religion, as a method or science of investigation, is still just learning to talk. If we divert its attention to the problems of theological synthesis, we are also turning it away from all the minute, delicate and difficult research which is indispensable for a precise knowledge of the religious fact.

Here I am swimming against the current. . . .[45]

As a matter of fact, the sketch traced by Leclerc should be viewed in the context of two phenomena which he fails to mention: on the one hand there is the real possibility of a sociologically oriented ecclesiology; on the other hand there is the emancipation of the Christian mind for social research that extends beyond the range of theological and confessional guidance. At the risk of speaking in barbarisms, we could say: on the one hand there is a sociologizing of theology, on the other hand there is a de-theologizing of social research. The first of these opens up the possibility for a sociologized theology; the second looks forward to an atheological sociology.

The socio-theology (or "theology of sociology") of Leclerc remains an ambiguous expression in which there are three elements still to be defined.

There is sociology as "social doctrine, a special branch of moral theology. This is the type of investigation described by Leclerc in the passage cited above. We shall call it a *social theology*.

There is sociology as an inductive arm for pastoral strategy. This is the type of investigation which, on appeal, has defined its field in broad terms and has given birth to a copious literature.[46] We shall call it a *sociologizing theology*.

There is also a sociology that is, potentially, a new theology.

This could be expressed more precisely as a mutation of deductive, authoritarian, normative theology into an inductive, communitarian, praxiological theology. It would be something like a re-activation of the so-called "positive" theology. We shall call it *sociologized theology*.

This third element has already been suggested by Marie Dominique Chenu.[47] It comes out of the very definition of theology. So long as theology is tied to series and hierarchy of traditional theological bases, it will indeed remain a deductive study as Leclerc supposed. ("The theological stance is essentially deductive.") *Omnis auctoritas de Deo.* . . . But insofar as theology recognizes that one of the foremost and most important of these bases is the life of God's people who have been gathered into the Church, isn't the door open for this theology to become what one might call inductive? *Vox populi, vox Dei.* Not only the social life of individual Christians, but also the Christian life of a given society provides this theology with a right to self-determination, to aspirations and aversions, along with the privilege of proposing, soliciting, structuring and re-structuring, all of which are immanent concerns of religious conscience and its future. Such is the physiology of the religious body, "tradition" *in statu nascendi.*

This religion that is lived, as Le Bras has so ably demonstrated in all his work, develops differently from prescribed religion, and investigation of this difference is the immense task to be accomplished by the sociography of religious practices.

But while it is being lived a religion develops according to its own system of internal and relatively autonomous logic which can never be reduced to the sum of the "non-theological factors" that supposedly are producing or have produced it—since, as always in sociology, the result is really something more than the sum of its component parts. Once more, Durkheim is to be cited:

> There is a whole world of feeling, ideas and images which, once they are born, obey laws of their own. They call out to each other, repulse each other, merge with each other, divide and multiply without any of these actions being directly ordered or necessitated by the underlying reality. . . . The life thus brought into being even enjoys a large measure of independence which sometimes permits it to take part in behavior that is pur-

poseless and completely useless, just for the pleasure of affirming its presence.[48]

It is from this *praxis*[49] of a confessional community that a "sociologized theology" will probably arise, first by recording this evolving life in all its breadth and manysidedness[50] or by granting to the physiology of a religious group at least as much attention as is given to its anatomy. Eventually, by using the *praxis* as a basis for defining or re-defining theoretical norms and by treating it as the material for a self-survey in an action research, one is recognizing the debt owed to this *praxis* in any future ecclesiological program.

> In the event that sociology is called upon to help the Church become aware of its own nature, what gives it this right and what is its scope? In the event that it is called upon to facilitate the Church's task in the world, what is this task? And does not working for a Christian society seem, at the moment, a hopeless enterprise? Even in this perspective the sociology of religion promises nothing but disillusion for the future and often offers the present nothing more than a distraction from difficult tasks and deep-felt worries. Perhaps at this promethean juncture it can only play *the role of what Newman called consultant to the faithful.*[51]

From this sort of marriage between theology and sociology there will be born—and is already being born, thanks to a conciliar and ecumenical ecclesiology—a clearly defined "sociology of religion." Its verso is nothing other than a positive theology transformed into a *consultative theology.*

5. Toward the Sociology of One Religion, of the Religion or of Religions in General

During the last twenty-five years one of the phenomena observed by this socio-theology functioning as a *consultative theology* has been precisely what we indicated by our second barbarism: a de-theologization of social action. The barbarism covers over a withering away on three scores.

De-confessionalization or the disappearance of confessional differences. In social action the hope is for a progressive recruitment not only of all the believers in a given religion but also the believers of some other religion to whom one has appealed on a pan-religious level, and even non-believers. In traditional or Mohammedan Africa the C.F.T.C. ("Confederation of Christian Workers") became the C.A.T.C. ("African Confederation of Believing Workers") and ended up as the C.F.D.T. (simply "Confederation of Workers").[52] The de-confessionalization of cooperatives in Quebec followed a similar pattern. There is no organized social action that does not, in the name of an exoteric necessity to expand, sooner or later come to question the esoteric nature of its confessional basis.

De-clericalization or the disappearance of clerical distinctions. Social action on the confessional level is often, at least initially, directed by clerics, pastors or chaplains who shift from their charter role of leader to the role of advisor. The more that theologians themselves propose "secularization" as an alternative to secularism, the more the laymen in the movement assume control over its programs and its fortunes.[53] In the end, a process of fission produces a dual filiation: a *temporal* strain in which there is decreasing clerical participation, and a *spiritual* strain in which laymen demand increasing participation in the ecclesiastical life of the Church itself.

De-sacralization or the declining importance of religious doctrine. In the *temporal* strain, problems lend themselves more and more to practical solutions (administrative, technical and economic) and the *theological* element is reduced to the dimensions of an ethic. The monolithic structure of the "Christian social order" crumbles away. The slogan "all of religion in all of life" is, to the surprise of all concerned, shunted down the well-known dead end of what Jakob Kruyt called "pillarization."[54] Indeed, "Christian social action" which is the password for social theology may well end up as its own contradiction, either as a state within the state (the "pillars" described by Kruyt), an esoteric society, something like a ghetto,[55] or as a check on political power in a Catholic state or in a state where the Christian party dominates the political scene—a "triumphalism." Can the Kingdom of God only appear in a theocratic or para-theocratic society? A first answer to this question is

implicit in the password of *secular* Christianity which proposes itself as a successor to *sacral* Christianity. The myth of the Third Path
(i.e., social Christianity as a third way between capitalism and socialism) is susceptible to pluralization and to the temptations of political action, and it quickly dies on the vine. Crypto-Christianity is
always suspect in the field of social action, even to believers who
want the game to be played aboveboard. The day of the crusades,
even non-violent ones, is past. The day of the Christian "mission"
is gone; it has given way to, or at least affiliated itself with, the movement for coexistence, dialogue and common action. Dietrich Bonhöffer has given us a clear portrait of this Christian whose Christianity is no longer a religion, and with it he offers a description of
the God who is magnanimous enough to have foreseen that the re-
cession of His realm would be proportional to the growth of a
Hominem humaniorem reddere. "It is before God and with God
that we are without God."[56]

During this series of changes an *initial* revision of the social ideas
in a dominant religion has gradually led to a *final* revision of the religious ideas in a dominant society. This holds, provided one admits
a reciprocal relation. At any rate, somewhere between this initial
point and this final point there has occurred a reexamination of the
material covered by what we call "sociology of religion."

It first appeared as a still undifferentiated combination (sociology
and theology) which was really nothing more than a theology of society. Although it was baptized "sociology of religion" one should
understand that it was intended to be a doctrinal teaching about
the nature, the purpose and the functioning of human, family,
economic, civic, national and international society. Thus there soon
developed a Christian sociology of the family, of work, of professional relations, and so on. Sometimes, when the secular nature of
the subject overshadowed the sacredness of the original inspiration,
this pseudo or pre-sociology would be closer to social philosophy
than to theology of society, but equally far afield. As Wach has
pointed out:

> Careful discrimination between social philosophy and sociology
> is necessary. There is no such thing as Christian or Jewish or
> Moslem sociology. But there are implicit or explicit Christian,
> Moslem or Jewish social philosophies. The totally unwarranted
> confusion of social philosophy with sociology is evident in the

normative concept of religion often styled "Christian sociology" which underlies most studies of the social implications of Christianity, valuable as they may be, and the few existing monographs on other religions. It is a mistake to assume, as was frequently done at the high tide of the promulgation of the "social gospel," that the sociology of religion should be identical with definitive programs of social reform.[57]

This statement already implies distinctions on several different levels.

There is the social doctrine (theology of society or social philosophy) of a church, a denomination or a religion which, when it stops posing as a sociology, reveals itself for what it is: a conception of human society consonant with the religious inspiration which gave birth to this particular church or denomination. It matters not whether this particular view is in competition or in peaceful co-existence with the conceptions that other religions and ideologies may have of the same human society.

There is a descriptive sociography of the religious society itself, a sociography that uses the methods of observation, quantitative analysis and measurement customary in the empirical sociology of any social facts. When a religious society applies this sociography to itself, the result is a sociologizing theology which we will find again later under the name of "pastoral sociology."[58]

Then, lastly—since this level exists only in vague outline—there is perhaps an inductive, non-theological ecclesiology which, when studying its own religious society, adopts methods of self-examination available to (but not yet accepted by) sociology in any human society.[59] This is sociologized (or "sociometrized") theology. On the one hand it admits that the *vox populi* is a determining element in theology, and on the other hand it envisions, at least as an ideal, a religious structure that will be completely congregational.[60]

If the term "sociology of religion" means a sociology proposed *by* a religion, then there are two principal domains involved and they can be defined with some approximation. However, if the term "sociology of religion" means a sociology *about* a religion, quite distinctive domains will immediately appear in profile, and all of these will have as a common base the principle that there can be no Christian sociology which is not at the same time a sociology about Christianity, since there is no sociology by a religion which is not a sociology about religions in general.

Whereas the first interpretation of the phrase opened the way for a sociologized theology, *the second points up the necessity for an atheological sociology*. It is on this level that discussion occurs in most of the basic texts cited in the brief bibliography included in the first section of this chapter.

At this point a much more refined psychological and linguistic analysis is needed if we are to answer all the questions that arise.

Why does one person use the term "religious sociology" while another calls his subject "sociology of religion" and still others speak of "sociology of religions"? Why does one person speak of "Catholic sociology" while another refers to his study as "sociology of Catholicism"? Why would the author of a "religious study of Catholicism" not expect his readers to think that he is proposing a "Catholic sociology"? Why do some accept and others refuse to use the title "sociology of Protestantism"? And why do others disagree on the possibility of a "Protestant sociology"? Why do some people speak indiscriminately of "Islamic sociology" and "sociology of Islam," while others understand these labels as indicating two different fields of study? Why do we willingly use the term "sociology of Judaism or of Buddhism" and hesitate to say "Jewish or Buddhist sociology"? Why is it that "atheistic sociology" and the "sociology of atheism," "Marxist sociology" and the "sociology of Marxism" so seldom coincide and so often contradict each other? Has not this been the problem and, for similar reasons, is it not still the problem in our use of the terms "religious sociology" and the "sociology of one religion or religions"?

Without answering all these whys, it has been necessary to elucidate a few of them. At least we have tried to do so.

As a provisional conclusion, let me propose the structure which must be induced for this atheological sociology about to be imposed on the various sociologies of religion.[61] It can be presented in three parts:

The part composed of sociographies.[62] These sociographies tend to be demographic, geographic or historical. As sociometrics they can be *static,* "taking into account all that can be counted," or they can be *dynamic,* taking into account not only everything that consents to be included in survey, but also what resists inclusion. This is a sociology of religion in its empirical phase, a stage that is indispensable for a purification of matrix in which doctrines, symbol systems, apologetics and polemics will appear. At this stage sociography, in practice as well as in theory, can look like a new phase in the sociology of religion, and is what Thomas Luckmann has called *neuere Religionssoziologie*—although he has rightly observed that if this empirical stage is not transcended the enterprise risks becoming marginal.[63]

The part interested in socio-geneses. This includes the *functional* sociologies which survey the dialectic implicit in the births, transformations and disappearances by which religion and society manifest themselves, challenge each other, or mutually protest each other's actions.[64]

Also included in this group are the structural sociologies which examine the recurrence of historical geneses and the repeated beginnings of man's search into the universal and impersonal mechanisms which govern them, their isomorphic traits and their differences. These sociologies even record the *elements* of the sacred (should we call them "hieremes"?) which, when combined together, might permit a deductive approach to the problem. This latter path is opened up only by typological analysis and, laterally, by borrowings from phenomenology.[65]

Perhaps this group also includes socio-analyses, at least if one follows Jean Piaget who believes that subsequent to the problem of function and structure one must face the problem of meaning.[66] In this case, sociology of religion would join hands with one of Wach's central concerns, hermeneutics, along with the present day controversies over the problem of interpretation.

The various *sociopraxes*—pointing in several directions. These are the social teachings (*sociogogies*) that open the way for sociology of religion to join hands with the basic principles about man explicitly affirmed (*andragogie*) by UNESCO and the world-wide ecumenical insistence on universal education.[67] This group includes *sociatrics* which, in the spirit of religion, sets itself up as a system for administrating the realm of the sacred, protecting its more vulnerable approaches and regulating both its cures and its ailments.[68] Also included in this group is a study of the *socio-urgies* observed in the liturgies of various *theurgies* and *demiurgies* as well as in socio-dramatic experiments.

It's a long way. In the chapters that follow I shall try to take a few steps down the road.

Chapter 2

From a Morphological Sociology to a Typological Sociology

Instead of looking at the gods, let us look at those who adore them; this is a condition of secular salvation for men—Gabriel Le Bras

"From Morphology to Typology" was the subtitle which Le Bras gave to the second volume of his *Etudes de sociologie religieuse.*[1] The title implies two different approaches to the subject and a progression from one to the other. One, on an international scale, had imposed quantitative measurement onto religious facts (morphological sociology in field work). The other, more and more, was proposing a qualitative evaluation of the measurements taken (socio-analysis in depth of recorded material).[2] First there was social measurement of religious behavior. Then there was the question: what have we measured or, more precisely, what is religious in the behavior thus recorded? Indeed, without this second step we would have measured something, but without knowing, religiously speaking, what we were dealing with.

To reflect on these questions and on the problems they suggest is another way of differentiating between several steps in the development of a sociology of religion.[3]

The Measurement of Religious Practices as the Sociography of a Participation

"There is . . . only one science which studies man in time and which constantly needs to bring together the study of the dead with the study of the living."[4] The response to Marc Bloch's proclamation is an invitation to examine "the faith of a people heretofore unknown to scholars, and of whom there are forty million now living and a billion, dead."[5] Is not the historian of canon law, who is a professional man of established religion, now obliged to become a professional in the field of real religion? "The historian of canon law develops a professional interest in the living world for which the rules have been made as soon as he is touched by these two truths: 1) that there is a living world, and 2) that both the present and the past are part of history."[6] This historian is implicitly postulating a sociological assumption and, in doing so, corresponds to the sociologist who explicitly hopes for a "conversion to history." "There is no such thing as a non-temporal sociology."[7]

Will we have "measured-history" or "slogan-history"? Christian France? De-Christianized France? What on earth are these things and how does one decide between the rosy prophetic view and its dark, no less prophetic, counterpart without wishing for "a chart tabulating the religious practices of all Frenchmen, in every parish, canton and province, as accounted for by some reasonably determined technique of measurement."[8]

We need a history of religious practices as much as, or more than, a history of religious theory, doctrines, theologies and dogmas. We need this history of religious attitudes to serve as the basis for a further exploration of the forms they have taken. And a field study like this would gather its data not from the actions of great men or virtuosos, not from the turbulent moments in the history of great events, but from everyday living, following the rhythms which characterize the seasons of the year and of life, and even the seasons of history itself. "We know of a thousand different doctrines and a thousand great men. Let us study together the religious practices and faith of a whole people."[9]

A history of people. A history of the masses, of those who, beneath the churning of events, exist and persist in the bonds of their institutions: "The Life of the People under Catholicism," "Understanding the Christian People," "The Mass of Believers." Such interests would probably not be unlike the enthusiasms of a Péguy,[10] the irritations of a Bakounine[11] or the reservations made by a Saint-Simon (who wondered why history had to be reduced to the biographies of those in power).

"Instead of looking at the gods, let us look at those who adore them." This transfer of attention seems so characteristic of the step taken by sociology, and the texts which comment on it are so persuasive and contagious that I feel justified in offering a brief anthology:

> There are abundant minute scientific studies on all the great events of religious history, but the greatest event of all, the religious life of our forty thousand parishes, has never been treated by an historian. (*E.S.R.*, 1, p. 2)

> Religious history has most often been studied from an outside point of view. Men have written, or tried to write, the history of ideas, institutions and knowledge, and studied the souls of the élite: but there are also things to learn about the ordinary mass of believers, about men who are not saints. (*E.S.R.*, 2, p. 137)

> The life of ordinary Catholic people is as little treated by historians of the Middle Ages and the monarchy as by those interested in the study of contemporary man. We have thousands of studies on doctrines, movements, illustrious men and their functions, notable baptisms in the Eighth Century and revolutions within the Church; but how many monographs on the religious history of the French people, of the piety or impiety of our forefathers, merit any more attention than a syllogism or a polished pebble, and how many of them explain any more of the unanswered questions? (*E.S.R.*, 1, p. xii)

> We shall concern ourselves only with the crowd, with the religious practices of crowds. (*E.S.R.*, 1, p. 220)

> All our attention has been focused on the great men and on movements considered as a whole. More than a billion Frenchmen have had to assume (there was no question of choice) an attitude towards Catholicism. We take them into account only when they are under arms and then only to document the actions of their leader or the effect of some propaganda! What these people knew, what they believed, how these thousands of men who rushed into baptism or into the crusades for or against the Church and the monasteries really lived we have refused to study. They remain the silent masses who built our country. (*E.S.R.*, 1, p. 227)

> When we consider the billion Frenchmen for whom were constructed the great systems of holy wisdom, the stone temples of prayer and the high walls of canon law, we would like to know what elements of doctrine were absorbed by these subjects of flesh and blood, by both the educated and the untutored, the lords and their underlings; we would like to know in what spirit they went to mass and, above all, what was the effect of the Church's moral and juridical precepts on their behavior. (*E.S.R.*, 2, p. 559)

> Dogmas and the rules of behavior have been studied with praiseworthy care and skill. It is up to us to consider the worshipers as well as the gods whom they worshiped. This is a condition for the secular salvation of men. (*Introduction à l'histoire de la pratique religieuse*, vol. 2)

In its later developments the sociography of religious practices assumed forms which, momentarily, lost sight of their origin in the basic premises of historical sociology. Synchronic correlations (in which professional status plays a dominant role) made any diachronic continuities appear occult, and stratigraphy became more important than the dynamics of social change. However, it was not long before this method of approaching the problem was caught short and performed an about-face which led it back to the original hypothesis—as is testified by an important inference made by F. Boulard, one of the first men to do a geographical study of those who practice religion: "It seems that the religious geography of a country should look for the secret of its particular physiognomy, above all, in history."[12]

This socio-history considers itself to be a sort of sociography of a participation in religion. And this participation is two-fold: On the one hand there is the people's participation in religious life. Criteria for measuring this are selected from the least disputable data available. Church attendance, especially in religions in which practices have been codified, is considered to be a social, public act formally required of believers by the religious authorities. Thus these believers are periodically called upon to ratify this requirement and, as has been said in other contexts, "they vote with their feet." Moreover, since there are varying degrees of strictness in applying the requirements or customs which regulate attendance at religious services, it is quite likely that, apart from ordinary absenteeism, attendance will be one way of distinguishing between the different classes of church-goers. By adjusting methods of procedure, this way of determining class differences can be applied to the country as well as to the city. And this is the type of investigation that has most commonly been followed.

On the other hand there is religion's participation in the daily life of the people: "The modern world, and even our western history, can only be understood if the role of religion in the life of the masses is clearly defined" (G. Le Bras). The sociography of this second kind of participation includes the first type, but goes beyond it to examine how a popular religion expresses itself not only in a dominant confession, but also in minority religions and dissidences, in latent religious traditions, and in mystery religions or even secularized forms of cultic auguries or myths. This exploration has made several promising contributions.[13]

FIRST TYPOLOGIES

The basic typology has been presented and commented on by Le Bras throughout his work. We know that it has four parts, but it is useful here to take note of his vocabulary.[14]

Type 1 "Outsiders" who are not part of the religious life; the "estranged"; the "dissenters"; the "detached"; those who have been "absolved."

Type 2 "Conformists"; "periodical conformists"; those who are "unconcerned."

Type 3 "Practicing"; "regularly practicing"; "observing"; "regularly observing."

Type 4 "Devout"; those who are "pious" or "zealous."

This amounts to using religious acts as the basis for classification.[15]

Type 1 Absence of any act whatsoever.

Type 2 "Solemn" acts related to the seasons of life: birth, baptism, first communion, passing into adolescence, marriage, death and burial. Or to the seasons of the years: Christmas, Easter, etc.

Type 3 Periodical acts: weekly attendance at mass, annual obligations, confession, communion at Easter.

Type 4 Exceptional or repeated acts: frequent confession and communion, pilgrimages, retreats, etc.

A few preliminary observations. First of all, this classification remains inside the practice of religion *ut sic* and is concerned with its greater or lesser intensity. It does not take into account religion's eventual extension into the larger field of social life, a movement which is currently expressed by the phrase "all of religion in all of life,"[16] or "the Christian life and political action,"[17] in brief, a "militancy." This militancy could be a criterium of classification in *Type 4* even though its zeal is often considered to be hostile to devoutness—just as a commitment to missionary work will later be called a forsaking of one's parish obligations.

Moveover, *Type 1* seems to include two subtypes: the person who ceased religious practices after a separation (the "estranged," the "dissident," the "detached"), and the "outsider" who did not have to cease religious practices because he had never subscribed to them in the first place.[18] The latter subtype would probably include a person who, in his own mind or in the mind of others, had been initiated into religious practices but had consented to do so only as a concession to a family or group custom. In this case it is not the practice of religion that he has abandoned, but a social mimesis.[19]

Moreover, since placing an individual in one or another of these types is "by force of circumstances limited to appearance" (Le Bras),[20] in no case may such a survey of religious practices be taken for an appraisal of religious intensity. "Religious practices are far from revealing the extent of religious vitality. . . . One must look beyond this" (Le Bras).

Despite these reservations, the new approach was so eagerly awaited[21] and the tasks it was expected to perform were so enormous that the socio-religious morphology thus set into motion soon engendered and is still engendering an abundant posterity.[22] But this progeny would use the four-part typology only with modifications.

For exploring rural religious practices it has been replaced by a three-part typology which no longer classes by acts, but by geographical areas. These are listed according to criteria determined by combinations of recurrent seasonal practices. It is generally recognized that in France Boulard was a major contributor to the elaboration of this idea.[23]

In the surveys of urban groups methodological difficulties have often led researchers to concentrate on a single act: presence at mass. After correlating the age, sex and socio-professional status of church-goers, it is possible to measure varying degrees of fidelity in church attendance and, in doing so, record the growth or diminution of religion in corresponding strata of society.[24]

Diocesan surveys, on the other hand, combine research in both urban and rural communities. This new approach which started with surveys in France[25] is spreading to other Catholic communities.[26]

FIRST LIMITS PLACED ON A GENERALIZATION

One of these limits has already been pointed out. In measuring the frequency of religious practices, one is certainly measuring something real; but one does not know precisely whether the thing measured is the religious element in what is obviously a social practice or whether it is the social element in an apparently religious practice. Since the religious rite from which sociography gets its data combines reactivation of natural religion (and its seasonal rhythms) with commemoration of an historical religious event and the legendary deeds of the founding fathers, it is difficult to discern what part of men's loyalty to this rite is based on the nature cult and what part comes from a faith in historical revelation.[27] This question becomes crucial if the religion based on revelation considers the nature cult to be "pagan" as in the title of a book about religion in Mexico, *Idols Behind Altars*.[28] Even if, in order to avoid gratuitous disparagement, one abandons the labels "pagan" and "idolatrous," there remain two different kinds of gods, or at least two different sorts of cults, each mobilizing the same people at the same time in the same place. When we add up the total of those present we are not adding up homogeneous quantities; they are not really addible and perhaps instead of attempting an addition we should be doing a subtraction.

This uncertainty is sometimes embarrassing for quantitative measurements, but it can be decisive when we begin to qualify the quantitative elements by assigning to them a meaning or simply a name. By postulating that the religious phenomenon is only a sublimation of a social phenomenon we are reducing the inconvenience of this uncertainty to a minimum, even though for a more precise analysis one could no more be satisfied with this minimum inconvenience than one can forget the fact that the postulate is only a postulate. The discomfort increases when one begins to interpret the results obtained by this means of analysis.[29] When the figures indicate a decrease in church attendance, what should we call this in our diagnosis? Should one use the terms of a society which is slipping away from religion, or the terms of a religion which is no longer performing a significant social function? When considering the religious practices of Christianity there is only one barbarous, but nonetheless widely used word for both of these processes: one speaks of de-Christianization, and in doing so one falls into an ambiguity of language that leads to dramatic controversies—in which, to name only one, the partisans of "sacral Christianity" are pitted against the pioneers of a "secular Christianity." The uneasiness caused by this ambiguity has been so great and the burden of its language has been so heavy that some scholars have been led to coin the word "profanization" to designate a "de-sacralization" or passing from the sacred to the profane, a process which is not to be confused with "profanation." The same fuss occurred in another area when other scholars coined another neologism and came up with the word "laicalization" to designate any "de-clericalization" which was not a simple process of "laicization." The new term was also used to designate the difference between a "theology of lay life" such as proposed by Yves Congar[30] and the notion of a secularized Church or a "religion for lay life" such as proposed by Charles Fauvety and others.[31] If these words refer to the level of experience that some have called "paganism" and others, like Heiler, have more precisely termed "the primitive and spontaneous religion of country folk" (i.e., a nature religion more or less disguised in the vestments of historical, messianic Christianity), then what exactly do they mean by "de-Christianization"? Are they talking about a loss of religious conviction or about the shedding of its vestments? Are they talking about a Christianization that no longer exists or about a Christianization that has never been? As Bergson would have noted, are they talking about a consciousness that has been nullified or a consciousness that has never existed? A man cannot cease being a Christian if he has never been one.

Thus progress in a sociography of religious practices postulates progress in a kind of formal sociology—the kind which refines concepts, terms and (if need be) the models to follow; the kind which later, like a boomerang, will appropriate for itself the vocabulary or procedures of the questionnaires themselves.

In recent surveys micro-sociologists have worked hard to effect these refinements. In one survey of ninety women living in a French-Canadian parish they tried to classify their subjects according to the presence or absence of certain traits held to be criteria for defining religious practice (weekly attendance at mass, weekly communion, observation of the first Friday of the month, participation in pilgrimages, religious processions and retreats organized by the parish, attachment to religious images or devotion to special saints, daily prayers or readings of holy texts, etc.). They ended up with a complex system of seven degrees of religiosity: "the devout," "the devout modernists," "the devout traditionalists," "the modal modernists," "the modal traditionalists," "the associate believers," and "the detached believers." The analysis uncovered a number of paradoxical facts: the "associate believers," for example, are those who are active in para-religious associations, but who remain marginal parishioners.[32]

Another survey, one of social psychology, proposed a typology not of religious practices but of religious experience on ten different levels:[33]

1. Traditional adherence to the Church.
2. Autonomous adherence to the Church.
3. Selective adherence to the Church.
   4. The believer.
   5. The militant.
   6. The liturgical experience.
   7. The type representing mixed factors.
8. Religious experience of low intensity.
9. A rejection of religious practices as a means of religious experience.
   10. A conscious rejection of the Church and of religious experience.
      a) Rejection of the Church.
      b) Rejection of all religious experience.

In his conclusion the author of this survey remarked: "We have learned that although the Church indoctrinates its members with a set of relatively structured and homogenous norms, and although the population studied was homogenous on the sociological level, our informants held a wide variety of religious views and attitudes."[34] His use of the category "selective adherence" disclosed a wide range of "implicit dissidence" which was not apparent in the first screening.[35]

Another limit to this scheme was approached by the Dutch sociologist Kruyt at the Sigtuna Colloquium in Sweden.[36] His study confronts us with what one might call the triangle of religious behavior: religious belief, religious practice and religious life.

Measurements of religious practice and auscultations of religious vitality have already indicated the combinations that are possible between those who believe and those who participate in the practices of religion.

1	2	3	4
Believer & Church-goer	Believer & not a Church-goer	Church-goer & not a believer	Not a believer & not a Church-goer

These combinations play a role in the results of surveys even when they are not retained as principles of classification.[37] In addition to the fundamental factors (belief and practice), Kruyt proposed a third: religious life. This could be religious life as manifested in the "piety" or "devoutness" stipulated in *Type 4* of Le Bras, or as manifested outside the bounds of any organized Church practices, or even outside any symbol system or definite creed—like the *nicht-kirchlich-Gebundene* which is quite similar to the third type outlined by Troeltsch and the libertarian type described by Herbert Spencer and Auguste Sabatier.[38] As soon as this supplementary factor is taken into account, the grid is pluralized and what was once a basis for empirical induction becomes a matrix of possibilities.

	Religious belief	Religious practice	Religious life
Type 1	+	+	+
Type 2	+	+	−
Type 3	+	−	+

	Religious belief	Religious practice	Religious life
Type 4	+	–	–
Type 5	–	+	+
Type 6	–	–	+
Type 7	–	+	–
Type 8	–	–	–

Some of the case types in this hypothetical and deductive nomen-clature have already been illustrated or exemplified by observations already recorded. Others could probably be illustrated by observations yet to be made. Perhaps for some of them there will be no possible corresponding observation. These latter types may correspond to some future combination in religious behavior. Also, we know that a table of data, if it is to be valid, must correspond not only to what really occurs but also to what is possible or even imaginable. At any rate, since the practices which concern us are part of a total behavior pattern we must structurize even if, in doing so, we will be recording our observations according to a system that is relative to our primary inductions.

There is indeed another relativization which any view assumed for purposes of comparison must take into special account: one must consider not only the possible nonreligious factors in the practices, but also what can be, has been or might be religious in the refusal to follow them. Thus, although baptism of children has always been one of the criteria for gaging the practice of Catholicism, it is a refusal to baptize children that marks the first step in the religious practices of the Anabaptists. To put it another way, it would be irreligious of the Anabaptists to practice child baptism. In other contexts it might be forbidden to construct churches or monasteries; indeed there was a warning against such activities in the testament left by Saint Francis of Assisi.

Some religious movements might be religiously iconoclastic. There is one Russian sect (the "nonprayers") whose basic tenet is a refusal to pray. The early Quakers, in the first stage of their movement, made it a religious obligation to cause disturbances during the services of the official church, and proposed that the only ritual be a silence propitious to the "Inner Light." Jesus doubted the value of the temple, Paul questioned the necessity of circumcision, Buddha cast doubts on the use of traditional holy writings, and in Christianity there is a whole spiritual tradition of salvation by faith which questions the religious significance of good works. And there is a contradiction in the basic tenet of Christianity itself: Jesus says that the way to perfection is to sell one's goods and distribute them to the poor, yet Paul tells us that ".... although I bestow all my goods to feed the poor . . . and have not charity, it profiteth me nothing" (1 Cor. 13, 3). There is probably not a single level or act of religious practice to which there does not correspond, in close proximity of time or space, another religion based on a refusal to perform this act—a religion that rivals or complements the one which requires the practice. As Bonhöffer has pointed out in unforgettable fashion, a behavior pattern of submission is buttressed by a behavior pattern of resistance. But if both the practice and the non-practice of a religion can be religious, if what is considered religion in one place is held to be non-religion in another and conversely, then, once more, the practices of a given religion are to be considered as only a "moment" in a life called "religious." And the sociology of this behavior, unless it is to be nothing more than a positivism,[39] becomes part of a wider sociology integrating this moment and its opposite in an ensemble[40] in which both a history and a sociology of religion would meet in an open-ended ecumenicalism

This was, approximately, the program proposed by Wach. "It is difficult to conceive how a theologican, especially if he is a sociologist and an historian, could end up with anything other than an ecumenically oriented theology."[41] The book in which he expressed this hope has a promising title: *Types of Religious Experience, Christian and Non-Christian.* But this promise was not well kept. At least it was less well kept in this work than in his *Sociology.* What stands out in this important book is the extent to which the thought of the author remains divided, and on certain subjects is split between two different typologies.

In another work we have already pointed out the nature of this ambivalence in Wach's analysis.[42] Any reader of Wach's treatise can discover this for himself by noting the frequency with which the author uses two terms or two groups of terms and how his turns of phrase are often characteristic of one or the other approaches.

A first series shows the religious phenomenon to be a reflection caused by a constellation of conditioning forces or by a socio-historical situation. In this series the religious fact appears as something in which a chunk of history has created for itself an ideal form—and this ideal is seen as reflecting the historical reality. Here are a few specific examples of this category of historical reflection, from Wach's *Sociology*.[43]

> In Egypt the cultic development is less determined by gentilic than by local differences, which are reflected in the political and religious structure. (p. 75)

> The superiority of the ruling group in power, property, and rank, often owing to previous conquest and domination, is reflected in an equally differentiated religious structure. (p. 209)

> Their vital interest in animals, so essential to their existence (the Eskimos), is reflected in mythology, cult, taboos, rites, and organization. (p. 220)

> The professional activities of these people (Toda) is clearly reflected in their cult. . . . (p. 221)

> It is interesting to note how the activities of these people (Yoruba) are reflected in the pantheon. (p. 231)

> Frequently, as in the religions of Nigeria and Oceania, this pattern reflects the influence of a higher civilization. (p. 252)

> The pantheon of early China or Japan, of early Iran and India, of the Etruscans and Romans, reflects a more advanced degree of social development than does the Aztec and Mayan. (p. 252)

> The religion of the pre-Columbian Mexican empire reflects clearly the dominance of a military organization upon the state religion in thought, cult and organization. (p. 256)

> In many religions the favorite or chief deity reflects clearly the most powerful or influential group in that society . . . Important social and historical changes are reflected in the history of some of these figures in their increasing and declining popularity. (pp. 252-253)

> The official Christianity of the early Middle Ages distinctly reflects the spirit of the two leading groups, the knighthood and the clergy. (p. 273)

Let's say that this series opens the way for what we might call a "sociology of functions."

A second series presents religious phenomena as examples, illustrations or concrete representations of abstract types that have previously been defined. In this series the religious phenomenon appears to be an historical example of a formal type, a living sample of a type conceived in the abstract. The following are a few of Wach's correlations:

Abstract Types	*Concrete Types*
"The preaching of a new faith . . . is addressed primarily to one group of people which may be more or less homogeneous. In culturally higher, differentiated societies the background of the converts is often very heterogeneous." (p. 36)	"The development of the early Christian church, of the Buddhist and Jaina Samgha, or of the Mohammedan and Zoastrian communities provides us with relevant material." (p. 36)
"A further consolidation of the unity of the religious society is achieved by the formulation of confessions and creeds designed to both express and to encourage the solidarity of those who are led and inspired by similar or identical experiences." (p. 38)	"Applications of dogma can be seen in the Christian creed, in the formula of the Buddhist Triratna, or in the Mohammedan Shadahah. The Jewish Shema and the Iranian confession of faith serve similar purposes." (p. 38)
". . . we might here point out the tremendous influence of locally influential theological schools . . . on the development of doctrine and on the life of the religious community at large." (p. 38)	"The history of such empires as those of the ancient Near East, Mexico, and Japan are cases in point." (p. 38)
"The variety of opinion and teachings set forth and discussed by . . . authoritative leaders and teachers . . . proves also to be of vital sociological importance."	"The history of religions supplies ample evidence for this statement. Pythagoras and Empedocles, Plato and Plotinus, the great Gnostic teachers, theologian-

(p. 38)

philosophers . . . in Hinduism . . . and in Japanese Buddhism exercised by their teaching and authority a most powerful influence upon their followers and, through them, upon their coreligionists in general." (p. 39)

". . . in spite of the presence of personal expressions of religious experience even in primitive religions, highly individual acts of worship do not play a part until a later stage in the development of religions." (p. 41)

"The Hebrew as well as the Babylonian religions evidence this fact." (p. 41)

1773434

"Cultic acts . . . are susceptible to a much larger variety of interpretations and so may frequently serve several purposes. . . ." (p. 43)

"a good example of such complex motivation is provided by a student of Pueblo civilization. . . . Such instances could be multiplied indefinitely from the history of every religion." (p. 43)

This two-column list could be extended, particularly by drawing on the author's admirable discussion of the typology of *dissent*. At any rate, in all these cases the concern is limited to a phenomenological typology. Eventually we shall have to raise the question of its possible extensions into a sociology which will confirm the effectiveness of this structure.

Sociology of religion and sociology of functions. Sociology of religion and sociology of structures. These will be the themes of our next two chapters.

There will be more pluralization of the sociological approach, since, whereas in the previous analyses sociologists made elaborate distinctions (*ex parte post*) between religion as prescribed and religion as lived, they will now raise questions about the nature of these prescriptions and their relations (*ex parte ante*) either with an historical, pluralizing function or with a formal, universalizing structure.

Chapter 3

Sociology of Religion and Sociology of Function

When we criticize or defend a religion how often do we take into account what is specifically religious in it?—Henri Bergson

In the excessive trust or mistrust accorded to the sociology of religion there is one dominant trait which, whether it be praised or disparaged, is always considered exclusive. This is the sociologist's tendency to reduce religious facts to nonreligious social facts, sometimes called "the non-theological factors of theological distinctions"—the sociologist's tendency to reductionism. This reductionist postulate has led to varied attitudes toward social changes: the polemicist hopes they will bring about a withering away of religious phenomena and the apologist looks to them as a sign of religious rejuvenation. This same postulate will be suspect to all those who, like Péguy, refuse to perceive the original meanings of a text after they have pulverized it and then reconstituted it to fit a personal interpretation. Generally, these are the people who, in art or poetry, invoke the idea of an indeterminism or self-determinism and do so in the name of a "grace" which stubbornly refuses the evidence of any determining factors, even when determinism is implied by the impersonal laws governing the structure of "grace" itself. Thus reductionism has been a fundamental step in establishing this sociology.[1] Yet, especially when this methodological reductionism is accompanied by a doctrinal *a priori* it has always run into a categorical refusal to argue the case.[2]

If one insists that the sociology of religion is a sociology of functions, one is obliged to conceive of this functionalism in terms of something more than a one-sided determinism. We hold this to be an accepted fact.[3]

Yet one is also led to loosen up this functional approach and accommodate it to the historical situations from which it draws its types and, as it were, variations on the theme. Basing our position on Durkheim's classic analyses, we would like to open up discussion of this approach by proposing that these situational variables be considered as a triptych corresponding to three functions: attesting, contesting and protesting.

It follows from this that if the sociology of religion is treated as a sociology of functions, this functional sociology should in turn be treated as a differentiating sociology.

It does not follow that this sociology of functions which we have looked at as both reciprocal (which we will not discuss) and differentiated (which we intend to examine) is the only sociology possible. In our concluding section, we shall return to this idea of a new relativization.

In the types, phases, variables and stages of this functional sociology, religion is viewed primarily as a function of a society that is acting on itself.

In a society that is affirming, confirming and testifying to its own existence, religion appears as an integrating function which we shall call *attesting*.

In a society that is examining its own premises and reorganizing its constituencies and antagonistic elements, religion appears as a differentiating function but stays within the limits of contesting the status quo. This differentiating function we shall call *contending*.

In a society that is denying, challenging and refusing its own right to exist, religion appears as a function of *protesting*, revolting and subverting.

In each of these cases the sociological approach is to treat the religious fact as a function of the social fact: a functioning part of society's self-affirmation, self-interrogation or self-negation. And, when all is considered, doesn't the first fact depend on the second, and can't it be reduced to this dependence? This is the question asked by functional sociology at every one of these stages.

Its answer, or at least the one we are commenting on here, comes in three parts: 1) generally, but especially in a synchronic context, the religious fact is a variable depending on the social fact; 2) yet, on the one hand, the social fact is also, reciprocally, a variable depending on the religious fact—and this was a definite dimension in Durkheim's analysis; 3) and, on the other hand, both the religious fact and the social fact can, especially in a diachronic context be variables quite independent of each other.[4] This is emphasized by

Claude Lévi-Strauss when he points out that "Any other line of reasoning makes it impossible to set up a necessary distinction between a primary function satisfying a *present* need of the social organism, and a secondary function which continues to exist only because the group refuses to give up an habitual pattern of behavior. To say that a society functions is a truism; but to say that everything in a society functions is an absurdity."[5] Moreover, as has been demonstrated by other analyses, in addition to this secondary function which diachronically makes yesterday's society operate in the society of today,[6] there is another secondary function[7] which, no less diachronically, assures the functioning within the present day society of an outside society or a society of tomorrow—or, using Karl Mannheim's terminology, assures that "incongruence" will function within "congruence."[8] The functional sociology of a present religious fact can no more be dissociated from a retrospective sociology or socio-genesis[9] than it can be dissociated from a sociology of the future—or from what one might call a "sociomancy."[10]

This play of functional variables will appear again in our analysis of the three types of situational variables.

1. The Function of Attesting

Society attests its existence through a religion. This is usually called the integrating function.

Religion is an integrating function. *Religio societatis vinculum.* The well-known aphorism has been paraphrased by Wach as "the paramount force of social integration." He does so, however, without a nuanced commentary on this social integration which religion produces, quite unintentionally.[11] It is *affirmed* integration.

There is also integration *used by special interests.* In one of his posthumous works Hugo Lamennais expresses this function in a vengeful fashion. "What is history? A long report of tortures undergone by humanity. Those in power wield the axe while the priest exhorts the patient. . . . On your knees, on your knees before the image of God! Who says this? The priest. See the people as they prostrate themselves. The king, for that is what they call him, uses them as a footstool. That is as it should be. A society is born."[12]

There is also integration that is *manipulated for special purposes.* "Religions! Religions! Oh children of men!" cried Napoleon. But he added to this: "Everytime I assumed power I immediately made an effort to re-establish religion. . . . Man's natural uneasiness is such that he needs this indeterminate something, this sense of wonder, that religion offers him. It is better for him to take it from religion than to look for it in Cagliostro, in Mlle. Lenormand, in all those fortune tellers and scoundrels. . . ."[13]

Lamennais gives us a vindictive description and Napoleon gives us a Machiavellian justification, but it is in the language of Durkheim that the thesis of religion's integrating function gets its most impressive commentary and most detailed explanation: "Religion is something eminently social"; "The aptitude of a society for deifying itself or creating gods"; "The religious surge is nothing more than a feeling which a collectivity inspires in its members, but this feeling has been projected out of the consciousness of those who experience it, and objectified. In this process of objectification, the feeling is concentrated onto an object which then becomes sacred"; "The principle of sacredness is nothing more than the idea of society, hypostasized and transfigured"; "The gods are only the symbolic expression of society"; "This reality which mythologies present in so many different forms but which is the objective, universal and eternal cause of the sensations *sui generis* which make up religious experience, this is society"; "If religion is responsible for all that is essential in society, this is because the idea of society is the soul of religion"; "A society can neither create nor re-create itself without at the same time creating an ideal image."[14]

Despite the force of the oft repeated leitmotif, it would be an error to interpret Durkheim as a pure and simple reductionist. For if there is a reductionism in his thought, it is two-headed. Religion is a function of society only because, in a different sense, society is or has once been a function of religion. In other words, *society only creates* a religion because religious experience permits society to *create itself.* This amounts to saying that before or without a professed religion, society is not a society. Religion and society are complementary functions in a total act. Society becomes itself only in a super-society (*sur-société*), the entrance to which is none other than the religious act or the source-act of all religion when this act has been assimilated into a cultural form of collective ecstasy. This assimilation alone permits the change from a prosaic society to an ideal society, from an "atonal" society to an "activated" society, from a cold society to a hot society—even if ultimately this ideal society can maintain its identity only by reactivating or commemorating itself in a society that has "cooled off" (and this is the basic purpose of both cult and ritual). Thus if religion is a "social thing" this is not because it reflects an already established society; it is a "social thing" because it is the "emblem" of a society that is being formed. This "being formed" is an act of self-creation and carries with it a profound emotion which is a cause, not a result, of the various sacred dramas that express it; it is a play in which the protagonists are at the same time authors, actors and spectators. In referring to it Durkheim uses expressions such as "heating up," "arousal," "revival," "abnormal plethora of strength," "intense passion," "frenzy," "transformation," "transfiguration," "encroaching," "metamorphosis," "extraordinary power galvanized to the point of frenzy," "hyper-excitement," "collective explosion," "psychic exaltation not unrelated to delirium."[15]

"Thus it is in these activated social milieux and in this 'activation' itself that the religious idea seems to have been born."[16] Religion is the act or state of being of an ecstatic society. This means that although it is congentially immanent in this society and is one of the society's functions, it also transcends the society since its special function is to open the way for society to go beyond itself and lose itself in order to find itself.

Thus in the beginning of a religion *a social experience of the sacred is identified with a sacral experience of society*. Its first forms are not, therefore, identical with subsequent forms of cult and ritual which later serve to channel, reactivate or commemorate the first or primordial experience—even when, exoterically, the religion is identified with these forms.[17] The primary forms are tied into a "socio-urgos" in which *society attests its existence as a society by the very act in which the sacred is differentiated as sacred*.

If the sociology of religion-as-function is to conform to Durkheim's canon, shouldn't it be defined, basically, as a "hierology"?[18]

2. The Function of Contention or "Protest Within"[19]

It is quite possible that the emphasis this theory places on the function of self-attesting underplays the function of self-protest, and that the attention it gives to primary and so-called "natural" forms (meticulously distinguished from any "naturist" interpretations) has diverted attention onto historical transformations.[20] To the extent that this theory gets jumbled together with the theory which views religion as a sublimation of (and therefore a submission to) established social order, it denies to religion the possibility of playing any "leading role" as an initiator of historical events or social change.[21] Like one of those philosophers of whom Marx said "they always appear just after the wedding," the religious movement only confirms or at most anticipates the social changes to which it will finally be reduced or in which it will be resolved.[22]

Now, the same reciprocal relation between perspectives pointed out by Durkheim for a society *in statu nascendi* applies to society *in statu mutandi*. In the words of Henri Lefebvre: "Historically, we may ask ourselves if materialism has really been the philosophy of the oppressed classes in times of revolt and revolution. A more attentive study seems to reveal that mysticisms and heresies have accomplished more and been more effective than materialism in stimulating and orienting the masses."[23] From a simple Marxist point of view, using the premises of its two classic writers, one could indeed construct a history of religions consonant with the hypothesis about the function of revolt.[24] It goes without saying that in this second perspective the significant part of religious behavior will be disagreements, sectarian deviations, "heterodoxies," "revivals," messianic missions, etc. But these are also religious facts and there is in them a tendency to reproduce the activated state which Durkheim analyzed in the primary forms of religious self-expression. It is as if a new experience of "hot" religion had grafted itself onto the former religion grown cold. Thus a new field is opened for the sociology of religion, the field in which it studies the function of disputes. Emblem is pitted against emblem; for just as there are religious facts through which society affirms its existence, there are others through which society examines its own premises.

Three of these facts seem to be particularly significant:

a. The redistribution of religious loyalties. Homogeneous, generalized and standardized loyalties are replaced by dual allegiances, shifts of position within the cult, decreased participation in the routine seasonal religious practices, conscientious objections, loss of sensitivity, relativizations, etc. The ceremony, cult or rite which has been the favored means of reactivating the religious experience becomes merely a means of commemoration in which social habit counts for more than does contact with a primary experience. And when the poles of attraction have passed from a maximal to a minimal religious experience, the pole of maximalization, no longer finding support in traditional loyalties, tries to replant itself outside of or along side of tradition. In any case, various religious classes appear and create a hierarchy in the membership: upper, middle and lower. This is the vast domain which the sociography of religious practices has undertaken to explore by classifying church-goers, semi-church-goers and non-church-goers.[25] On the other hand, bipartisanship of the clergy and the laity[26] and even tripartisanship of the clergy, the monastics and the laity,[27] are themselves likely to produce a radical redistribution of functions[28] in the various religious roles, even when these variables occur within a binomial or trinomial constant.

b. Intramural contention ("la contestation interne"). This is what Wach calls "protest within"[29] and what Bonhöffer covers in his notion of "resistance-submission."[30] The contending can either come from an individual as in prophetic or para-prophetic types, or it can take the form of a collective action more or less formalized by a dominant personality. It may be opposed to a tradition that is considered obsolescent (this is the cry of "modernism"); it may also be directed against progress held to be pernicious or perverting (the cry of "traditionalism," "fundamentalism" and radical religious conservatism).[31]

In each of these cases the disputation will tend to emphasize the need to set up a special privileged area within the dominant but disputed religion. It may even demand that its reservations be recognized in a kind of *ecclesiola in Ecclesia* such as is found in "movements," study groups, schools of thought, fraternities, missions, institutes, cults, rites, self-governing activities, congregations, orders, etc. In a second stage this "protest within" will use its acquired position to act as a *reformatio* of the dominant religious order or, at the very least, it may act as its *aggiornamento*. If it does not suc-

ceed in this endeavor, the tendency will be either to wither away or
to deny the validity of its society instead of just interrogating it.
When the latter occurs, protest from within changes into protest
from without. This may be protest by a sect, even when the sect
evolves into a denomination and that denomination itself ends up
as a new church, or it may be a generalized religious dissidence
moving toward civilization.

   c. *Total displacement*. This kind of protest cuts deeper into the religious pattern. It reacts not only against the dominant religious
phenomenon but also against a coalition of the religious structure
and the social structure such as "Church and State" ruling over all
of society.

   Despite appearances, this kind of protest does not propose a macro-
sociological upheaval in the system. It allows things to stay as they
are, but becomes indifferent to the system from which it is alienated and, by refusing to follow religious practices and directives,
it tries to set up a micro-society distinct from the macro-society.[32]
If social classes, castes or racial discriminations exist in the macro-
society, the contending group does not deny them. It simply affirms
and practices their disappearance or withering away in the confines
of the newly formed social islands which it has established within
the old society. Without trying to destroy them socially, this group
makes them religiously inoperative. Thus Buddhism appeared in a
caste society and Buddhism does not call for the suppression of
castes except in the *sangha*.[33] Thus the Greek mysteries and early
Christianity appeared in a slave-master society, yet they did
nothing to suppress this class distinction except within their own
cults and churches. However, especially when this religious micro-
society tends to become a complete micro-society[34] eventually
destined to break away on its own, the seeds are planted for a kind
of protest that leads to a general sociological displacement not only
in religion but also in the larger society. Displacements of this sort
may well wait several decades or even centuries for conditions
favoring its maturation in the world of events.

   In all of these phenomena the way in which religious changes
accompany, precede or follow changes in society probably conforms
to a pattern much like the one outlined by Durkheim for the birth
of a religion and the birth of a society.

   The binomial vocabulary of "protesting-infrastructure" *versus* "protested-superstructure" is not sufficient to indicate these changes when they occur. These double-barreled terms describe only the vertical dimensions of the dispute. Also involved is a relation between the two disputants on the level of two contesting superstructures. In this case it is a relation between two phenomena, two sets of convictions, two patterns of behavior, both of which are equally religious, and this gives the dispute a dimension which could be called "horizontal." *Crux sociologorum.* Thus we have not only a dispute between a religious phenomenon and a socio-economic phenomenon, but also a dispute between the two religious phenomena. In this crisscross game of vertical and horizontal disputes, the second dimension can be a cause as well as an effect, although it is more generally both cause and effect; and even when the vertical contending is responsible for the appearance of the horizontal, one wonders if the vertical without the horizontal could ever become aware of its own existence or if it could even be considered as contention. Since, as Durkheim pointed out, a society can become a society only in and through a larger society, the question arises: would any society ever change if the changes were not bound to and by an over-all change of which religious changes and the contending they imply are one of the major manifestations?[35] This question opens up one of the principal domains for an historical sociology of religions which might well turn out to be what Comte was hoping for, a religious sociology of history.

3. The Function of Protest

This is what Wach called "protest without." It occurs when the function of protest is pushed to the point at which it becomes a schism, a secession, and eventually subversion and disintegration.

Protest of this sort is already present when societies begin to question the principles of their own existence. If this self-interrogation stimulated by a reactivated religious experience does not find a satisfactory answer in the dominant religion which is commemorating itself, and if a coalition of "Church and State" suppresses internal dispute, the disputants tend to join forces with *the enemies of the allies of their own enemies,* producing a radical protest which may develop into open social revolt.

The primary stage is a strike. It starts as a strike against the cult. This is a strike against the particular religious society and its basic acts; yet it is also a strike against religion and as such it involves a refusal to respect conventional manifestations of the sacred (either iconoclasm or rejection of all images); a refusal of sacred personalities (relativization of the cult of saints); a refusal to respect sacred buildings (temples and churches);[37] a refusal to honor holy days (the meaning of the sabbath is questioned); a refusal to pray, as in the Russian sect of "non-prayer" or the Quaker cult of silence and the "inner light";[38] a refusal to follow ritual (such as circumcision); a refusal to attend services in church.[39]

This strike against religion can also spread wider and wider until it becomes a strike against society's customs and institutions. When this occurs there is a refusal to use the civil courts; a refusal of cultural facilities such as schools, music and profane literature; a refusal of recreations, such as gambling; a refusal to be counted in a census; a refusal of certain forms of property or ownership; a refusal to participate in industrial production; a refusal to consume meat (be it as a vegetarian, a non-pork-eater or a prohibitionist); a refusal to marry and bear children; a refusal of life which pushes the ritual fast to the point of complete self-denial as in the Cathare *endura* or in suicide by fire as seen in the Raskol's collective suicides and the Jainist holy suicides as well as in the self-immolation of the Bonzes and Bonzesses in present-day Viet Nam. In sum, there is a strike against the contemporary society with a more or less millenarian hope that this strike will be extended until the whole system collapses. Such is the social and even class content which sociology will have to point up in the endless proscriptions produced by religious movements past and present.

A second stage is coexistence. In one way or another the new religious group begins to consider itself as something distinct from the rest of the religious body. It may become an overt rival in a competitive coexistence, as in a crusade or religious war; it may undertake a missionary effort to proselytize its adversaries; or, more subtly, it may preach a conciliatory peace which, more often than not, is a cover-up for religious war. In any event the new group makes secret alliances, both offensive and defensive, against a third party who is the enemy. In each of these cases the sociologist will have to harvest a crop of "non-theological" factors, and these will have to be tied into the various theogonies and ideogonies.

At the same time that it is competitive, this coexistence can also be secretly and laterally cooperative to the extent that each of the various religious strains tend to claim, channel and remodel the same system of values. Sometimes the new group will consider the old religion to be a prefiguration that prepared the way and will simply absorb it as a stage in its own development.[40] Sometimes the old religion will maintain its dominant position by interiorizing a protest that was born on the periphery and thus neutralize it by transforming an external rivalry into an internal difference. This last is what Troeltsch called the "ecclesiafying" of a sect, and he saw in it the origin of certain religious orders.[41]

A third stage is *social revolt* combined with a radicalized religious protest. This stage includes peasant revolts that are ignited by a re-activated or dissident religious fervor. The most recent of these to be noticed was the peasant revolt of the Moslems in Indonesia which was preceded by numerous Mahdisms.[42] The Indonesian revolt is just one example of a whole geography of socio-religious uprisings observed in North America (the Indians) as well as in South America, black Africa, Oceanica and Asia.[43] This geography of revolt corresponding to the geography of colonization and underdevelopment, has its counterpart in European history which produced a similar number of socio-religious upheavals.[44] Chief among these would be the German peasant revolt under Thomas Münzer, an uprising that Mannheim called "the orgiastic chiliasm of the Anabaptists" in which, according to him, "chiliasm and revolution were structurally united."[45]

Whether it be by attesting, protesting from within, or protesting from without, according to this view here is religion acting as if it were a social function in a society that is affirming, questioning or denouncing itself. The task of functional sociology is to show that the whole structure of a society is involved in each of these religious phenomena and vice versa.

From these preliminary remarks we can draw a brief conclusion.

If sociology of religion is treated as a sociology of functions, it follows that this functional sociology must be viewed as:

Reciprocal: Durkheim has already established the frame of reference for this reciprocity.

Differentiated: we have outlined this differentiation according to three types (at the same time continuous and discontinuous).

It does not follow that this sociology of functions is the only possible sociology of religion.

According to Piaget, whom we have already quoted, religion as a function presents only one of the three great problems facing those concerned with a scientific study of man. His triptych, as he presents it, includes function, structure and meaning.[46] This amounts to saying that, above and beyond a sociology of religious functions, there should be a structural sociology, and that this structural sociology should be superseded by a sociology of religious hermeneutics. Piaget's trivium can be amplified, for the trivium should be a quadrivium. How indeed can one overlook the sociology of religion as it is practiced and taught—a sociopraxis?[47] Thus, sooner or later, we must return to "sociogogy" if only to uncover the fundamental pedagogical demands that fathered sociology;[48] and we must even return to the study of "socio-urgy" if only to bring the great body of confessional litanies into the purview of scientific thought[49] and, more precisely, to locate the religious origins of theatre[50] and understand the theatrical destinies of religion.[51]

But these are questions which we will discuss in later chapters.[52]

Chapter 4

Sociology of Religion and Sociology of Structure

A religion is a closely knit system of beliefs and practices having to do with sacred things.—Emile Durkheim

Throughout his most important work, Durkheim was ill at ease with the anthropological approach.[1] "This school does not try to see religions in the social setting to which they belong and differentiate them in terms of the various milieux to which they are tied. Quite the contrary, as is indicated by the name they have chosen for themselves, their aim is to go beyond national and historical differences and discover the universal and truly human bases of religious life. . . ."[2] To this goal Durkheim objects: "Social facts are a function of the social system in which they occur; they cannot be understood when separated from it."[3]

In his objection is not Durkheim giving up the quest for a definition of religion in general in order to analyze its multiple manifestations? Is he not renouncing the essence in order to deal with particular appearances in particular situations? However, Durkheim did not really renounce this quest. Quite explicitly, he asked himself questions about the nature of religion in general;[4] and, in order to close in on his subject, he proposed a preliminary definition[5]—a method which is not without begging the question.[6] *"A religion is a closely knit system of beliefs and practices having to do with sacred things, which is to say things that are separated and forbidden, beliefs and practices that bind all those who adhere to them into a single moral community called the church."*[7]

This definition can serve as an Ariadne's thread leading to an eventual, more precise, formulation. The risks, if there are any, are hardly fearsome, since, structurally speaking, what Durkheim proposed is not so much an abstract definition as it is a working model that can somehow be dealt with.[8] He is not proposing that we look for a generalized religious language, the minimum or optimum common denominator for all religions which so many scholars have hoped to find.[9] He is, rather, proposing a grammar with a morphology and a syntax that can be applied to all actual and possible religious languages.[10] At least this is what he hoped for. By talking about a "closely knit system" Durkheim was, in a sense, foretelling its existence.[11]

The starting point lies in the need to account for the repetition and recurrence of the same religious phenomenon in social circumstances which are discontinuous and dissimilar in respect to both time and place. Thus Robert Harry Lowie asks the question: "Are there any undeniable examples of repetition independent of cultural phenomena?" and he answers in the affirmative by pointing to the messianic cults of primitive peoples as "irrefutable proof that cultural traits can appear independently within great cultural areas."[12] But whatever may be the case, in this or in other examples, the diffusion in space and the transmission through time of a particular model phenomenon does not constitute a plausible explanation of the identity observed any more than they account for the differentiating traits behind which the identity was perceived.[13]

To explain that these identical results come from identical conditioning factors does not help bridge the gap between the concrete preciseness of the results and the abstract generality of the conditions supposed to have produced them; and the explanation is even less helpful when these identical conditioning factors can also be observed in other lateral phenomena where they may produce indifferently this result, some other result or no result at all. Thus the particular religious phenomenon which Lowie was considering, the social frustrations of an oppressed people, can produce a messianic revolt in one place and a cultural acclimatization in another; it may also produce an ecological or professional migration; and there are instances in which it produces nothing at all except degeneration and extinction. This brings to mind Sartre's remark that just because Valéry was a middle-class intellectual does not mean that every middle-class intellectual is a Valéry.

As for Lowie's "psychic unity of the human species, a unity which everywhere produces similar reactions,"[14] these terms are too loose and too vague to provide a real grid of "those temporal modalities of the universal laws which constitute the unconscious activity of the mind."[15]

Thus repetition and recurrence seem to imply a certain continuity and necessity in a phenomenon which appears, nonetheless, to be discontinuous and contingent. The contradiction is sometimes flagrant.[16] It can be overcome only when the demand made by a discontinuous and contingent reality corresponds to the offer made by a recurring model or series of models combined together and when, in the cross fire of this simultaneous offer and demand, a substance takes on form, and a form by becoming substantial ceases to be just a possibility in order to become something real.

The basic principle is quite simple. It is like the one proposed by Alfred Radcliffe-Brown: "Try to re-introduce diversity into any conceivable order. Behind that diversity you will certainly discern a limited number of general principles which have been applied and combined in diverse ways."[17] Or like the one proposed by Lévi-Strauss: "We only want to extract from an empirical diversity which will always exceed our attempts to observe and describe its riches, a few constants which recur in other places and other times. . . ."[18]

Since it concerns religious phenomena, a project like this is not overlooked in Durkheim's premises. True, Durkheim was always bothered by a certain confusion between the elementary and the embryonic, as Bergson has pointed out. But when he theorized on the possible combinations of religion, on the one hand with the sacred (auspicious or ill-omened) and on the other hand with the cult (positive or negative) and considered each of their variables as well as the parallel variables of beliefs, Durkheim nevertheless obtained something resembling a sociological matrix for the phenomenon of religion and its manifestations in a diversity of time and space: an identity in a diversity, a universality in particulars, an invariable in variations.

Before discussing this matrix, we can trace the stages that a sociology of religion must pass through as it heads down this road. They are modest and are what one might call "preparatory,"[19] generally limited to the level of phenomenology at the bare beginnings of the structural level itself.

1. On the Level of Typology

This is a possible first stage. Perhaps, as Jean Guiart suggests, it is inevitable.[20] We have already discussed the typology of religious practice as it was initially drawn up for a particular religious milieu, western Catholicism. But Le Bras, the pioneer in this field, has many times suggested the possibility of refashioning the code and extending this typology to other Christian denominations or other religions.[21] Roger Mehl is presently trying to remodel this typology so that it may also apply to a sociology of Protestantism.[22] But whereas in Catholicism, given the extent and precision of canon law, a sociologist like Le Bras could consider religious practice as the measurable element in Christianity, "in Protestantism there is no element of canon law." Mehl explains that "this absence of an organized canon law reveals Protestantism's built-in fear that the various acts of religious practice may take on a value in themselves and become units of measure for religion itself, quite apart from sociology. Thus the sociology of Protestantism cannot operate on the same basis as the sociology of Catholicism."[23] These reservations do not prevent Mehl from making sociological analyses of Protestant religious practice[24] and affirming that they are sufficiently consistent to permit a basis of comparison and even allow him to outline a "typology of cults" (Protestant, Catholic and Orthodox).

In a preceding chapter we have already discussed Kruyt's hypothesis that the big variables of practice (presence and absence) can and should be considered together with the variables of belief and/ or religious life. Durkheim, in his definition, retained two elementary factors (belief and practice) and these were already sufficient to give him several combinations: believing and practicing, believing and non-practicing, not-believing and practicing. To these three he added a fourth: not-believing and not-practicing. But there is a third factor to be considered: an inner life which may be unconsciously religious and may even refuse to be called religious,[25] an inner life with no participation in religious practices or adherence to dogma.[26] And, with the addition of this factor, the pluralization is doubled (see above, Chapter Two). At the very least, this offers a first typological cluster; for, as we shall maintain, typology is built, cluster by cluster, although it never automatically furnishes the cluster of clusters since that over-all cluster would be as great and possibly greater than the totality of clusters observed. As for the cluster proposed by Kruyt, it obviously suffers from an uneven elaboration of its component parts since, although the factor of "practice" supplies its own variables, the variables of "religious belief" and the variables of "religious life" remain incompletely worked out.[27]

Among the variables of "religious life and belief" Friedrich Heiler fixed on prayer and tried to work out its typology, but the result was probably still too closely tied to historical and comparative classificatons and to the product of theological conceptualizing.[28] He cites one of Bergson's definitions for religion as "the worship of the gods one prays to,"[29] and he raises a pre-structural question: although a life can be religious without participation in cult and ritual and without belief in dogma, can there be a religious life without prayer? To this question Auguste Sabatier and William James reply: "Without inner prayer there is no religion." Others have stipulated that prayer is the "life" of religion (Adolf Deismann), the "act" of religion (Thomas Aquinas), the operational "manifestation" of religion (Shleiermacher and Novalis), its sign, its criterium, its characteristic trait.

This amounts to saying that a typology of prayer, once it has been sociologically worked out, would lay claim to areas of study often attributed to or coveted by a sociology of religious vitality.

There are other typologies, such as the one suggested, implicitly or explicitly, by Wach. We have already explained how Wach regularly alternates between a functional approach and a phenomenological approach in his treatment of religious phenomena.[30]

At times in Wach's analysis the religious phenomenon appears as an idealization of a reality, and it often appears so even in those cases where the dominant religion is defined as the religion of the ruling class; Wach even uses a favorite Marxist term, "reflection."[31] This is a functional approach. At other times in Wach's analysis the religious phenomenon appears to be the realization of an ideal, an historical case of a formal type, a concrete example illustrating an abstract type.[32] He even considers the idea of a nontemporal present which would be valid for all possibilities of past and future, such as the *in illo tempore* so often found in myths.[33] But there is more in Wach than these implicit typologies, *currente calamo.* Although his *Types of Religious Experience, Christian and Non-Christian* does not live up to its title, the *Sociology of Religion* does offer several clearly defined typologies.[34] His two-part typology of religious *expression* (as something distinct from religious *experience*) restores Durkheim's duality of beliefs and cult.[35] His typology of "religious attitudes towards the world" explores some of the paths opened up by Max Weber's analyses.[36]

Wach's typology of *native* religions and *elective* religions corresponds approximately to a classification first proposed and probably taken up again by Mensching.[37] There is a three-part typology for relations between religion and the state and a typology for religious leaders.[38] And one should neither forget nor underestimate his typology of "protest."[39]

As for Wach's typology of religious bodies,[40] naturally it owes much to Troeltsch's prestigious classical analysis with its dialectic of *Kirchentypus* and *Sektentypus,* a dialectic of breadth and depth.[41] Yet one should note that Troeltsch's dialectic is really tripartite, not bipartite, since it involves a third term which is Christian experience outside Church and sect.[42]

Other typologies have been attempted, such as that of messianic types.[43] Others look tempting enough to try, such as typologies of religious orders, sects, ascetisms, interdictions, holy days, ecclesiastic organizations (other than "religious bodies"), levels of expression, etc.

It soon becomes apparent that there is no word used by any science of religion which is not also used with unreflective spontaneity (or, as often happens, inflected to suit the purposes of a dominant ideology) and that all of these words can be isolated, distilled, pluralized, "modelized" by a typological treatment. Admittedly, this treatment is often still summary and, even when it does produce a type, the type produced is still conceived as a simple genre within which the species are to be classed. Yet this is a first step, and with it comes a new dimension of reflexion moving toward a meta-empiricism. Sometimes the types thus induced are already tied into inductive elements. But, instead of moving toward an abstract universal, we are headed toward a grid of factors whose multiplicity of combinations resembles more and more the all-inclusive character of a concrete universal.

2. On the Level of Phenomenology

Typology is differential classification. Phenomenology, following
close behind, distinguishes the essences of what typology has
labeled, and arbitrates disagreements between the terms. This is an
ungrateful task and often renders phenomenology suspect, especially to historians or sociologists who worry lest the particularity of
the facts evaporate into a nebulous universality. After asking what
constitutes a fact in its *hic et nunc,* one is less astonished by (and
perhaps less curious about) what makes it *istud* or *ille.* The gladi-
ator with a sword backs away from the net wielded by his adversary the retiarius. To the sociologist, phenomenology often appears
to be only a hyper-theology (which, for him, is not enough) or an
archetypology (which is too much).

However, despite what others have said on the subject, it is difficult not to include this phenomenological approach in the series
of formal approaches which have been leading the sociology of religion, step by step, toward a certain structuralization.[44] Of course
some people will consider phenomenology to be an inadmissible
or outdated alternative. Certainly, its tendency to make hypotheses can seem gratuitous and its demand to be comprehensive can
seem fallacious to the sociologist who is baffled by his own reductions and at a loss to follow his own explanations. But sociology
is also learning that its "reductions" can no more be unilateral
than they can be exclusive, that its own explanations gain by becoming comprehensive, and that it must have an objective understanding of what it has understood subjectively.[45] It is in this sense
that a few phenomenological steps can be recommended to the
sociologist looking for a well-defined landing from which to operate. Should this landing open up the vista of a grammar, phenomenology will probably have little to tell him about syntax, but it will
certainly afford some useful training in morphology. It might even
contribute to the development and sharpening of a sociological
vocabulary.

Moreover, a dose of phenomenology can help free the sociologist
from an empirical approach to the objects he studies. For, if structural analysis postulates that one can never understand an object
taken as a whole except by understanding this whole as part of a

real whole (as one of the *membra disjecta* in the well-known structured complex), then, in this sense, phenomenology does indeed free the sociologist from the empirical view and it does so by relativizing: sometimes by unifying what was given as plural, sometimes by pluralizing what was given as unified.[46]

After all, even if phenomenology's positive contribution to sociology were only an assimilation of a negative theology (something like the *coincidentia oppositorum* or the *Divine Names* of Pseudo-Dionysius for the positive theologian), it would be no small thing to be engaged in a dialectic like this in which terms are related in a way that assures the invariability of the variants. Although it runs the risk of becoming artificial and being sublimated into an archetypology, could not phenomenology become really pertinent if it were sharpened to serve as a structural conception? After all, did not Marx do his apprenticeship in the phenomenology of Hegel?

3. On the Level of Structure

This level is still only a possibility. At one time it was thought that documentary analysis would prepare the way.[47] For, although this approach is tied to classified facts, it did offer a chance for structural considerations, and the attempt which, unfortunately, was abandoned, is now being taken up again.[48] It may well end up bringing together the inductive approach initiated by the typologies and the deductive approach foreshadowed by Durkheim.

The instability of the inductive approach should not be concealed. As we have pointed out, it can only operate in terms of clusters. And each cluster is potentially dependent, horizontally, on another cluster and vertically, on a cluster of clusters. Any particular typology, however ingeniously it may be presented, will always be in suspension, existing uneasily under the Damoclian sword of the re-evaluation which must come as soon as a particular typology is considered as part of a larger typology. The typology of religious practice becomes invalid as soon as it is paired to the typology of religious belief, since practicers and non-practicers of religion do not consti-

tute two species in the genus of religious believers any more than
believers and non-believers constitute two species in the genus of
those who practice religion. Each of these terms can be both genus
and species: they cancel each other out. In the same way, the
typology of monastic life is reshuffled when it is coupled to the
typology of priesthood. The typology of sects upsets the typology
of utopias, and utopian typologies interfere with typologies of
messianic movements. And yet, as a working hypothesis, the sociologist is obliged to assume that each of these groupings he has
chosen to examine (practicers, believers, monastics, priesthoods,
sects, utopias, messianic movements, etc.) represents a recognizable
type of behavior. Thus there is a contradiction between the desire
to be definite and the certainty that any definite statement can be
rejected as merely provisional. These problems are aggravated by
the destructive effect of typologies that are lived (*typologies vécues*)
on typologies that are conceptually assumed (*typologies conçues*).[49]
This aggravation is increased by the fact that it is necessary to pass
through the first of these in order to reach the second.[50] And, even
when they are conceptually assumed, the typologies inductively
conceived are not prefabricated materials made to fit the structural
pattern which will integrate them. If they are to be refined and
made into models, the inductive process which spawned them must
pass through a deductive filter.

In this way the mounting architecture of typologies will be both
spanned and relayed by a descending architecture, and observations
that have been classified by induction will be subject to reasoned
hypotheses grounded in more general and generating categories.
To the empiricist who fears an intrusion of ideology, one can always repeat what the metaphysician says about the naturalist: as
soon as he (the naturalist) uses subjects and verbs, terms such as
"to be" and "to have," prepositions such as "with" and "without,"
he is spontaneously bringing into play the very categories which the
metaphysician proposes as the object of reflective thought. In the
same way, as soon as the most modest parish or sectarian mono-
graph uses words like "religion," "God," "divine," "sacred,"
"church," "priest," "cult," "rite," "myth," or "belief," it is
spontaneously proposing a vocabulary and even a grammar which
would constitute the object of reflective thought for a sociology

examining religion on the level of structure. More precisely, this spontaneous consciousness of structural elements is grounded in the subconscious and impersonal problem of the terms themselves, of their recurring content (morphology) and of their dialectical relation to each other (syntax). This is the order of problems which the structural approach, like a maieutic pedagogue, would bring to the threshold of consciousness. Until something better appears, this sociology of structures can and should provide a sort of grammar for dealing with the sacred, a provisional set of rules governing the structuring, destructuring and restructuring of what might be called "hagiemes."[51] In any case, the question for sociology of religion is not whether or not there should be a grammar; it is whether or not that grammar shall be rational or nonrational, whether or not it shall be conscious or subconscious, ordered or whimsical.

Rudolph Otto, who has contributed more than anyone else to a "constructed model,"[52] argued that such a grammar would lead to a genealogy of the sacred quite different from the embryology of elemental or primitive religious forms, quite different from an evolutionary type history of religions. It would provide a matrix for evaluating all religious phenomena, from the most primitive to the most evolved, from the most apparently reasonable or clearly reasoned to the most aberrant and irrational. This brings us back, as expected, to the analyses of Durkheim whose *Formes* constitutes a first sketch of just such a genealogy, something which had, until then, never been known.

At the top of his deductive scale, Durkheim proposed a first triad:[53]

> the religion or the "religious person"
> the god, the gods or the "divine"
> the sacred

The order of presentation in this triad is approximately the order in which the sociologist observes them when he makes the field of religion his object of study, asks himself if all religion necessarily is directed toward a god, and wonders whether this god "tele-commands" man to cultivate a sensitivity to the sacred or whether it is the experience of the sacred which makes man treat the god as a god. In other words, once these categories are granted a phenomenological autonomy (their *époké*), the question arises about their relationship to each other. Which one first appears in the genealogical structure?

Durkheim's answer is well known. He said that although there may be religions without gods, there is no religion without a sense of the sacred. And then, flanking each of the three terms with its own opposite, he transcribed the three categories into a three-triangle configuration and represented them in the diagram in Figure 4-1.

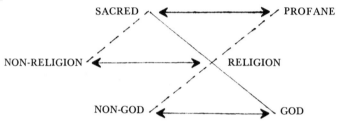

Figure 4-1. Durkheim's Configuration

Durkheim's choice of categories can be disputed, even though their diagrammatic relations were meticulously controlled by experiments designed to detect them and ground them in empirical observation.[54] But one cannot escape what he affirmed anymore than one can avoid facing, all over again, some of the questions he raised.[55] Let us examine a few of these affirmations and a few of these questions.

First, a remark on the alternative proposed: religion assumes an experience of the sacred and is consecutive to this experience.[56] This is a leitmotif throughout Durkheim's work. One of his followers even wrote: "Religion is the administration of the sacred," even though when one says *religion* this is not the same as saying *a religion;* the simple addition of the article *a* changes the meaning of the word and the sense of the statement.[57] But there are other, more fundamental, questions to be asked about the point designated as "sacred" in Durkheim's triangle:

Although nothing is religious unless it is related to the sacred, cannot there be a sacred which is unrelated to religion? This would be a nonreligious sacred such as found in art and its *monstres sacrés.* The question is far from vain, since men as different as Wagner and

Lenin had plans for using the theatre as an alternative to the conventional religious act.[58]

Another question: is all religion a religion of the sacred? or, through a process of de-sacralization, is there not also the possibility of a religion of the profane or, at least, of "profanization?" The question is not utopian: Jacques Maritain launched a religious movement based on the theme of "sacral Christendom"; Max Weber and Richard Tawney treated the Protestant ethic as the animating force for a certain kind of capitalism, and, in doing so, suggested a transference which brought the sacred from the world-beyond into the world here-and-now. Emile Durkheim treated the ambiguity of the sacred and specified its contagious character, its propensity to sacralize the profane, but he might just as well have spoken about the opposite kind of contagion, the propensity of the profane to "profanize" the sacred.[59] How can we expect to explicate the nature of secularization, one of the most complex problems confronting contemporary sociology of religion, without first clarifying our ideas on the inner workings of these opposites, alternatives and ambiguities?

Another affirmation: religions can be religions without being the religions of a god or gods. Buddhism and Jainism are both religions without a god;[60] and "there are rituals without gods and there are even rituals in which gods are created."[61] Phenomenology confirms this by speaking of "atheistic religions" (Gerardus Van der Leeuw). Comte sought a pattern in which there would be a presence of religion and an absence of god. There is no need to enumerate all the patterns in which diverse ways of representing the godhead infinitely pluralize his structure.[62] Turning the question around: just because we sometimes observe the phenomenon of religion without the phenomenon of a god does it follow that everywhere we find the phenomenon of a god there will also be a religious phenomenon? Do we not sometimes find a structure in which the presence of the god-phenomenon is not accompanied by the religious phenomenon?

If the phenomenon of "religion without god" is observable, does this mean that "god without religion," even if it were not observable, would be impossible? Simply by reversing Karl Barth's postulate *Religion ist Unglaube* one can see that this is, indeed, a possibility.

One could continue indefinitely with these questions raised by
the conjunction of Durkheim's three primary factors (sacred, religious, divine) and their three opposites (profane, without religion,
without god) and their three interlocking triangles.[63]

These questions could be multiplied in view of the fact that, although the sacred does indeed seem to be the stem of this cluster,
it may well be, at the same time, the stem of other clusters. Durkheim pointed out other pairs: sacred purity and sacred impurity,
the sacredly auspicious and the sacredly inauspicious, attraction to
and withdrawal from the sacred . . . all indispensable for a clarification of religious terms as fundamental as "consecration," "ministra-
tion" and "sacrilege." And, according to Durkheim, the sacred goes
through cycles, passing from sacred exaltation (*in statu nascendi*)
to sacred reactivation and sacred commemoration. All these distinctions are also fundamental for any interpretation of cults and rites.[64]

And on the subject of the triangles, what has become of the
three-term pattern: religion-god-church? Durkheim's answer is perfectly clear: although religion does not necessarily assume the idea
of a god, "it is, on the other hand, inseparable from the idea of a
church."[65]

Question: is this not an arbitrary definition of the word "church?"
On the one hand the word has been enlarged to cover any informal
system socially polarizing the religious phenomenon (is not Islam a
religion without a church?)—meaning it implies no precise distinction between church and society. On the other hand the word has
been narrowed to a point at which it excludes, as speculation about
the future, "those personal religions . . . so frequently encountered
in history and which today make some observers (like Spencer and
Sabatier) wonder if this is not destined to become the highest form
of religious life and if there will not come a day when the only cult
is the one each man freely composes for himself in his heart."[66]
This is, undoubtedly, a weak link in Durkheim's definition of religion.
One wonders if his hypothesis of religion as a "social thing" has not
led him to slip into an arbitrary sampling, into some debatable as-
similations, or at most into a unilateral sociogram. For, just as he
affirmed, religion can be a "social thing," but it can be so in a sociogram of self-refusal as well as in a sociogram of self-acceptance; it
can be so in the actions of a community stirred up into a paroxysm

of religious passion as well as in the non-action of an individual probing the depths of his own solitude. And certainly the last thing we
should abandon is a promising possibility that offers *a fortiori* a
type, especially when this type is something we have already observed.

No doubt we shall have to accept the fact that there will be further bifurcations. There will be religion *with* and religion *without*
a church; and, in the case of religion without a church there will be
the variant of a church which exists but is ineffective because it has
been assimilated into society, and the variant of a church which has
already ceased to exist. In this last case, there will be two more variants corresponding to categories 2 and 3 of Troeltsch's analysis—
the one in which this nullification of the church was due to a collective dissidence (the dissent of a sect), and the one in which it
was brought about by an unorganized, unfocused group of individuals, all of whom are equally religious and who may or may not
be the precursors of what Spencer and Sabatier were waiting for.

Shall we add a few of the other questions related to this same
triangle? If, *dato non concesso,* there are no religions without
churches, does it follow that there can be no churches without
religions? Or, to complicate the matter even further, are there any
churches with a god but no religion, or churches with a religion but
no god? And so on.

Since we are now asking questions rather than working out long-
winded answers, let us focus on another triangle, one which seems
more specifically ecclesiastic. Durkheim touched on it in two of
his terms.[67] In this triangle we meet, once more, a triad of the basic
religious characters: the priest, the monk, the layman.[68] It offers a
good example of a partial typology which, as Troeltsch pointed out,
cannot be considered without canceling out the *Kirchentypus* and
Sekentypus typology.[69] Let us concentrate on the transformation
systems which produce subtle changes in the relationships between
the three terms. What a syntactical maze is created by the crisscrossing of this morphology!—the clericalization of monasticism;
the monasticization of the clergy; the secularization of the cleric,
which Marx claimed was often only a clericalization of the layman;[70]
the monasticization of this layman, which Weber suggested could be
one characteristic of pietism;[71] the secularization of monastic life,

producing lay institutes for the church . . . And we still have not mentioned intra-ecclesiastic secularization (the call for lay participation) and its opposite which is anti-ecclesiastic secularism coming from outside the church.[72]

Already this amounts to saying that the triangle of religious characters is related to the quadrilateral of religious organizations and its four points of reference:

> centralized (or papal)
> episcopalian
> presbyterian
> congregational

and that this quadrilateral is not unrelated to Troeltsch's dyad of *Kirchentypus-Sekentypus* (there are both congregationist churches and sects ruled by pontiffs), nor is it unrelated to Wach's triad of church-denomination-sect.[73]

To the list could be added Durkheim's dyad of *cult* and *ritual,* the much disputed dyad of *myth* and *ritual,* or the one of *positive* and *negative* cults (along with a table of what the faithful are forbidden to touch, eat, behold, say, wear and do).[74] But, in adding to our list, we would only be reaffirming a set of problems which exist, if at all, only in vague outline and in verbal disputes. This is the problem of how to make a structural analysis of the religious phenomenon when it appears to be, simultaneously, *the whole* in which recurrent parts are subsumed, a *part of the whole* that is assumed when there is polarization of the sacred, and perhaps (when religion is being treated sociologically) even *a part of one or more wholes* which are not assumed by the idea of the sacred.

In his discussion of the structural approach, Jean Cuisenier refers to an analysis by Robert Carneiro.[75] This analysis of nine North American societies concluded with a scalogram representing the presence and absence of eight selected cultural traits in these nine societies. The final chart ingeniously reveals a "definitive" pattern and even suggests a matrix.[76] Naturally, it is not possible to repeat this tempting experiment in the vast field we have been considering here. Our subject is too complex and too unreliable. Yet, as a provisional hypothesis, we can use this principle of analyzing the presence or absence of certain characteristic patterns in a given religious group.[77] The phenomenon of religion (or "religions") would then be presented in terms of *plus* or *minus* signs, depending on the presence or absence of the trait being considered (see Table 4-1).

Table 4-1. Presence or Absence of "Religious" Traits

TRAIT	RELIGION	
	Present = + = with	Absent = − = without
Sacred	sacralizing	desacralizing
God	theistic religions	atheistic religions
Church	ecclesiastic organization	either non-operative or nulli-fied (de-confessionalization)
Priesthood	clericalizing	de-clericalizing
Sacrifice	blood or liturgical sacrificing	neither blood nor liturgical sacrificing
Cult	cults of the dead, of saints and of images	no cults other than an awareness of the Inner Light
Myth	mythologizing	de-mythologizing
Monasticism	monks and religious orders	neither monks nor religious orders
Beliefs	dogmas	no dogmas
Practice	social or religious	neither social nor religious
Etc.	. . . . .	. . . . .

The very least one can say about this table is that with this nomenclature it would be difficult to set up any accurate hierarchy of traits.[78] Nevertheless, once the vocabulary is sharpened, a scale of this sort could lead to a closer accounting of traits in a given religious society as well as an accounting of societies having these traits in common. It could also have an affect on certain studies in comparative religion. At any rate, it should relativize the religions of *yes* to the religions of *no,* and throw the *yes* and the *no* of each religion or religious phenomenon into a reciprocal perspective. It does away with verbal monopolies and terminological blocks by affirming the necessity of a pluralized approach. And indeed it indicates a way of combining the conceptual tools which, for better or for worse, are often overused in sociology of religion research. Finally, and above all, it dialecticizes the object: a-religion is no longer a marginal or teratological phenomenon; it has its place in the religious structure as part of the definition of religion. Of this religion and this non-religion one could say what Hegel said of being and nothingness: "The being of a finite being is to have within itself, as the very principle of its being, the seeds of its own disappearance: the hour of its birth is also the hour of its death." Nicolas de Cues spoke of a *coincidentia oppositorum*. It would be no small contribution if a structuralizing sociology of religion could make the empirical so-ciologies recognize the burden of fears and fascinations attending a presupposition like this.

Chapter 5

Sociology of Religion and Sociology of Origins

*We must admit that at the beginning of the evolution called
history of religions there are certain strange things which
precede it in time and which, although outside it, later
exercise a profound influence on it.*—Rudolph Otto

Even when clearly defined, the historic-functional and the formal-
structural approaches are not irreconcilable. This is admitted by
certain of their proponents, some of whom even tend to think of
these approaches as systematically complementary and, in doing
so, treat a given social fact as belonging to a "whole" that is both
single and double: a *functional whole* of an all-inclusive society: a
structural whole of an aggregate of related parts.[1] If these are not
two keys for the same latch, they are at least two keys for a double
latch on the same door. Perhaps this is why, for a given religious
phenomenon, the functional and structural factors are likely to
offer different explanations of the same trajectory; the first explaining it in terms of a propelling force, the second explaining it in
terms of gravitational pull.[2] Does not every social impulse trigger-
ing a religious phenomenon turn out to be some form of biological,
then social, energy finding expression in the act of a supra-society
(*sur-société*)? And is not every structural combination like a numerical figure or orbital formula governing the recurring force of a gravitational pull? A comparison never explains anything. Moreover, this
particular comparison is inadequate since (by using a ballistic image)
it assumes successive and distinct moments of intervention for each
factor (with the launching determined by the firing charge and the
trajectory determined by gravitation) whereas in the case of sociological phenomena these two factors are contemporaneous and inseparable from each other. Perhaps this analogy could be rounded
out by some other comparisons: organ music which is a conjunction
of two determining factors, the bellows supplying the air and the
chord pattern composed on the keyboard; or the melody produced

by the synchronized movement of two hands on a violin, the right one maneuvering the bow and the left one setting the sound pattern by varying the length of the strings which the bow has caused to vibrate. Or else, perhaps, we could use (as another approximation) the old Aristotelian formula of material and formal causes which, when considered together, explain that *this is*—and, in doing so, explain on the one hand, by weighing on the active force of the verb, that it *is* what it is and, on the other hand, by emphasizing the quiddity of the thing itself, that *this* is *what* it is. . . . Or else consider the telephone on my desk; as a means of communication it involves two factors: the electric current passing through the wires, and the number I dial and the fact that this number corresponds to a particular line. After all, the energy detected by functional analysis is something like a "current" and a pattern detected by structural analysis is quite comparable to one of the possible combinations of numbers on the telephone dial. So it is like an electric current, like the firing charge of a rocket launching a satellite into space, like the bellows of an organ or like the movement of a bow across the strings of a violin. And, at the same time, it is like a number, a code or the combination for opening a safe, like an equation for determining an orbit, like the organizing pattern of a musical sound pressed on the strings of a violin or the keyboard of an organ.

Do such comparisons exhaust the possibilities for analysis of religious phenomena? Alas, or rather fortunately, no! "Here's your party," says the telephone operator. But although she has put you in touch with him, there remains the question of what you are going to say and the act of saying it. In this case, who does the talking? Who "emits?" To explain that what is *exists* and then to explain that what exists is *what it is* does not do away with the need to explain *what makes what it is what it is*. After the material and the formal causes come the efficient causes, to continue with our Aristotelian vocabulary. Perhaps this means that, after sociologies of function and structure, we come to a sociology of action.[3] At any rate, we come to a sociology of those who act out the religious drama and, finally, to an "actionization" of its sociology.[4]

The problem of who speaks is obviously solved *a priori* by a theology of revelation: it is God who does the speaking. The speaker is the god. But there are religions in which there is no god; and, even in those religions which do have gods, any apologetics either offers or calls for reasons for believing in them; any spirituality assumes the ability to perceive spirits when they appear, and the ABC's of every exegesis postulates a theory of literary expression. Indeed, when the sociologist, even when he is a theologian, asks "who is speaking?" and gets the theological reply "this is God on the line," this answer, once it is refracted, de-theologized and described as an audible phenomenon, can be nothing more than an action: "he says he is God."

Once again we come to Durkheim's sociological hypothesis: the voice is that of society acting as if it represented a supra-society (*sur-société*).[5] This role leads the actor or actors into a dual and ambiguous world which is both sacred and profane. On several occasions Durkheim points out the religious essence of theatre and the theatrical essence of religion that lie at the heart of this role-playing which is also an action or "drama" wherein a god reveals himself to men and does so through men who are acting out their role of men in front of a god—even though that god himself was initially nothing more than their own supra-natural playacting (*sur-représentation*).[6] Durkheim seems to have had no hesitations in accepting the exclusive claims of this theory about the volcanic genesis of religion. Just as in geology the present configuration of the earth depends on past eruptions and pliations and on what has been supporting these changes or eroding them, so it is that every religious phenomenon, however distant from its original cause, can be traced back, through an agent or through an agent's agent, to some sort of sociological eruption. This eruption was not the religion itself; for the religion is nothing more than a collective action undertaken to buttress the changes caused by the eruption and to combat their erosion.[7] Religious liturgies are nothing more than commemorations, reminders, reactivators, mystical initiators or mimers of an original soci-urgos.

This is a promising hypothesis, but perhaps it should be examined more closely. We have already quoted Sartre: "Valéry is a middle-class intellectual. But every middle-class intellectual is not a Valéry."[8] Although it may be true that religion is really the immediate or ultimate product of a social milieu which has started to break out of its mold, does it follow from this that every social milieu in ferment has produced a religious phenomenon? One cannot overlook the hypothesis that religion is only one possible product of this ferment, even though it is evident that this is what has been produced in vast areas of history and social geography. Another product of this ferment could well be an inhibition, and in that case we would have to look for the explosive primitive phenomena hidden behind the repressions which subsequent collective memories have created to control it. And these repressions will be strongest when the ferment described by Durkheim (and he points this out) is accompanied by irrational, meta-moral, deviant, convulsionary behavior and when the established society takes pains to occultize, obliterate, moralize or sublimate this behavior—even if (with emphasis on the *if*) the society looks favorably on the group for whom this deviant behavior seems essential.[9] In the last analysis, will not the established society eliminate not only the behavior, but also the group itself?

But if this experience of ferment could either produce or not produce a religion, there is still another possibility: it could produce either a religion or something else. For although the frenzy of this "super-natural" society (*sur-société*) can be observed in other groups experiencing a ferment strikingly similar to the phenomena from which "the religious idea seems to have been born," the ferment in these other groups does not necessarily produce a religion. Durkheim clearly saw this possibility but called it a secondary effect.[10] But this secondary effect could very well turn against itself and become a primary effect, block the way to a religion, either by forming a nonreligious cult[11] or by an obsessive nostalgia for the collective frenzy as a value in itself, thus inducing a choreographic orgy which would be the Paradise Lost of all religion.[12]

Certainly in the latter case this Dionysian element calls forth its Apollonian counterpart.[13] Alfred Métraux points this out in his analysis of voodoo: "The dances themselves are executed with a sense of rhythm and admirable grace which are in no way Dionysian; they are more like difficult exercises which one performs with all one's being without ever allowing the movements to become disordered."[14] But isn't this because without the voluntary discipline there can be no undisturbed enjoyment of the involuntary trances? Saul could quiet his demons only with David's harp, and a Shaker writer has left us a description of a similar therapy in his cult:

"From that time on, we saw that the quickest way to experience peace of soul and delivrance from the jerks and the barks was to take part in the organized dance."[15] The experience of the god is unbearable and leads to complete collapse. Religion, like the nonreligious lyricisms of theatre and dance, is indeed "an administration" for this state of being possessed, something like a remote control, a way to live the unlivable, touch the untouchable, and in this it is both similar to those lyricisms and one with them. But since this religion and these collective forms of lyricism are derived from the same event and since, in the context of this event, they remain undifferentiated, the question is: cannot this initial act produce *either one or the other* of these manifestations?

Pushing ahead, but still basing our reflections on Durkheim: if the act of the supra-society (*sur-société*) in ferment can 1) produce or not produce a religion, and 2) produce a religion or something other than a religion, then there remains a third question to be answered: can religion be produced by something else beside this frenetic or collective action?

a. *The frenetic action:* First, how can one ignore another well-defined tradition of religion *in statu nascendi*: the tradition of ataraxia found in social milieux that are, systematically, not in ferment and in which all such frenetic activity is considered suspect? The sociogogy of religion does indeed operate in two traditional lines: there is the exoteric line treating cultic or festive gatherings celebrating a primitive religious experience and dedicated to its diffusion, commemoration or reactivation; but there is also the esoteric line which is selective, methodical and specialized, treating the producers or reproducers of the experience itself.[16] This second strain has given birth to observable group types: orders, monasteries, meetings, congregations, communities, etc., all of which are laboratories for religion. Whereas the "frenetic" tradition produces something like wild religion or religion in its natural state, this second, specialized tradition is a deliberately *cultured* religion—using the word as in the expression *a cultured pearl* which is, nevertheless, natural and quite distinct from the synthetic pearl. This tradition is quite different from the tradition of cults given to religious seizures. Certainly it does, in one sense, gravitate around those wild cults, and that is where Durkheim placed them: either before, in the early ascetic stage of a negative cult, or after, in the liturgical stage of ceremonial commemoration.[17]

Thus, in one sense, Durkheim did sharpen the differences and even the distinctions between them. But is this enough? Just as the cultured pearl does not grow from a natural pearl that has already been formed, but from a physical state in the oyster before this formation occurs, so the ataraxic tradition does not necessarily grow out of acts of frenzy, but out of a collective state of mind or situation anterior to frenzy, and can lead the people to various forms of religious seizure (or, to use Durkheim's vocabulary, *ecstasy*) which are not simple repetitions of what is found in those dionysian cults. This state of mind may even be opposed to ecstasy, just as the behavior recommended by traditional ataraxia is opposed to the frenetic tradition. The latter exteriorizes, the former interiorizes; the latter explodes, the former concentrates; the latter exalts a society, the former deepens its sense of solitude; the latter induces paroxysms, the former creates an impassive serenity; the latter polarizes by totalizing behavior, the former is caught in the net of Nirvana; the latter splits men's consciousness, the former deems this split in consciousness to be unseemly, equivocal and affected—something like the behavior of an actor who lives his part so thoroughly that he has become alienated from his own personality and no longer knows who he is in real life. Everything considered, this alienation is something like what Marx-Engels described as "retraction": "We who have self-doubts as soon as we begin to become generally accepted. . . ." The tradition of ataraxis is basic and no less religious than the other one; it thinks that collective exaltation involves alienation and sees sacred magic as a sign of mystification. In its view participation in the supra-society (*sur-société*) involves an underground personality. This explains the ingenious efforts of sociogogues to combine a maximum of interpenetration (in order to catch on their loom the threads of social behavior) with a maximum of interiorization (in order to draw these threads tight on a woof of personal experience); certainly this envisages a communal life such as is realized in no other society, but it is a communal life bound in the framework of sacredness, silence and journeys through the inner wilderness. Whereas one tradition allows religion a volcanic and incandescent origin and a life of what might be called "evaporation," this other tradition gives it a chilling genesis in icy solidification. On the one hand there is the mounting smoke of sacrifice; on the other hand, the *en-soi* of an eternal black stone. Unless these two traditions are merged into one, does not each of them become a substructure for the other? And, in that case, the structure suggested by Durkheim becomes not the sole genesis, but one among the possible geneses of religion.

b. The collective action: The foregoing duality of individual frenzy and collective action does not mean that we must fall back on Bergson's hypothesis of two sources for religion, but that this hypothesis raises a last question to which our consideration of "two sources" has progressively been leading us. Indeed, an examination of the frenetic and ataraxic traditions, each of which is in its own way "ecstatic," brings into focus an ultimate relativity in the sociology of religion which Durkheim proposed in his definition of the religious actor. The actor in this religious drama, he said, is, essentially, the collectivity.[18]

Durkheim's affirmation leaves open the question of whether his religious actor is a *creating* or a *created* collectivity. In other words, in this religious drama does the collectivity play a major role and create its own secondary characters, or does it have a minor role called into being by the major character or characters of the play? The question of this major role (which can be either that of a character who creates a collectivity or of a collectivity which creates its character or characters) arises in both the frenetic and the ataraxic processes of dramatic creation. Despite a few of his stylistic hesitations, Durkheim seems to have left this question wide open.[19]

It is precisely on this point that there are many objections. According to Nathan Soederblom, "psychology of religion will not make any progress until it concentrates on the great geniuses and probing souls in the realm of religious piety." According to James, the religious life of the masses is probably no more than a second-hand religious life, modeled on the religious experience of those "virtuosos" (Weber) who represent a first-hand religious experience that has been recognized and collectively transmitted. And Heiler emphasizes the idea that "so long as the science of religions persists in understanding and explaining primitive religion without invoking comparisons with the religious life of the great religious leaders, it will be fumbling in the dark. . . . By great religious leaders we mean those whose spiritual life reached a climax in the religious experience, who were absorbed into it, and who subsequently played a creative role in religious history. . . ."[20]

It remained for Bergson to follow this path as far as it would go. He did so in two ways.

He first considered static religion (the one which merges with the social demands of a closed society) and granted it a dual function: on the one hand it buttresses society's refusal to bring about its own dissolution; on the other hand it supports the individual's refusal to minimize his own importance. From this came Bergson's final definition: "Religion is a defensive reaction of nature against what might be depressing for the individual and dissolvent for society in the exercise of intelligence."[21] This is not far from the idea of a collectivity playing a leading role and creating individual secondary roles, even though these secondary roles may be less and less secondary. . . .

Then he designated two sources for two religions: first, there is static religion in which a social religion determines the individual religions by binding them in a closed society; then there is dynamic religion in which a personal religion (or mysticism) tends to determine the social religion by evoking the idea of an open society. In this second case, changes are brought about "through the medium of certain men, *each of whom thereby constitutes a species composed of a single individual.*"[22] In part, this is what Troeltsch meant by his third type, the one which he called, variously, "free individual religiosity," "spirituality," or (a word also used by Bergson) "mysticism."[23] "Mystical doctrine interiorizes and offers immediate experience of a universe in which ideas have been hardened into dogmas and cults, and does so in order to experience them as a true personal and intimate possession. Thus it can bring together only free-floating groups and aggregates structured solely by personal allegiances. Moreover, these groups reject as superfluous all ties born of cult, dogma and history."[24]

Troeltsch expected that these brotherhoods of individualists, all orphans in matters of religion, would remain unorganized. He did not envisage the possibility of a new mystical experience that would be formalized by a posterity which sees in it the forerunner of a new kind of religion.

In Bergson's analysis of the two sources it is not a question of two distinct phases separated by an unpassable line of demarcation. In the religion of a closed society there are elements of open-society personal religion; and, in turn, an open-society religion will survive its ecstasies and initial "creative emotions" only by inscribing itself in a universe of closed-society religion. The preexistence of the second in the first depends on the survival of the first in the second, and does so according to the pattern of relationships already proposed for accommodating matter and the *élan vital.* Negotiations for an accommodation between the first and second phases can give rise to the many variants already evoked in our discussion of the sociology of protesting and contesting. Here is where we find a few of the ways in which "these two religions remain antagonistic yet combine together," from the moment when "the second religion attempts to lodge within the first, preparatory to supplanting it," until the time when there arises "a mixed religion, implying a new direction given to the old, a more or less marked aspiration for the ancient god who emanated from the myth-making function to be merged into the God who effectively reveals Himself, who illuminates and warms privileged souls with His presence."[25] This new religious species may be either a new religion or a new religious consciousness within the dominant religion (as in the founding of new religious orders, congregations and spiritual families); but both alternates will be a mixture of unequal doses. Bergson's image of overlapping supports his thesis but does not allow him to deal with cases in which the new message passes more or less victoriously right through the old one.[26] We know that this has often occurred and we have seen cases where the new message, after being defeated or suppressed, has persisted either among marginal heresies or in the catacombs of social neglect.

In a word: "We hold religion to be the crystalization caused by a learned chill in whatever it is that mysticism has deposed in the burning soul of humanity." "In this sense, religion is to mysticism what popularization is to science."[27] Similarly, in the context of Durkheim's thought, Hubert stated that "religion is the administration of the sacred." And there are even more similarities between the two approaches. Both Durkheim and Bergson look for religious experience in a society that is acting as if it were a society beyond society (*sur-société*). Both think of this religious act in terms of a ferment or an upheaval. Both deem popular religion to be the product of this initial ferment after it has been channelized.

But whereas for Durkheim the collectivity is essentially responsible for this act of channelizing, for Bergson the collectivity has no more than a fabulating function, inventing the myth of *nature naturée;* Bergson's act neither contains nor suggests anything more than itself; it is a latent mysticism which has made itself felt in certain privileged individual experiences and in certain new emotions which are the cause, not the effect, of new religious images—even if, in order to formulate these new images, one has to seek out "some ready-made ideas expressed in words that already exist, in short, segments of social reality."[28]

In Durkheim, there is the search for the fundamental, first and final, creation of religion in a primitive society that has been isolated for study. In Bergson, there is the search for a continuous, ever rebegun, never-ending creation—a continuum of creative activity[29] which began with a creation of creators of religion.[30]

Bergson's manner of stating the problem complicates (fortunately) the pattern of religious transmission by grafting it onto the pattern for new religious emissions. But an unrepentant sociology will bring up the old questions once more: if these are the conditions under which new emissions occur, then what are the conditions for receiving the messages—messages that, for the most part, are interpreted either as refusals or as attempts to convert the listener? If this creative evolution of religion offers the key for deciphering new religious messages, then what is the key opening up the new audiences who are supposed to receive them? And, if this offer to explain is not met by a corresponding demand to know, how is communication ever to be established? Although, looking at it from Bergson's point of view, the offer to explain seems to dictate the demand for an explanation, from other points of view does not the listener's demand for an explanation dictate the kind of message that is offered?[31] It is the expectations of the clientele which determine the behavior of the merchant-supplier, not only in respect to how the merchandise will be used, but also in respect to how it is to be designed and produced. Are we supposed to look for the sociology of beginnings in the psychology of the beginner, or, conversely, should we look for the psychology of the beginner in the sociology of beginnings, or does the source of each lie in the other?

Yet this Bergsonian sociology is as irreplaceable as the sociology of an Engels, a Weber, a Troeltsch, a Durkheim or a Wach, to mention only those who are no longer active. Alongside those who uphold religions, Bergson has made a place for those who promote religions. To the study of what is social in religion, he has added the study of what is religious in religion.[32] And who knows whether or not his theory of freedom[33] will not offer what Charles Péguy was pleading for, a basis for some sort of sociology of grace, and this is a contribution which a sociology of religion owes to a sociology of action.[34]

Finally, Bergson's sociology spotlights a latent distinction between two religious levels, the level of repetition and the level of innovation. This is what James called second-hand and first-hand religion. It is what Lévi-Strauss calls secondary and primary functions.[35] It is what Durkheim saw as marking the way from the initial frenetic *presence* to the institution of religious rites *representing,* miming or commemorating it. It is what Bastide has recently indicated by his categories of *lived religions* and *living religions.*[36] The door is open for a dialectic: on the one hand, innovation within repetition—revivals, illuminations, missions, messianic callings, etc.; on the other hand, repetition functioning as a system for constraining the innovations—liturgies, canons, standardizations, cults and beliefs, hierarchical roles, etc. Once one overlooks Bergson's weakness for imagery, once one accepts the literary genre he uses, the Bergsonian contribution is a step forward in the sociology of those who have created or are creating the religious play which religious practice is performing, the play which, when functionally analyzed, refashions the theatre and which, when structurally analyzed, destroys the whole scenario.[37]

Chapter 6

Sociology of Religion and Sociology of Practice

The question of whether man can achieve an objective unity by intellecutal processes is a practical, not a theoretical, question. It is in practice that man must prove the truth.—Karl Marx

In this chapter we would like to assume that somewhere there must exist an apology corresponding to the classic *In Defense of the Study of History* (*Apologie pour le métier d'historien*); only in this case it would be "In Defense of the Practicing Sociologist," for sociology must not be limited to a simple discipline taught by professors of sociology to students of sociology in order that the young may take up the torch and become, in turn, professors of sociology teaching a new generation of students of sociology who will, in turn, etc. . . . Furthermore, as it becomes a practicing science, sociology must not degenerate into a utilitarian empiricism, a tool for social work, social service or social action; and, even less, must it permit its energies to be channeled into "psychological action" at the service of decision-making centers which would use it for their own ends. Caught between the Charybdis of academicism and the Scylla of agit-prop, the practicing sociologist tries to trace out a path which will lead him from a sociology of action to an "actionization" of sociology—which will not only permit praxis to be deduced from theory, but will also assure that theoretical horizons continue to be induced from praxis.[1] For, since free and creative acts do intervene in the course of history, this praxis cannot be like a piano recital in which the player follows a preestablished score, as if his hands were obliged to execute only what his eye has seen. But even for a musician praxis becomes improvisation every time a free act explodes; and when this occurs it is the musical score which is subsequent to the recital. It is as if the touch of the player's hand has given birth to a melody or harmonies which will later be transcribed for the eye on the printed page; the act has imposed its own reasons for being. We have already quoted Pascal on this subject: "M. de Roannez used to say: my reasons come to me afterwards; at first encounter, a thing pleases me or shocks me without my knowing why; I don't discover the reasons until later. And I really believe that when I was shocked it was not for those reasons that I found later, since I only found those reasons because something had shocked me." Sartre used to give this definition of a man: *Faire et en faisant se faire et n'être rien que ce qu'il s'est fait* (He makes and, by making, makes himself, and is nothing except what he has made of himself). Maurice Blondel's first "Action" was devoted to rehabilitating this idea of man.[2] Bergson broadened it. And, in a remarkable study, Sertillanges showed that, after all, this reaffirmation of creative freedom, reasons and values simply resurrects an interpretation of Thomas Acquinas that is not only possible but also necessary.[3]

But this is not the place to set up and examine these arguments. For our purposes here, it suffices to outline the problem of "practice" (along with its political implications) and indicate how it is intimately related to scientific sociology. And in this sense we agree with the basic principle proposed by Alain Touraine:

> The movement which made a scientific sociology possible also gave it a political role to play. This is not to say that the sociology of historical acts should take part in political struggles, but that it can exist only by destroying all forms of reification in social life and so must combat every effort to dispossess man of his creative role . . . in the interest of material or spiritual forces which, because they claim an inner logic and sovereign design, confront the human actor with a given which can be accepted or rejected, adored or hated, but not accommodated.[4]

This problem reappears in the sociology of religion.

We have already indicated (at the end of Chapter Three) a few of the possible orientations for this sociology as it develops into a practicing science: sociatrics, socio-urgy, sociogogy.

For a discussion of sociatrics in the field of religion we naturally refer to Bastide's admirable *Sociologie des maladies mentales* which gives an historical account of the relation of this discipline to other studies of mental disturbances. In his conclusion Bastide specifically relates mental disturbances to an analysis of the sacred: "To a great extent madness is a sacred disease." This is an upside-down version of Durkheim's view that the sacred is an expression of religious ferment approaching a state of frenzy.[5] It also restores the *fascinosum et tremendum* which Otto saw in the practice of the sacred. Finally, it also commits sociology of religion to making a new differentiation and recognizing something which might be called a depth sociology or a sociology of the unconscious.[6]

As for a study of socio-urgos in the field of religion, we have already indicated that the raw materials for this can be found in Antonin Artaud's religious program for the theatre and in Alfred Métraux's theatrical interpretation of religious seizures in cults such as voodoo. Some research has been done by the C.N.R.S. to prepare the ground.[7] And, naturally, the studies made by Jean Duvignaud are becoming more and more important.[8]

We shall not pursue these approaches any further here.

We are especially interested in the third approach, the one more or less misnamed "sociogogy." Why has this name been chosen? Doubtlessly, because of its resemblance to "pedagogy" or even to "androgogy," this neologism was recently accepted by UNESCO as a term for "continuing" education and education of adults. The word reflects a change in attitude. Since we have abandoned the idea that education is something limited to childhood and adolescence and begun to envisage education as something which, although not necessarily continuous, can continue during the entire life of a man, including his "third age,"[9] it seemed best to substitute for the old word "pedagogy" (with its limiting sense) a new word which would cover the entire field of education. In the main, let us say that sociogogy would include all those educative, didactic or initiatory interventions which render humanity more social or society more human—thus picking up what appears to have been another strain in Durkheim's thought.[10] At any rate, here (as in Comte) we find religion recognized as one of the major educative enterprises, both didactic and initiatory, in the framework of universal education for mankind. Once again, let me quote from Paul Arbousse-Bastide:

> Research done by a sociology of religion interested in the origins and transmission of beliefs would conform to what one could prudently call the latent requirements of Comte's positivism. At the end of this research one would come to the

vast domain of religious education beyond confessional and institutional limits and even beyond the limits of a sociology of "continuing" education insofar as this education is used to transmit a message and integrate values considered legitimate in a religious universe. Need I remind the reader that this enterprise is not an irresponsible fantasy, since the whole of Comte's thought is, in the last analysis, dominated by a concern for total, continuing and universal education as the sole road to human salvation. . . .[11]

Finally, this sociogogic orientation of an eventual practicing sociology is identical to the approach which seems most immediately plausible to theoretical sociology.[12] To the sociology of religion it is also the one which seems to offer a maximum of entries and documentation for reflective and critical analysis.

Times have changed. Not so long ago there were people who boasted about a "new sociology of religion" that had cured scientific sociology of the positivist infection which has afflicted it "ever since the days of Auguste Comte and Emile Durkheim." They thought that the field had been open for "men of religion" of whom "more and more were turning to sociology in the hope of seeing more clearly and thus acting more effectively" (sic).

In an article now become a classic, Le Bras showed that this shift was really not a take-over or a substitution; it was a bifurcation into two methodological developments, each of which saw its origin in the common trunk.[13] That this common trunk is firmly rooted in a supply of sociographic descriptions has once and for all been confirmed. That this supply of raw material, if it is to be refined, needs to be treated conceptually in the manner of men like Comte and Durkheim, is probably still contested by certain scholars who evoke the erroneous and paradoxical alibi of their pseudo-irreligion. Yet it is true, as Arbousse-Bastide has tried to show, that this conceptualization was of real concern to Comte. A similar brief has been made (see above) for Durkheim's position, and the definitions recently proposed by Duvignaud strike me as a remarkable argument in support of Durkheim's insight on this matter.[14]

Be this as it may, what terms are we to use for the two strains of this bifurcation? Should we call them "scientific" sociology and "pastorate" sociology, as Le Bras proposed? Or, as other colleagues have suggested, should we call them "basic" sociology and "applied" sociology? Or, as I am tempted to propose, should we use the terms "independent" sociology and "confessional" sociology? Each of these labels has its own drawback, just as there is a special drawback to the terms "Marxist sociology" versus "bourgeois sociology" proposed by our colleagues in the East.

One of these labels, however, seems to have been generally accepted: pastorate sociology. It has to its credit an imposing array of operations and publications.[15] For our purposes here it suffices to note that this pastorate sociology has a tendency to expand and include not only the parish (the most active) but also the missions (including missionary parishes and parish missions) and, more recently, it appears as an ecumenizing sociology within this strain. One can already detect a duality of characteristics in its submission to the authority of a confession or an interconfessional order, however removed this may be from the methodology used in its surveys. In practice, it is utilitarian rather than praxiological. Indeed, its studies, whether they be descriptive, analytic or typological, are related to a more or less continuous intervention, and are tactical rather than strategic.

As for the nomenclature of the companion term, the adjective "independent" would have two connotations quite different from the other terms suggested. It would connote independence of all authority and confessional or interconfessional agencies, thus freedom from all ecclesiastic control. It would also connote independence of all practical application and a determination to remain dissociated from the interests of any future intervention.

Beneath their seeming obviousness, these crisscrossing strains are nevertheless quite complex and ambiguous. This recently became apparent to me when I was examining a sample of pastorate sociology in a report which must be representative of the genre since it had been considered important enough to be translated from German into French. The report treated a text by Bernhard Haering.[16] In order to underline the complexity and ambiguity of this crisscrossing, I quote a review of this work as it appeared in French.

> *Macht und Ohnmacht* (Power and impotence of religion). This book is, in fact, a manual in which sociology of religion is

treated as if it were a science of the pastorate: "a social pastorate committed to Christianizing society with the help of solid sociological research"(p. 6). "A sociology of religion enriched by theology can indeed trace a sure path for a pastor of souls as well as for those who share his concerns. The one presented here proposes, above all, to establish a theological basis for the participation of laymen and to bring the role they play into sharp relief. This represents a systematic effort to Christianize social life, particularly in centers of influence" (p. 7)

Haering's clearly defined commitment to the pastorate is the subject of comment throughout the work. On the last pages (pp. 288 and following) it is described as a "missionary sociography" and distinguished from a sociography that is scientific. "Scientific sociography is concerned with recording all the facts, processes, structures and relations that one finds in the social domain, but does this for a purely scientific purpose. Religious sociography, such as we understand the term, is motivated by a missionary zeal and apostolic determination to achieve the goals of our pastorate" (p. 288). It would be unfair to conclude from this that the religious or missionary sociology proposed by the author is necessarily non-scientific; and it would probably be unjust to say that it is bound to the rules of an ideology, since it does firmly plead for empirical research (pp. 296 and following). The difference between these two sociologies ((1) scientific, (2) missionary) are probably to be found elsewhere: the one is independent and therefore polarized by a meta-ecumenism, the other is dependent and therefore polarized by an apologetics (or, as its adversaries would say, by a need to market the product): this gives an advantage to No. 1. But there is also an advantage for No. 2, in which dependence and concern for apologetics permit an active sociology of action-research and development-research; and this is something that is practically never allowed to Approach No. 1 in which independence can easily harden into academicism unless there is an ecumenical or meta-ecumenical concern opening the doors for its own action-research. This makes for an interesting debate, but it is like the final plays of a tennis match which one would rather see neither player win.

This *status questionis* is reminiscent of discussions that once occurred in a group interested in the sociology of religion. Those discussions were fumbling and given to approximations now out of
date. But, since they apply to the same set of questions, they may
well serve as an introduction to the origins of the problem under
consideration here, and I shall quote at length from the transcript
with no apologies for the cursory, debatable, purely documentary
character of what was said.

> Central to our research is the distinction we propose between
> scientific and pastorate sociology. We consider them to be two
> distinct approaches, one of which is extra-confessional, com-
> parative and directed toward pure research; the other, con-
> fessional, subservient to theology and polarized by practical
> concerns. On this, all agree. But we should expect questions
> to be raised about our terminology. And, sooner or later, we
> shall certainly have to take part in the debate which has long
> been simmering at the heart of all sciences of religion.

> I would like to state clearly my position on two points which
> raise doubts about the clear cut distinctions that we have been
> using: 1) the non-scientific nature of pastorate sociology; 2)
> the non-pastorate nature of scientific sociology.

> I

> First, I note that this terminology contains an implict judge-
> ment against the "pastorates." For, if the "scientifics" are de-
> fined by the fact that what they are doing is not pastorate
> sociology, then, inversely, the pastorates must assert that what
> they are doing is not scientific sociology. This can be harmful
> to their position. And needlessly so.

> The term "pastorate" does indeed, at first sight, have several
> connotations: 1) It can be an empirical expedient perfected by
> a procedure that is more or less approximative; 2) It derives
> from an absolute based on the self-interpretation of a confes-
> sional group; 3) It is intimately tied to an intervention, an ac-
> tion. . . . In brief, it connotes *empiricism, confessionalism, in-
> terventionism.* Yet we must look more closely at what is non-

scientific in this approach. On this first point I now find myself alternating objections with answers to these objections.

1) Empiricism

It is probable, and even certain, that the sociological approach
as practiced by the pastorates will remain empirical, approximate, ill-adapted, uncoordinated. . . . Certainly, other reproaches
could be added to this list. But at the same time one must
recognize that, elementary as it may seem, it does represent
amazing rational progress on the part of "pastors" who only
a century ago were accustomed to explain their allegiances
and disaffections by appeals to virtues and vices, grace and sin,
the historical intervention of Providence or the perversity of
demons and their votaries. The introduction of social factors
into the manicheism underlying their struggle against Satan and
his array has caused a real upheaval. And we should not be surprised to note that this upheaval was accompanied by a withering away of many arbitrary notions related to their original
position.

But this does not make these pastorate approximations any
less plausible and scientific, provided they are not treated or
understood as ends in themselves. But that depends on the two
following characteristics:

2) Confessionalism

Here, as with empiricism, definitions are in order. There is a
sharply defined confessionalism (salvation within, perdition
without) which cannot fail to affect seriously and deplorably
all observations of religious facts both *ad intra* and *ad extra.*
This confessionalism makes all sociology of religions impossible;
only religious war (or a crusade) is possible and in it sociology
is hardly more than a tool for psychological action. The same
could be said about a dogmatic atheism in which sociology of
religion would be only an added refinement in the arsenal of
agitation and propaganda.

But alongside this crusading confessionalism there is a
missionizing confessionalism calling for communication and
dialogue (with all that is implied by this recognition of others

either in the domain of missionizing or in the field of ecumenism, comparative religion and, in the long run, comparisons between religion and "the world"). It does seem that this confessionalism, with its windows if not its doors open onto the rest of the world, is responsible for developing the ecclesiological views to which the sociology called "pastorate" refers. Here, too, undeniably, there has been rational progress. By declaring that this pastorate is non-scientific we are denying that this ecclesiology can also be a science of religion. At the same time, bit by bit, we are eliminating from the field studied by science of religion all theology and ecclesiology, since they both imply confessionalism. It may be that in the sciences of religion we are still so far from attaining the definitive precision of a system that we must accept any of the various routes which follow a common set of rules—rules which were themselves empirically determined. At this phase we will run into many blind alleys before finding a single open road. But the open road will not be found unless the blind alleys are explored. Both open roads and blind alleys play a role in scientific research.

Having said this in defense of confessionalism (not only in defense of the researcher, which goes without saying, but also of the research itself, which is open to more objections), I am not persuaded that the relation between what is scientific and what is confessional in an enterprise like this will turn out to be a happy one. This relationship (in matters sociological) has been concretely set by Mgr. G. in a formula which affirms that the *raison d'être* of confessional sociology is to learn how the leaven can be put into the bread—and not just stored up on the side. In other words, confessional sociology is a sociology of bread, not a sociology of leaven. The result is a pastorate procedure to which we shall return later. For the moment we need only point out the dichotomy of interest.

We have all deplored how, following the line of least resistance, this procedure leads to a sociography of populations at the expense of a psycho-sociology concerned with how a people's cultural and spiritual experiences are represented in religion. Using G. Le Bras' terminology, one could say that this diversion leads to hypertrophy in the sociography of "realities" (in religion) and atrophy in the sociology of "system" (in religious law or the religious system proposed by the authorities). Or, borrowing the terminology of testing, this sociology of "bread" mobilizes its analyses around the facts of religion as lived (and latent) and ceases any critical examination of the religion as prescribed (and formal).

In pointing this out, one becomes aware of a curious cross-fire between religious sciences and sociology. The religious sciences are most often concerned with religions other than the one of the observer. More often than not, they are so concerned with the analysis of systems, texts, prescriptions, ritual formalities, etc., that when someone asks for information about the people who live under these forms and how they are affected by this imposed order, he seems to be raising an almost unheard of question. On the other hand, in the case of pastorate sociology, one notes that its recent origin (1931-1933) is directly tied to a plea (first formulated by Mauss and then presented by G. Le Bras) that research be transferred to the field of the major religions ("ours"). Recalling this paper (read, I think, at the *Institut de Sociologie*), I.M. emphasized the deep effect that the outline of Le Bras' program had on university people present at that meeting. It was not long before the confessional publications took note of this new effort and soon hailed it as a "conversion" of sociology and an end to the conflict between Durkheimians and believers. But for the next twenty years this investigation was going to move in a sense contrary to that of the other sciences of religion (especially the history of religions) by limiting its studies to the facts of religion-as-lived and latent and, for a long time, by further limiting itself to a study of those facts which apply to people organized in official religious groups, each with its own criteria and clear-cut standards of measurement. In doing so the investigation abandoned, at least provisionally, the sociology of "system" and prescribed religion, and, therefore, the sociology of religious prescriptions in general (revelation, traditions, cults, etc.). This continued, despite the appeals of G. Le Bras for a sociology (I think I quote these in order of appearance) of religious vitality, liturgy, dogma and atheism.

More generally speaking, one might say that a sociology of

the pastorate (by which I mean a sociology which a confession practices on itself) is subject to the same suspicion that plagued its antecedents and their dubious motivations: but it avoids this suspicion insofar as it persists in a dual approach to the religious fact: one approach aims at what is deemed accessible and amenable to reasoned analysis; the other approach aims at what is thought to be inaccessible and, by nature, irrational. The line of demarkation between these two parts varies according to who is doing the research. It sets the limits for: cultural or folkloric implications (facts relative to Christendom as distinguished from facts relative to the Church); certain canonical disciplines; schools of theology; spiritual traditions; definitions of dogma; revealed truths. If one examines terms used for theological concepts, one notes, as M. Cano has pointed out, that the closer confessional sociology comes to a central concern of theological thought the more reticent and reserved it appears to be—or, to use Mgr. G.'s vocabulary, the more it looks like a sociology of leaven, not of bread. This is understandable since it is the nature and logic of sociological treatment not to reduce its object but to relativize it; and it is psychologically normal for this principle of relativity to lose its cutting edge when applied to facts or values considered to be absolute. One remembers that when the other sciences of religion (particularly history and Biblical exegesis as taken up at the *Ecole Pratique des Hautes Etudes* in the years before 1931) were applied to Christianity they addressed themselves immediately to the question of revelation as recorded in the Old and New Testaments and attempted to treat the scriptures as a quasi-sociological work. Thus, even though one may dispute his beliefs and his conclusions, one finds a strong dose of sociology in Loisy's refutation of Harnack in his *L'Evangile et l'Eglise;* and if there is ever a sociology of millenarianism we shall have to recognize its debt to this work. But to do so, we shall have to pass from a sociology of bread to a sociology of the leaven which made it rise.

This sociology of leaven is, I believe, an open question, even for us. On this score, one of G. Le Bras' texts strikes me as very *à propos.* I refer to the introduction he wrote for F. Boulard's *Itinéraires.* "There are areas of religion that the Catholic is forbidden to investigate, such as the Revelation. For, whereas the myths of ancient peoples may be an invention, an explanation or a response (or, if you like, a hypostasis) produced by the tribe or clan, the Christian mysteries have been dictated to man by God, and man is limited to translating them into his own language. Man's contribution begins with exegeses and schools of theology, and these arise in observable places and reflect a few of their particular characteristics. A cult is even more closely linked to the habits, aspirations and structures of the human society in which it is born. And this is even more true of canon law." This analysis enumerates *loci theologici* which are not open to sociological research precisely because they are central concerns. I don't know what attitude to take toward this reluctance. It is rooted in one man's experience. Joachim Wach had a similar experience, although he seems to have drawn the line of demarcation quite differently (closer to the experience of religion *ut sic* than to the experience of Christianity as such).

And these experiences are tied to the tradition in which religious experience resists efforts to rationalize its own nature: some refuse to take a census of the faithful, some refuse to put revelations in writing; some refuse to translate them into the vernacular, and some refuse to pronounce the name of God, even mentally, and *a fortiori* to represent Him in a graven image. I think it would be an error to liquidate this question by arbitrarily declaring that these are taboos and that in pursuing them we risk volatilizing a religious experience which is probably in its formative meta-rational or meta-moral state. . . . *Hagia Sigè!*

I repeat this to myself over and over again, yet the sympathies of my own thought go to another text, also by G. Le Bras. "The conditions of human life are in part set by nature, but, even more, they depend on society which conquers its habitat, forms its men, establishes relations, creates an economy *and, to some extent, its gods*" (*Etudes,* II, p. 798). It is I who have underscored this "*and to some extent its gods.*" To some extent:

quodammodo. Any clarification of this *quodammodo* opens
up the whole quarrel between confessional and non-confessional sociology and, beyond that, the dispute between the religions
of those who believe God created man and the atheisms of those
who believe men created their gods.

It is into this no man's land that I wish to introduce my own
present position and hypotheses.

I am inclined to think that no sector in the field of religion
can be shut off from sociological research. All the facts of religion can be humanly thought in terms of man's relation to
nature, to society, to the social conflicts growing out of religious
conflicts, or, in parallel fashion, to a social stability correlated
with a religious stability. . . . The history of the gods is part of
the history of mankind. The only gods are the gods of man.
I am also inclined to think that all non-religious, lay or profane
sectors of society are tied, at least genetically, to religion. In
other words, there is not one sector accessible to sociological
investigation and another sector reserved for religion. Everything is accessible and yet at the same time everything is reserved.

I would not be reluctant to accept a radically sociological approach to a question such as the origin of Christianity. To argue
that the origins of Christianity imply a discontinuity in the net-
work of historical and sociological factors strikes me as an ob-
struction to any serious research on the subject. Is Christ an
historical figure who has been sublimated by a subsequent religious tradition? Or is he a symbolic figure who has been
historicized by some other tradition? Are these traditions related to each other? Do they conflict? If symbolic, what is the
figure's relation to gnosticism? If historical, what is his relation
to peaceful resistance (the Essenes) and to the partisans of force
(the Zealots)? Etc. If Christ was selected from among many
such figures in holy writings, figures which had in turn been the
result of some previous selection (and therefore of a discrimi-
nation), what is the sociological substructure of this selection?
Etc. These are questions which confessional sociology tends to
leave untouched. How can the unrepentant curiosity of a

straight-forward sociology leave its confessional colleagues in this state of suspense?

And, conversely, when we face the question of atheism and its origins, I would want sociology of religion to be as unrepentantly curious about this irreligion as the sociology of non-religion should be when treating religion in general. Provided, of course, that we do not stay at the platitudinous stage of what theology calls "truth gone mad." Moreover, there are so many different kinds of atheisms, so many different religious meanings given to the word. . . . I would say the same thing about the origins of laicism and the difficulty we have in discerning the difference between it and a lay religion, or between it and laicology. . . .

Both cases imply the hypothesis that an historical sociology of this type is necessary and sufficient for de-mythologizing the cult of religion as well as the politics of atheism. Without this hypothesis we are left with either the politicizing of the cult or the cultification of the politics. There was one moment in the speech of the Polish delegate (Ossovski) which touched on the importance of this problem.

Does this mean that a radicalized sociology of religion (if indeed this radicalization is necessary for its development as a science) will automatically be opposed to confessional sociology? Let me propose another hypothesis: there is a contradiction between sociology of religion and *certain* theological presuppositions of the Christian confessions, but this contradiction involves a question of fact and not, perhaps, of nature. It is a question of fact: making the *god of the men of God* appear as the *god of mankind* can, at first hearing, only seem sacrilegious to mankind, especially so long as the two divinities remain rival candidates for a single place in the sun. We have learned all we want to know about this kind of competition from the still burning controversies over the first appearance of man. The dispute will be twice as bitter and the levels of accommodation will remain esoteric even longer when the question is the appearance of a divinity (for example: how "true" are the children's versions of the Gospels?).

Still speaking for myself, I would like to add that this
competition and this hostility is due to a theology. Perhaps
it is not due to every theology. Or perhaps it is. If indeed one
examines the evolution of theological thought over the past
fifty years, it becomes evident that, at least marginally, this
process of theological integration is already underway. There
is a Biblical theology based on critical exegesis, Church history
and history of churches, history of dogma, history of theologies,
without mentioning Bultman and Bonhöffer. . . . We are a long
way from the traditional Discourse on Universal History. Nor
are there any more attempts to make a religion look like the
"whole" of the world without at the same time showing it
as a part of the whole thing. Can we push this further? Can
we ask if an approach treating all gods as products (in the complex sense of that word) of a society would eliminate the fundamental religious act of adoration? Affirmative answers to
this question have been given by both religion and atheism.
It is safer to state that we really don't know, since even if we
did eliminate the act of adoration (or seemed to do so) there
would not be much evidence for a causal relation between this
and a sociological rationalization. Personally, I do not believe
that any such relation exists. I even believe that this sociological radicalization occurs as a logical development in
theology, and that it is because of an eclipse, interior migration or exterior transfer of this development that a religious
faith and sociological knowledge appear to be contradictory
or mutually impenetrable. For, in the science of religions as
in the other sciences, the key to coexistence (or *convenance* as
the Scholastics used to say) lies in an *intellectus fidei* which
is, precisely, what defines the theological enterprise. If I have
a predilection for Wach it is because his thought leads me up
this path.

Perhaps this has been a digression. Returning to my subject,
my only conclusion (perhaps a very personal one) is that
scientific sociology and confessional sociology are not incompatible. This may seem paradoxical since it is apparent that I
have been arguing against an ill-informed confessionalism and
for a better informed confessionalism, and since the theological

position favoring this evolution has long been considered a "marginal" deviation and, as such, suspect to both the system and the authorities responsible for maintaining it. Even so, it is wrong to hold as absolute and definitive an incompatibility which is, perhaps, only relative and provisional.

3) Interventionism

Another scientific liability weighing on sociology of the pastorate is the fact that its intervention is generally occasioned by some practical, calculated objective. This is the opposite of the disinterest which characterizes pure research. On this subject F.I. replied to Z. by distinguishing pure research from applied research and by pointing out that he did not wish to discriminate against one for the benefit of the other. We should reflect on this and on the fact that a diptych of *basic and applied* research is probably at first sight more useful than a diptych of *scientific and pastorate* sociology.

A propos of this duality I would like to make two remarks concerning the pastorate.

The first of these is negative. I have already presented it in an article pointing out that, whether we like it or not, the techniques of pastorate sociology can be understood as an aspect of the managerial revolution and are therefore related to the departments of social psychology in big business. In other words, the body of believers constitute the object or field of intervention: this group is not (or at least not significantly) the subject of the study. If we apply the distinction between the leaven and the bread to the ecclesiastical domain, we get: leaven = pastor = clergy; bread = flock = laity (when laity is defined as the body participating in the Candlemas procession of the flock, a well-known definition which is nevertheless rightfully disputed by the more informed theology of the laity). At first the faithful flock (*laos*) tends to participate only incidentally in the work of pastorate sociology when, individually or in teams, it does the leg-work for a survey; but after the survey has been completed these field workers become the field to which the results apply. Embedded in this process (not always, but often, and in any case the principle remains the same) there is an esoteric exploitation of the survey by interested authority and sometimes there is even a determination by the clergy to conceal the results. I refer you to the conversation with D. about the researcher's obligation to keep secret the results of certain surveys.

In addition to this clerical esotericism, quite naturally, there is an esotericism of confessional interests as such. This issue was discussed during the seminar at M. following J.M.'s paper on the psycho-sociology of those who do research. Let me restate here what I said at that time: no matter what religious body is being surveyed, it is as if there were a tacit game of give-and-take being played between the researcher and the person being researched. The first can have no knowledge of the second until the second acknowledges that the first is, more or less, actually or potentially, one of his kind. Neither archives nor mouths will be opened unless the inquirer is a partisan, a sympathizer, a convert, or is treated as such. One hates to admit that the researcher must act like a proselyte in order to obtain data for his research. When L., who is doing research among the Pentecostists as an observing "participant," complained that he would never be able to "speak in tongues," he was touching the Gordian knot of sociological procedure. Lévy-Bruhl once said in a colloquium at the C.E.S. that "there is no need to be a mystic in order to understand mysticism. *Quite the contrary. . . .*" Yes, of course, we know what he means and we are reminded of the old proverb: "One need not have laid an egg to know whether or not it is fresh." We all know that real knowledge, the kind that can be conceptualized, requires a certain exteriority *vis-à-vis* its object. But the problem is not positional. It is one of method. It concerns the preparatory phase during which, willy-nilly, even before considering the ethnological demand to share the life of the people under study, one must acquire from them at least some documentary knowledge of their religion's written sources and oral accounts. Naturally, such knowledge can be obtained indirectly, like a report from an information bureau. However, there is a limit to this kind of knowledge and the sociologist is usually not a detective. At any rate, he is not what Sartre once called "a cop." Thus, since access to the sources is normally a matter of good will, it will be difficult for the sociologist to procure his data unless he is or appears to be a member of the group and can use the pronoun "we." This "we" becomes even more important when one considers how often the sociologist's curiosity appears to be abnormal or importune.

The dilemma is not absolutely new. Perhaps it is sharper when one is studying a religious group, but it can be found wherever there is a need to penetrate an enterprise, a section of town, a labor union or a family group, etc. I am astonished that so little is made of this problem in discussions about sociological methodology. Perhaps this is because the relation between the person making a survey and the people being surveyed has always been considered in terms of **A** observes **B**. Perhaps it is because the surveys of religion have been devoted to religions that are distant in both space and time, although this does not necessarily exclude some backlash as was demonstrated in a recent colloquium of ethnology when a black African took the floor and presented an aborigine's reaction to what had been said. Yet we can at least retain the principle that no sociological field survey is possible without some sort of cooperation between the researcher and the people he is researching, and that this will occur before, during and after the research operation and will not occur without some sort of recognition between the two parties. This required cooperation closes the doors to observers who are *personae non gratae* and it generally supposes that those whose credentials have been accepted are in some way part of the "we" being observed.

To these two esotericisms (confessional and hierarchical) one can eventually add a third which is characteristic of authoritarian religions, at least during their period of growth. During this phase of an authoritarian religion it is psychologically impossible for an adherent to distinguish between the religion-as-prescribed and the religion-as-lived without being excluded or excommunicated from the group. Naturally, there can be a tacitly accepted laxness, especially in matters of religion practice (for example, the Paschatins). But during the growth stage the problem of religious content is especially acute. In practice, beliefs that are lived coincide strictly with those that have been prescribed, even when this living is no more than a stereotype, as is often the case. When asked questions about content, a believer will give answers which he thinks match the catechism, for he will have difficulty in distinguishing between the interview for a survey and an examination for confirmation in the Church. For example, imagine the answers we would get if we administered a questionnaire such as the one on the personal beliefs of American ministers and students (relative to Revelation, hell, the Holy Ghost, etc.) and applied it to a micro-authoritarian group such as a sectarian brotherhood or a macro-authoritarian group such as a large traditional parish in a place like the Quebec of thirty years ago. It is probable that if this particular questionnaire were distributed to the Church-going population of Quebec it would not produce any significant data; moreover, one can hardly imagine questions like these being asked from the pulpit. And, even if the questions were presented outside the walls of the Church, one can imagine the complaints of its priests about this intervention in "their" people's lives. If any answers did come in from such a questionnaire, at the most they would probably only reflect opinions prescribed by the established system for the "realities" on which it is the authority. The same problem does not arise when we are dealing with an authoritarian religion in its declining phase. This is what makes it possible to get meaningful answers in surveys such as the one on the I.F.O.P. in which the results clearly showed a discrepancy not only between what is prescribed and what is lived (something always observable in objective attitudes) but also between what is prescribed and the people's interpretation of this prescription. Knowledge of these opinions and, consequently, of the discrepancies, is essential to sociological research. It presupposes a referendum on the symbol system (in this case, the articles of the Credo), something which hardly seems possible without establishing a procedural methodology, a development which the conflict between scientific sociology and pastorate sociology makes improbable.

These diverse esotericisms (organizational or psychological) do indeed limit the clear understanding that "scientific" sociology needs to establish between the researcher and the researched. But, on the other hand, the intervention of pastorate interests does entail one element which can be called "scientific"; this is the fact that pastorate knowledge is tied to pastorate action. This observation leads us directly into the second part of these remarks.

II

The second part of these remarks is devoted to the non-pastorate character of "scientific" sociology.

In the first part I presented the pastorate-scientific diptych as analogous to the confessional-nonconfessional (or supraconfessional) diptych. I tried to point out that there is a two-way conflict between these terms, and that the serenity promised by non-confessional sociology is in methodological trouble. I admit that I should have organized my analysis better and that I have given free reign to my pen, jotting down ideas as they came into my head. Despite the risks involved, I shall do the same thing again as I try to clarify my position; however, this time the concern is not the nature of religious experience, but the nature of sociological procedure.

From the point of view of scientific sociology the necessity of a non-pastorate approach is, initially, self-evident, and the advantages it affords are too obvious to be explained. Its objective attitude toward the results obtained by apologetic and polemical analyses undeniably lend its operations a quality of disinterestedness. The absence of concern for practical consequences gives this research the disengagement necessary to pure research. I know all too well the various arguments that can be drawn from this theme. And yet I ask myself a question similar to the one Péguy raised about the philosophy of Emmanuel Kant ("Kant's hands are pure, but he has no hands"). Do the hands of research stay pure just so long as research has no hands?

In the light of this question the diptych "scientific-pastor-ate" is no longer the equivalent of the diptych "pure-and-applied" research; it becomes the equivalent of another diptych composed of academic sociology and applied sociology. And this raises the fearful question of the nature of sociology and its importance not only as a science of history but also as a practice (in the widest sense of that word, meaning that sociology must have a praxis if it is to qualify as a science).

It is in this sense that there may be a recto and a verso to the word "pastorate." The recto of its confessionalism has as its verso, if not the reality, at least the immediate possibility of a "praxis." As soon as one admits this, one is involved in a tangled problem. In a disordered fashion, let me attempt to untangle a few of the strands.

1. I note that when a sociological analysis is undertaken to satisfy a demand this does not necessarily mortgage the analysis to the demand that called it into being. All things considered, a sociological analysis of confessional population density, present and future, made to guide the clergy in locating new churches, may well be more closely related to market research than to depth sociology. A distinction must be made between the scientific value of the procedure and the moral value of the need that it serves; we must not automatically suspect the first just because we are suspicious of the second and those who implicitly hope that the scientific procedure will validate their moral need. Whatever the case may be, this respect for the validity of a procedure does at least shift our attention onto a praxis, an action. The same would be true of other analyses which grow out of practical needs such as: a reorganization of administrative divisions, a redistribution of the clergy, a re-evaluation of teachings (for example, an inquiry into Christian anti-semitism), the restructuring of youth groups, changes in the catechism (for example, inquiries on the preparation for first communion), etc. In all such cases, one could indeed accuse those making the survey of not having pure hands. For example, the basic principle of building new churches on what are, sociologically, the best sites could be considered an ir-

rational project by a free-thinking rationalist or an irreligious project by a mystic of the Inner Light. But no matter who evaluates the survey, he would have hands. The needs that have been detected, measured and analyzed may be morally fallacious, ambiguous or blown-up out of proportion, but they do represent predictions about the future needs of the consumer, and these needs will be the criteria for judging what the survey produces. If the analysis leads to the construction of a church and the church remains empty, the empty church will suffice to invalidate the analysis. As Engels used to say, the proof of the pudding is in the eating. Certainly this is not a sufficient proof. Specifically, a full church does not prove the validity of its message any more than an empty church invalidates that message. Analyses of the ecclesiastical market are not concerned with such questions of validity. They operate in a well defined field within which they find a rare reciprocal relation between theory and practice. I do not mean to suggest that all pastorate surveys result in such concrete and practical enterprises. I am saying that: 1) They could lead to such enterprises; 2) The confessional character of the inquiry does facilitate this; 3) The practical purpose of a survey should not be interpreted as disqualifying its scientific respectability; 4) The observations of this practicing sociology (*praxisation*) can be transformed into a group dynamics whether or not the observer participates in the concern of those who called for the survey in the first place; 5) This transformation corresponds to a scientific quality one often looks for in sociological research.

2. On the other hand, one wonders if this "scientific quality" is not lacking in an academic type of sociology of religion. The academic type implies unquestionable, methodological privileges: the open door, a free hand, absence of all controls other than self-criticism and mutual-criticism, etc. Yet one notes that its disinterest in application and practice is only relative: it writes reports on research, publishes reviews and circulates them to a special list of subscribers; it produces articles and expects them to be criticized, etc. All these activities attest to the fact that a cultural circulation is taking

place. And this circulation is already an action. If the action profile seems somewhat blurred that is because its form remains esoteric—as do the profiles of those large periodicals devoted to the sciences of religion. But it is an action: enough of an action to be considered a full-fledged praxis, not enough of an action to be culturally accepted or rejected as a large scale representation of the objective serenity one strives for in the confines of a laboratory.

3. One wonders what the eventual consuming public for this kind of research would or could be. One wonders not only what would be the market for such research (after all, it would be negligible), but also what need to read would correspond to this desire to write, or what need to intervene would correspond to these theoretical explorations of the field; in brief, what kind of interest corresponds to a decision to do research. If I am not mistaken, this question must be cleared up immediately. . . .

Roughly speaking, where is one to find such a public outside the group of five hundred specialists who are the natural clients for these laboratory reports? Or, reversing the question, where are the consumers for a sociology of religion which is not a confessional enterprise?

a) One gets the impression that during the Durkheimian period of sociology there was an audience in the French normal schools for such reports, with the result that this particular sociology of religion was part of a macro or quasi-macro cultural experience. On a professional level, this public remained interested in all research pertaining to humanistic studies of religion.

b) During the period of sociography of Catholicism, there was an ever growing audience with a confessional concern. This represented a break-through and it was accompanied by a more or less large-scale interest which spread laterally to meta-confessional concerns.

c) As for any mass consumption of religious culture, this is what happened: On the one hand, courses in religious culture were introduced in the schools as alternative non-theological courses for children and adolescents. On the other hand, here and there, in books, on the stage, on the radio, in films and in the press, there were outcroppings of interesting data from religious history.

But in the last analysis, the significance of scientific meta-confessional research was never really grasped by this larger public. Apparently, on the level of mass consumption, there is nothing that corresponds to the interconfessional and inter-religious character of such research and no understanding of the respect which it presupposes for believers and non-believers alike or of the meaning of scientifically controlled data. What comes nearest to this would be the ecumenical movement, but even it is still two or three notches away from the ecumeni-cal or meta-ecumenical attitude that science calls for.

4. This is why there is a problem of "practice" for the soci-ology of religion. It is the problem of a void, of work done in the void. If the sociology is "pastorate" its consumption is assured, but its production in doubt, tied to a mortgage. If the sociology is "scientific" its production is guaranteed, but its consumption remains esoteric. In this second case I would add: there is a void between the emission and the reception. The laboratory functions as a broadcasting operation, but there are almost no receiving sets around to get the message. I know that messages can be carried by relay, and that even confessional sociology uses this method of spreading the word, as does independent sociology more and more frequently. It remains none the less true that in the sociology of religion, as in the other sciences treating religion, there is a problem of esotericism; and, as a result of this, the subject is left untouched on the level of primary and secondary education. The child, the adolescent and the adult are all caught in the same alterna-tive: either confessional education or no religious education at all. I do not mention those countries where the dilemma takes on an even more radical form: either confessional edu-cation or no education at all, since the schools will admit only those who submit to their credo (which in other countries

might be anti-credo). UNESCO has discussed at length the problem of a basic education. It is evident that a common human culture will remain impossible until we reach a formula for some such basic religious instruction. It will not come as a common denominator for religious diversity or as a set of sublimations of the kind Vivekananda proposed to the *Parlement des Religions*; it will only come after a widespread apprenticeship, on the level of everyday language, to what is entailed in this diversity (of non-believers as well as of believers) and with the development of a manner of speaking that does not imply a cold war of words and ideologies.

To achieve this we must not only maintain our efforts to be scientific, but also find a way to amplify the scientific effort so that it becomes consumable in the daily life of the people. According to this view, the least we can do is conduct research on the problems of teaching religion, of diffusing these teachings, of assimilating them and of exteriorizing them. This is the minimum *praxis* presupposed by a science. And the problem is a crucial one since, at the present time, it seems as improbable as it is necessary that this minimum will be realized. Must we believe that the chips are down and that in the face of the trusts which religions have created to monopolize feelings for the sacred and which ecclesiastical organizations have then created to monopolize religions, there remains no alternative other than the one most followed in modern societies: a total rejection of churches, religions and the idea of sacredness, all those things we lump together and label "atheism". . . .

I am aware of how ridiculous this cry of woe must seem. One is always exposed to ridicule when one plays the *vox clamantis in deserto*. But in order to be granted shelter in the shadow of Kierkegaard does one have to sign his name Johannes de Silentio?

The "complaint" of this latter day Johannes de Silentio is, indubitably, dated. Over a decade ago (already!) the questions he asked were similarly treated in two remarkable, but little noticed studies which poured both vinegar and oil on the debate by advancing stubborn methodological demands which were countered by a no less stubborn theological silence.[17] But then one must recognize that theological literature is more and more self-sustaining in its effort to formulate in bold, even imperative, terms the double problem tied to secularization of religious studies and the laicalization of institutions concerned with them.[18] A German editor has recently announced the publication of a magazine *die dem Dialog Zwischen Glaubenden un Nichtglaubenden pflegen soll* (which should promote the dialogue between believers and non-believers). He even intends to have his writers criticize each other's articles and proposes to exclude all apologetics and polemics from the publication. At the present moment a cartel of socio-religious institutes, both Catholic and Protestant, is proposing a "colloquium on inter-disciplinary confrontation and its contribution to the dialogue between the Church and the World." The bridges between confessional sociology and independent sociology seem to be multiplying.[19] On certain points they have even touched on the content of catechisms. And there is, of course, a long procession of conciliators walking hand in hand, hoping to bring together their various confessions, religions and ideologies.

Along with this effort to create a dialogue there should be a more methodical exploration of the possibilities in the field of mass communications. During the past few years thousands or even millions of spectators at the theatre and at the movies have enjoyed the fruits of long and patient scholarship on the story of heresy: John Huss, Thomas Münzer, the Albigenses, to say nothing of the Jesuits in Paraguay. Religions long dead have taken on new life in popular literature dealing with their monuments as well as with the documents they left behind. A serious religious drama can raise a storm (as did the film made from Diderot's *La Religieuse*). "Virtuosos" of the dominant religion play and replay their parts under the spotlights: Joan of Arc, Judas, Luther and even Jesus. There is an enormous supply of studies, novels, tragedies, scenarios, songs, films, phonograph records, leaflets, costumes, choreography . . . whose relation to sociology of religion has hardly been noted by the cataloguing librarians at confessional headquarters. They represent an enormous social praxis in which religious functions and malfunctions, archetypes and structures are resurrected in images which animate or reanimate individual and collective minds, and even influence behavior and convictions. There is then a diffuse but massive social experience which only awaits appropriate treatment to become sociological data.[20]

The task of bringing together this material, either formally or informally, challenges an independent sociology of religion to become a practicing sociology in its own right, and, even more important, to develop its own sociogogy (although, in meeting this challenge, it does risk losing its birthright for a mess of potage). In doing this, it can make common cause with the other sciences of religion if only these sciences which have for so long been identified with the History of Religions will accept its company; it can even make common cause with theologies and ecclesiologies insofar as, under the impact of an ecumenical revival, these disciplines become interested in a science of *homo religiosus.*

This sociogogy depends on the existence of departments of sociology of religion in the universities. On this score, France is a few steps ahead due to the fact that in the nineteenth century such a department was created to replace the old schools of theology. This department has not been without its difficulties, as Emile Poulat has related in a recent article written with his customary erudition.[21]

The case of France seems to be an exception, as one can see by examining other continents and other cultural threshing-floors. At times, when discussing this project of an independent department of religion with our non-French colleagues, it has often appeared to be *fascinosum et tremendum.* Either it seemed inconceivable to operate apart from a department of theology or it seemed impossible to set up because of objections from supporters of a powerful lay tradition. However, in both cases, the project seemed to be the key to progress in the field. And we can attest that this was the opinion of tough-skinned non-believers (*nicht kirchlich gebunden*) as well as of believers, pastors and theologians aware of the cultural mutations occurring in their peoples. General acceptance of these chairs and departments throughout the modern world will certainly be one of the first contributions that the sociology of religion makes to a meta-confessional practice of contemporary ecumenism.[22]

On the other hand, even if these departments existed, we would

still face the problem of their exoterization either in the systems
for educating the young or in the programs for "continuing" extra-
academic education of grown-ups. After all, whatever may be one's
personal option in religion or non-religion, practice, semi-practice
or non-practice of religion, the religious thread (and, even more so,
the thread of the sacred) is woven into the cultural fabric of mankind; and although one may rightfully deplore the failures of
physical and artistic education in an obstacle course of exams
which relegate them to secondary importance or make them something merely optional, one should also deplore a system of religious
education which has not even succeeded in finding a common basis
for all religion. For want of this, we get either unilateral education
or no education at all. This is a paradox, since for a long time
peaceful coexistence (the postulate of recent ecumenism) has been
the guiding principle for research in the sciences of religion. Thus,
bit by bit, there appear signs of an educational movement mindful
of the demands for peaceful coexistence and an ecumenism of
"life and work"; slowly we move toward an international organization which will define the role of religious culture in the basic education of a citizen of this world.

In this context we meet the half-dozen questions which will
eventually have to be asked by a sociology of religion and a sociology of education.[23]

Can the practice of sociology of religions as developed over
several decades in the laboratory be extrapolated into this field?

Under what socio-cultural conditions can the sciences of religion
give up their esoteric serenity and move, no less serenely, into the
exoteric fields opened up, on the one hand, by an institutionalized
program of social sciences for adolescents, and, on the other hand,
by the demands for information about the religious phenomenon
in a system of continuing education for adults (with its international variants)?

How can we pass from an esoteric science of religions (not to be
confused with a science of esoteric religions) to a scientific exoteri-
cism without first going through the stage of an esoteric or crypto-
religion of science?

After ceasing to be academic in order to become operational in
the immense field of what Comte dreamed of for the universal edu-

cation of mankind, how will the sciences of religion be able to find in this operation itself the conditions for doing action-research? What will be its rules of scientific procedure?

What will be the content of this non-ecclesiological, non-confessional, non-ideological education offered to the adolescent and the adult? Will it remain independent of all authority, convictions and orthodoxies of an ecclesiological, confessional and ideological type?

And by what procedures would this sociology of religions (committed both to its own independence and to the demands for a universal education) define itself methodologically, structurally and praxiologically as a sociology that is both applied and self-activated?

When we ask questions like these, we confront the upper limits of practicing sociology, a realm beyond our grasp, since the answers to these questions can hardly be deduced from an analysis. They can only be induced in action by specific actors. They will take form in behavior that sociology can ausculate but not produce on its own. Perhaps it is there, beyond this border line of action, that lies this domain which transcends sociological reasoning.

An educational movement like this is something that the sociologist of religion cannot, could not and would not want to create. He can only diagnose its absence and delineate the empty place. This infirmity he has in common with his colleagues. The sociologist of rural life does not know how to and would not want to create experimental towns satisfying his optimal ratios. The sociologist of industrial life has a similar attitude toward pilot factories. Likewise, the sociologist of literature or cinema will not create fiction or direct films. This principle is, at least generally, accepted. Just so, we shall probably see a division of work develop between the sociologist of religion and the socio-practician who would animate a religious evolution. Because it was allied to a religious actor (the pastor), pastorate sociology early in the game was able to take the measure of its possibilities in practice, but its lot is not entirely enviable. As for the "independent" sociologist, he is obliged to wait for the future appearance of cultural mutations which he can only predict; in the present his action is limited to unmasking imitations and, here and there, pointing out indications of things to come. Like Rimbaud, this "independent" sociologist has to "arm himself with a burning patience," but for him there is no assurance that "in the morning he will enter into the cities of splendor." At any rate, he is certain of one thing: the kings will not become philosophers and the philosophers will not become kings. The pastorates and the independents follow different paths even if they come down a common road before reaching the fork, and even if, after this bifurcation, their respective ways do crisscross each other or move in parallel directions. By eradicating the distinction between them one does not even get an *Ideal Typus*. It is better to think of this distinction in poetic terms:

The tree of knowledge is not the tree of life.

And as for one's personal thoughts, they will vary according to whether one is an optimist or a pessimist: "Sorrow is knowledge" or "the *gai Savoir*"—one can choose between Byron and Nietzsche. But whatever choice one makes, one will sooner or later confront a fact already confronted by three of the great French pioneers in the field of sociology of religion, Saint Simon, Comte and Durkheim: the fact that religious action is not deduced from knowledge. This probably explains why each of these three men sooner or later tied his sociology to a meta-sociology of an adventist type. The first of these men awaited,[24] the second announced[25] and the third expected[26] something like a new religion. . . . But musicologists are not necessarily musicians. And conversely.

Chapter 7

Sociology of Religion
and Sociology of Development

. . . the bloody struggle between those who attack God but defend his works and those who defend God but undermine his works by opposing human progress.—Père Enfantin

The reflections in this chapter represent a reworking of material already commented on in a published article and a book.[1] Their bearing on traditional sociology of religion can be verified by consulting N. M. Hanson's subtle observations on the ideas of Weber and their significance to the problem of economic development.[2] His basic principle is that "ideological and religious values which were formerly belittled as irrational and therefore devoid of any positive significance for economic growth, can in many cases serve as positive motivations for rational economic behavior."[3] This may not be the answer we are looking for, but at least it implies a basic problem which is more and more coming to the foreground.

Hanson sets the problem approximately in the following manner: The initial economic problems are undeniably material and practical: how to survive and live, eat and live, work and eat, acquire instruments for work, exchange or sell what is produced, assure the means for subsistence, find the funds necessary to buy equipment as well as consumer goods. These operations are all familiar to anyone interested in development and they are the basic problems for anyone interested in economic cooperation: consumption, supply, distribution, credit, equipment, etc. All these operations are politically and religiously neutral, but through them increasingly pass other operations sometimes called "energizing" (*animation*) and through the latter we get religious implications. The implementation of these projects for development does indeed occur according to a plan. The plan demands the support and participation of the people, a sort of psychological mobilization in depth in the name of their national destiny, its historical role and present situation. This mobilization cannot be achieved without respecting these motivations in depth, for they intervene, either positively or negatively, whether or not one likes it, knows it or wants it. As Hanson points out, "There is a marked tendency in economic thought to neglect the importance of religious values in underdeveloped countries and to under-estimate the difficulties involved in attempts to radically alter existing institutions."[4] His general conclusion seems beyond dispute. "No matter what the system may be, religious or ideological motivation is one of the fundamental conditions and presuppositions for economic development."

This is a relatively recent problem.[5] The strategy of economic development has often been characterized by an over-weening confidence in economic techniques with no allowance made for the play of cultural elements in a complex social structure. The attention given to the transmission of this self-confident technique easily obliterates curiosity in how the technique will affect various elements of the structure in which it is to be employed.[6] Moreover, in this socio-economic structure the religious element has too often been considered negligible or of no concern, and has thus been isolated from the problem of economic planning.

The neglect of this religious element has been pertinently analyzed by Arthur Niehoff and Juanita Niehoff in their recent study of 203 cases in which they were able to pinpoint how the acceptance or rejection of a technological message (sanitation, pedagogy, agriculture, etc.) induced a crisis in belief or traditional religious faith.[7] Their hypothesis on the positive and negative effects due to the transmission-reception system of a technological message is not unlike Hanson's:

> Any important part of man's culture is potentially influential on the process of socio-economic change, if for no other reason than that the different parts of any cultural system are inter-related, and change in any one section can potentially affect other sections. No men are willing to give up their accustomed way of life for economic advantages alone. Economic considerations may be paramount but if they disrupt too much the non-economic aspects of the culture, they may still be rejected.

> Some aspects of culture are considered to be more of a hindrance to economic change than others. The body of beliefs and practices we are here considering, religion, has probably been considered to have a hindering effect on modern change much

more often than it has been considered to have helped the process. This is particularly true of the religions of the non-industrialized, developing countries. From a purely secular, "rational" point of view, this generalization is probably at least partially true. Modernizing change is disruptive, and religion tends to emphasize continuity and tradition. But the basic fact is that no one has methodically studied the religions of the world in this regard. No one has studied them in the context of actual efforts to bring economically advantageous economic changes to the believers. The so-called hindering effects may be far less than believed. . . ."[8]

These remarks illustrate the point of view from which the following comments are made. My observations were conceived out of my own experience with the practical problems of development economics, in this case the development of cooperatives in a program which has long been a corollary to my theoretical studies of religious ideologies. Let me explain briefly that our theoretical research led us to put together cooperatives somewhat the way Paul of Tarsus wove his tents, and perhaps we did so for the same reasons. Plying the two trades at once affords a two-way perspective with certain advantages once known by Hylas and Philonis.

I. Outmoded Monisms?

In discussions on the relation between religion and development economics we note references to two distinct kinds of monism. The first is an apologetic monism which, to put it crudely, considers that religion favors development; the more religion, the more development will take place. The second is a polemic monism which generally considers religion to be incompatible with development; the more development, the less religion there will be.

These monisms seem to have been outmoded by events, as is evidenced by the survey cited at the beginning of this chapter.[9] There have been and there still are religions which slow down development, those which still teach patience at a time when sources of social energy are already preaching impatience. There are also religions which would accelerate development too rapidly; it was an account of Münzer's vision of social change that led Engels to devise a method for diagnosing forecasts which, though brilliant, are premature and, in the long run, traumatizing.[10]

Conversely, the classic accusation of religion as "opium of the people" (which is to say, "an illusion in a situation needing illusions") cannot be countered so long as religion is radically unilateral. Skipping over the dialectical reflections of Marx-Engels,[11] one still cannot ignore the warning set forth by Togliatti in his *Testament:* "The problem of religious belief, its content, its roots in the life of the people, and the way of moving beyond it must be approached in an entirely different manner from what we have known in the past."

II. Pluralized Interrelations

An abstract table of these interrelations could be set up in the following manner, with plus and minus signs indicating the favorable and unfavorable implications of religion for development and of development for religion:[12]

	Religion's effect on Development	Development's effect on Religion
1.	+	+
2.	–	–
3.	+	–
4.	–	+

1. A religion favorable to a development which, in turn, is favorable to the religion. Weber tried to show that this was the reciprocal relation of the Calvinist ethic and the development of capitalism. Is there a similar reciprocity between any other religions and other forms of development? This question was asked at the Fifth Congress of Sociology.[13] Hanson mentions a few possible examples of these, drawn from various sources.[14]

2. A religion unfavorable to a development which, in turn, is unfavorable to the religion. This is just about the case of old Quebec in French-speaking Canada where a Catholicism based on rural parishes was unfavorable to the development of an urban industrial society which threatened the sociological and cultural foundations of the old Church. The question is still being debated.[15]

3. A religion favorable to a development which is, in turn, unfavorable to the religion. A religion gives birth to the development; then the growing child suffocates the parent who gave him birth. This was the situation deplored by John Wesley.[16]

4. A religion unfavorable to a development which is, in the end, favorable to religion. Immigration to the New World was for the most part a flight from the Old World (at that time the "developed" world); certain sects even believed that this exodus had an apocalyptic significance corresponding to the Biblical flight of the "Woman in the Wilderness." Yet this New World was soon supra-developed and, paradoxically, now offers statistical curves indicating an apparent growth of religion, just as if it were a country favoring a certain positive religious feeling.[17]

III. A Constellation of Prime Importance

In the contemporary struggle with the problem of underdevelopment and, more specifically, the emergence of young nations to political and economic independence, a constellation of factors has taken on a special importance. This is the constellation of nation-class-language-religion.

In their sociographic surveys Western sociologists of religion have tried to correlate the religious factor with grids set up to show social differentiations that depend on differences in the various socio-professional systems. Some researchers have already pointed out the relativity of this correlation as far as the West is concerned, and they emphasize the important role played by historical factors in the vicissitudes of family, regional and national life.

In the case of young nations, the change in national status be-

comes a fundamental factor and the role of religion in the movement leading to independence becomes a determining factor. This
religious factor is even more important when the nation moving
toward independence thinks of itself as a class dominated by another nation which, on the whole, acts like a ruling class.

The religious factor is still more important when these two nation-
classes speak different languages and when the major religions in
these nation-classes are in some way tied to this difference in
language.[18] In his study on three Southeast Asian countries, Fred
Robert Von der Mehden points out the importance of this type of
constellation.[19] Examining Burma, Indonesia and the Philippines
in the light of this *religious-nationalist movement* hypothesis, he
arrives at the following diagnosis:

> . . . a major influence on the nationalist movement was the
> unifying force of religion. The presence of a single faith as a
> catalytic agent was particularly significant in areas where there
> were no other coalescing factors such as language, culture,
> history, or past common territory. . . . Religion was the one
> unifying factor among the conquered; it divided the ruler
> from the ruled and in doing so provided an emotional basis
> for nationalism and a tool for ambitious political leaders.[20]

According to the author, in Burma this was the role played by
Buddhism against the religion of the British and, in Indonesia, by
Islam against the religion of the Dutch; whereas in the Philippines,
which was the only region where the religion of the conquerors
(Catholicism) became the religion of the conquered, the imposed
religion tended to split into two segments, differentiating the
Christianity of the conquered from the local version which either
developed into a Philippinized Catholicism or produced dissident
anti-clerical, nationalist Catholic groups.[21]

One concludes from this that the way to characterize a religion
sociologically is not to be found in its essential content, but in
how it appears to one or the other of these poles of tension. In
one perspective a religion may look like a means of national identification and cultural liberation; in another (for example, a nation
with a proletariat),[22] this same religion will appear to be an instrument of political alienation and cultural servitude.

IV. A Possible Cleavage

This line of thought suggests a cleavage which runs through and threatens the peace of contemporary ecumenism. Demographers, statisticians, economists, all warn us of the widening gap between the economically dominant civilization of a demographic minority and the economically dominated civilizations of a demographic majority. In general, Christianity is the religion of countries representing the dominant civilization, and the religions in the countries representing dominated civilizations are non-Christian. Therefore in those dominated countries an affirmation of their religious identity is tied to a protest against an international division of labor which classifies them as "proletarian nations." Just as during the Reformation in the sixteenth century an intra-Christian Protestantism abetted the emergence of certain Western nations, there is in the world today a kind of extra-Christian Protestantism which is abetting the budding nationalism of extra-Western regions.[23] Since these budding nationalisms are either socialist or leaning toward socialism, the relation between socialism and religion in these lands is usually the opposite of what this relation has been in Western history, especially during the nineteenth century when religion and socialism were generally in conflict.[24]

V. The Necessary Pluralization of a Religion

One should not infer from the foregoing that in the history of socio-economic development Christianity should be considered as monolithic and unchanging. The tensions which affect the other forces in the constellation also affect Christianity itself.

In some areas the cleavage occurs along confessional lines. This is what is happening in Canada where the cleavage between social groups follows differences in language and religion (English-speaking Protestants polarized on the upper-upper and French-speaking Catholics polarized on the lower-lower). This explosive mixture leads, in one form or another, to assertions that there are really two Canadian nations.

But the cleavage can also occur within the same confession. And when one writes of the religion of certain countries in South America one wonders if it would not be more accurate to refer to Catholicism in the plural.

Observation and interviews with the people in one of these South American countries, for example, led to a report on four distinctive forms of Catholicism in the area:

1. The established Catholicism of landowners, who are conservative and aristocratic.

2. An explosive, eschatological Catholicism among the peasants who are illiterate, millenarian, subversive, and moving toward the confiscation of property by the landless poor.[25]

3. A social Catholicism originating in the enlightened part of the ecclesiastic hierarchy. It is socially aware, cautiously interventionist in the field of economic and cultural reform, and is held in check by Christian social doctrine and submission to Church authority.

4. An alienated, protesting Catholicism of those who intend to reform both the Church and society with the support of both Christians and non-Christians.[26]

It is true that, ecclesiologically, these diverse Catholicisms are all part of the same Catholic Church. But, sociologically, there is an undeniable and perhaps incoercible tension which sets these strata against each other; and the strain is all the stronger because, parallel to it, similar strata are being set up in other spiritual families or ideological groups. Beyond a certain degree of tension there is a point at which the vertical ties binding the various strata within one of these families or groups tend to be counterbalanced by the horizontal ties which bind strata of the same level in two or more groups. This is especially true on the level of social protest.[27] Here is the cross which contemporary ecumenism bears, and its importance should not be minimized.

VI. Religious Differentiation within a Single Culture

This issue brings together all our previous remarks and lays bare

the operational problem which these religious implications raise for
programs of economic development.

Our example is the South Sahara region in Africa and our documentation is taken from a survey now being made in that area.[28]

Religious differentiation in this cultural area has been surveyed
by Bouaké and reported on at international meetings.[29] The following table gives his break-down.

A) Traditional beliefs	1
B) Imported religions	
Islam	2
Catholicism	3
Protestantism	4
C) Syncretisms and messianic religions	5
D) Non-religion[30]	6

We have on file classified reports representing each of the six
types of voluntary affiliation. There can be no question here of
examining them in detail. We are only interested in drawing from
each case a characteristic that approximates a constant in its category.
Whatever type of religious affiliation is claimed by the person in-
terrogated, it seems to be an affiliation with certain reservations:
I am a Catholic, but . . . ; I hold to the value of traditional beliefs,
but . . . ; I am a Protestant, but . . . ; I am not religious, but . . . ;
etc.

Here are a few of the interviews on file:

INTERROGATION OF A TRADITIONALIST

From the age of four to the age of five, I lived in a village which is
mine. My village is self-respecting and is one hundred percent
fetishist. This fetishism is apparent in the villagers' devotion to the
god of the earth (Assié) and the god of cheese-makers (N'Gnin).
Everyone worships the same gods, has the same ceremonial obligations and recognizes the same religious authorities. It is a very
serious matter to dispute their decisions. One runs the risk of socially isolating himself. . . . There are some negative aspects to this religion which have to be attenuated. I much prefer the word "attenu-

ate" to the word "eliminate" because I am completely against the spirit of innovation which, in this domain, runs the risk of creating dangerous splits in the population. So long as the villagers agree to one ceremony a year instead of two, so long as they agree to send their sick to the public dispensary and fish in the only near-by river instead of waiting for the *kapoques* of the cheese-makers, so long as they agree that the cow and the zebu shall be the only offerings made to the gods and not make competing offerings of sheep, goats and steers . . . we manage to attenuate the negative effects of this religion.

In my village even if I spent a whole month explaining the principles of collective responsibility to those who administrate the co-operative there would still be no group solidarity. For what they need is something else, something more concrete; and I find this in the old idea my people have of the gods. I tell them that although the god N'Gnin needs to eat a zebu in order to be strong and fight better, he will certainly have to gather his ponies together under the same social and economic roof in order to see how much stronger he has become. Instead of explaining to our administrative committee that each man has a responsibility to the collectivity, I show them that the loyalty which induces villagers to pay their taxes is the same as the force which makes them pay ceremonial respect to the gods: this motivating force is not something in a written contract; it is the result of the villagers' will to survive, since an angry god never pardons anyone. As far as the men in a community are concerned, if the social welfare organizations decide to set up a cooperative, that is because the god of earth and the god of cheese-makers want this to happen. . . . Religion can co-exist with the will to economic development, but it must be channeled into a certain way of thinking. . . .

INTERROGATION OF A PROTESTANT:

I am a Christian Protestant. I became one after weighing the importance of my decision. I am a member of the Christian Association of African Protestants. My friends and I joined this religion because we recognized its value, but we also joined in order to shake up Protestantism and make it more dynamic and more likely to survive. . . . We belong to the category of under-developed countries, those countries which even before colonization had experienced the winds of religion in many different forms. . . . We did not wait for Western religions to appear to discover and develop the beatific and mystic force of our faith. For many years my ancestors practiced fetishism. To your way of thinking this was paganism, but for them it was a way to grasp the superior forces residing in matter; the soul of material things. Theirs was a patient and moving search. . . . In certain missions, especially those of American Presbyterians, we witnessed a wave of religious McCarthyism, as if everything was a struggle between a mentality judged to be evil and its replacement by a value system without flaws. . . .

INTERROGATION OF A CATHOLIC:

Catholic religious instruction has often brought with it general education, and it has even taken over a large section of primary education in rural areas. Circumstances have often made it promote economic and social progress. The Youth Movements it created permitted young people to come together in groups to study the problems of their own social milieu . . . and ways to solve them, such as evening schools for illiterates taught by volunteers and the creation of savings banks and banks which make loans.

But this does not prevent us from seeing that only too often the Catholic hierarchy has refused to recognize our own personality and has tried to mold us in its own way, throwing a curse on those who dared to resist its authority. Moreover, its interests have always been too closely tied to the interests of those in power and have supported their capitalist tendencies.

INTERROGATION OF ANOTHER CATHOLIC:

As a former pupil of the Jesuit fathers I saw how energetically they tried to make the best students become choirboys and then go on to the seminary to serve God. . . . Back in the village my grandfather had worked on a cocoa plantation called the Pope's Plantation because its profits went the the Vatican to pay for the robes, the chasubles and those things which the missionaries need for their masses. My grandfather, who was a chief, had to give up all his wives except one so that he could be baptized and married religiously and send my father to secondary school to study administration under the Jesuits.

I finished secondary school and I belong to the Catholic Youth Movement. One of my relatives is a Catholic priest and last autumn when he returned from the Council I discussed this subject with him.

INTERROGATION OF A MOHAMMEDAN:

Islam creates a community of views and ideas, a keen sense of solidarity and mutual aid. Its moral code aims to harmonize the relationships between individuals. Its sense of organization encourages the faithful to be disciplined, obedient, respectful of their rights and obligations. It has made it possible to develop a national conscience. . . .

But its doctrine encourages a steady struggle against those who refuse to accept this law. . . . There are many sects, each of which considers itself to be authentic and preeminent. This leads to mistrust and misunderstanding among the masses. Islam could become a class instrument in the hands of the marabouts and religious societies who oppose all projects and tend to proliferate strict rules and negative taboos.

INTERROGATION OF ANOTHER MOHAMMEDAN:

(After enumerating the reasons for forbidding children to attend the modern school) . . . because they will not learn the faith of the prophet Mohammed. . . . My own position is that so long as Mohammedans continue to believe these arguments I fail to see how the Mohammedan religion will ever serve economic development, and I say this as a faithful Mohammedan.

INTERROGATION OF A SECULARIZED MOHAMMEDAN:

My religious faith is the mark of my childhood and my youth. It impregnates me like the odor of herring in the herring barrel.

I was born in a family with a long religious tradition. From my grandfather I inherit the tradition of the warrior; from my mother's family I inherit the tradition defending the faith. When I was five years old, the age at which in my family one decides on a trade, destiny designated me for religion. For seven years, far from my parents, I learned the Koran, worked the land, and often traveled on foot through most of the regions in the country. I suffered physical hardship, poverty and spiritual distress. My religious convictions, such as I had been taught, made me see irreligious people everywhere I went.

Once, on a trip to F. . . , chance brought me to a French school Children were playing in the courtyard. What I saw there gave me a strong desire to do what these children were doing. I decided to leave the Koranic school and enter the French school.

That was not an easy thing to do. At my *Medersa* the master beat me when I told him what I intended to do. I had to run away to go from F. . . to L. . . , my village. My family met in council to discuss my case and decided to send me back to F. . . , but my mother's stubborn opposition to this decision made it possible for me to stay home with her and attend the French school. But there was a condition attached to this victory won by my mother's enthusiastic support: I was to attend school, but also I was supposed to continue my studies of Arabic. Every day before going to school I had to spend a few hours at the *Medersa* and learn a few verses by heart before obtaining permission to go on to my other school. That is why quite often I arrived late.

The schoolmaster refused to understand my explanations. He, too, punished me with beatings. I continued to endure these punishments until about 1943.

At that date, because our neighbors thought so highly of me, I was sent to an Arab high school in D. . . . There I found the same bad pedagogical methods. My memory was well developed and my brain was filled with verses of the Koran, although they never touched my heart, since I did not know what they meant. In the local mosque, despite my young age, I was admitted into a group of older people. Suddenly, I was grown up. This close contact with adults made me understand that the religion they preach is not at all the same as the religion they practice. They make it into something like a political party. This explains the lively and sometimes violent quarrels between the different sects and religions.

That, very briefly, is a resume of how I reached my convictions. I am not hostile to religions, but I deem that they have not fulfilled their mission which is to unite men and make peace reign among them.

A recent African novel has portrayed what it calls "the ambiguous adventure."[31] It offers more examples of ambiguous partisanship, atheism with reservations, attesting-protesting, agreements-disagreements, and reluctant fidelities. In it, once again, we meet the theme of a generalized Protestantism.

Rather than prolong this commentary, perhaps we should simply suggest to all those who make up closed questionnaires that this *sic et non,* this *yes and no,* is a typical category of religious loyalty. On a larger scale, it also applies to belief and non-belief.[32] Ultimately, it even applies to the supposedly fateful question of theism and atheism, of God and non-God. . . . There is a Russian proverb (already quoted) which expresses one reaction to a prickly problem like this: "Thank God, God does not exist; but what if God really existed?—May God preserve us from that idea!"[33] After all, if there were enough of us, even a great many of us, who think like this proverb, wouldn't there be a needle's eye (or just the hole in a punch card) through which we could pass into the Kingdom?

VI. A New Dimension?

The crisscrossings of these different approaches have not passed unnoticed. In Manila, June 1963, there was an international conference on *Cultural Motivations to Progress in South and South-East Asia.*[34] Commenting on his own resume of this conference, Robert Neelly Bellah stated that if it were possible to put into a single sen-

tence the problem raised by his report and by the conference which
preceded it, he would say: we discussed the "modernization of the
soul." The very incongruity of this phrase reveals the complex,
paradoxical and unpredictable nature of a subject like this. After
all, religion deals with eternity and ultimate truth. How could it
ever become involved with change, modernization and progress?
How could it ever be judged in terms of its "potential for modernization?[35]

Yet long ago this problem was raised by Saint-Simon and his
school[36] and it is still a problem for specialists in rural development
for whom psychological mobilization appears more and more necessary as a preliminary step not only for participation in the planning
but also for organizing and for gathering the information on which
both the planning and the organizing depend.[37] The significance
of discussions such as the one in Manila is that they underline the
role of religious values in this problem of how to animate the moral
forces needed for a socio-economic development.

Soedjatmoko calls them "developmental values."[38] After emphasizing that these values are usually found on more specific and deeper
levels than those manipulated by politicians, he adds a decisive remark explaining that the basic difficulty is that the developmental
process is not self-justifying. He points out that in many cultures
the possibility of raising the standard of living and creating greater
material wealth is not a sufficient stimulus to unleash motivating
forces in the traditional sectors of society. And so Soedjatmoko
concludes that in order to stimulate a sufficiently strong force of
persuasion it is necessary to relate developmental projects to other
projects which, in terms of the culture, represent worthwhile values.
Rostov had already drawn attention to this fact.[39] And R. Buron,
in a colloquium on African development, has stated it in other
terms:[40] "What is normal in the history of mankind is not development, but non-development; what we call 'development' is a fever
for growth which has affected a thin slice of human history and
geography; everywhere else the life of mankind is dominated by
the universe of repetition under the archetypal symbols of an eternal
return. . . ."[41]

Without returning to Weber's classic analysis of the ethical and religious conditions for a capitalist "take-off," we now have an ample

supply of data and theory on the possible correlations between religious systems and the various stages or rhythms of economic development.[42] Out of these come many questions, some of which
it may be well to ask at this point.

The first of these is: how should we take into account the socio-
cultural dimension which parallels the socio-economic dimension
of development? For many years a half-digested Marxism has
emphasized the priority and primacy of infra-structures, as if the
socio-cultural levels (known as superstructures) followed along,
more or less automatically as their consequences; at any rate it believed that these socio-cultural levels were a soft wax on which the
marks of technical progress would be stamped. It was only after a
few disasters that we have come to (or come back to) a view which
takes into account the reciprocal relation between economic and
cultural changes. As Louis Althusser has argued: it is one thing to
treat the needs of an economy; it is something quite different to
satisfy the needs of a culture; and the determining factor in development, even if it comes as a last resort, is not necessarily the one with
which we were first concerned.[43] Just so, in many cases, a concern
for the religious phenomenon is woven into the actions of agents
or agencies who were once exclusively concerned with the economy.
It is at this point that the sociology of religion[44] has an impact on
the sociology of development.

Willem Frederik Wertheim has raised another question in a book
which brings together the problems of sociology of religion and the
sociology of development.[45] This is the question raised in his last
chapter entitled "Betting on the Strong?" Should we bet on the
strong or bet on the many? This is a question of strategy similar
to the one faced by a practicing sociology, since if one chooses to
bet on the many (as Wertheim thinks we should) the choice can be
validated only by an intensive program of education, therefore an
exoteric androgogy.[46] Lest this formulation seem too abstract, let
me give a concrete and even operational example. Imagine a sociological mission as follows: "The bishops of Latin America, who
were summoned by the Celam to Argentina, have proclaimed that
the socioeconomic structures of the continent are unjust and that
it is imperative to change them immediately. Although the new development agencies want to be human, they foster a development

that has inhuman consequences: the rich grow richer and the poor grow poorer." By simply ending this description[47] with the question "why?", we would be back in Wertheim's dilemma. Moreover, we would be pinpointing a sociological phenomenon as important as the emission-and-reception of the encyclical known as *Populorum progressio*.[48]

One last matter reveals how the sociology of religion is caught between two other poles of socio-economic development: the pole of ethnological interest and the pole of revolutionary demands. It is evident that the value of development as such has been over-estimated and often slanted, unilateralized and hyper-occidentalized—until it has become something that ethnologists might disdainfully denounce as "the greatest mystification of the twentieth century." Indeed, only too often, development can be described as the rule of those who are *doing* over those to whom it is *done*: the reign of the developers over the developed, of the planners over the planned, of the teachers over the taught, of the aiders over the aided, of the motivators over the motivated and (why not?) the evangelizers over the evangelized. It is as if there were no reciprocity in this relation. It is as if "development" means only the transference of a prototype or application of a model, both of which have been brought in from the outside.[49] It is as if the only solution for a people being developed is to define themselves in the language and project themselves into the culture of the developer.[50] In some cases we find the complementary problem of a colonized people who appear to have no chance to be religious except through and in the religion of the colonizer. This is why the developer is caught in the crossfire[51] of the ethnologist who is concerned with local cultures and has always resisted the pseudo-hierarchies imposed on them by a ruling culture, and the theoretician (or practician) of radical change for whom "developmentalism" is only a subtle palliative or device for evading the basic problem.[52] For the ethnologist, development is uselessly traumatizing; for the revolutionary, it is a vain attenuation.

This is why, as Soedjatmoko says, socio-economic development is a "challenge to religion."[53] It requires the activation of more fundamental and specific forces which are indubitably part and parcel of the cultural-religious matrix in a society; and this mobilization becomes possible only when the motives are drawn "from the well-spring of religious life itself." This gives a new urgency to the old conflict between traditionalists and modernists, and perhaps it requires the expertise of specialists in something which one might call the "maieutics of development."[54] Such expertise would add a new dimension to a sociology of religion concerned with religious differences. We shall have to define its possible effect on the relation of this sociology with the other sciences of religion, such as ecclesiology, missiology and ecumenology.

Chapter 8

<u>Sic et Non:</u> Sociology, Christian Theology and the Sciences of Religion

The day is coming when the West will not only have to know and understand the cultural universe of non-westerners, but also value it as an integral part of human history. . . . for the encounter (or collision) between civilizations is always, in the last analysis, an encounter between two spiritual forces, even two religions.—Mircéa Eliade

We have already pointed out that what is called sociology of religion or religions was first created and developed under the influence of a religion which was considered to be dominant because it was the religion of a people who dominated the world. This was Christianity in its western forms: Protestantism and Catholicism. Thus sociology of religion emerged in a field already covered by Christian theology.

However, this same theology, in this same field, had already witnessed the emergence of other, non-theological, sciences of religion—although not without upsets and controversy. This meant that sociology, as a new arrival in the field, had to carve out its own field of action in an area between the sector traditionally claimed by theology and the sectors already held by the modernists of non-theological sciences. Our observations in this last chapter will deal with the crisscrossing of these various strains. By noting the interrelations between "Christian theology" and "sciences of religion" one can, quite neatly, draw a line around the material studied by sociology. But in setting this up, there are three precautions to take:

a) Our nomenclature which plays a singular (theology of religion) against a plural (sciences of religions) may seem to be what the Anglo-Saxons call "biased." Why couldn't we reverse the game and speak of Christian theologies (in the plural) and science of religion (in the singular)? Some people would certainly feel more at ease with this second configuration. For indeed how can we speak about Christian theology without pluralizing it according to the schools and historical phases which marked the cleavages within each of the great confessions? And, since men have still not succeeded in determining the essence (*das Wesen*) of Christianity, this pluralization would even seem to be necessary. However, must we speak of sciences of religion in the plural? It would seem more plausible to do so. On preceding pages we have just pleaded the case for pluralizing one of these sciences: sociology of religion. It is none the less true that, although there are several different sociologies of religion with diverse ties to several different sciences of religion (such as history, phenomenology, psychology, anthropology), there does persist a nostalgia for, if not unification, at least a concerted effort to achieve something resembling an interdisciplinary front; independent sociology of religion and the other non-theological sciences of religion have even postulated a common base of interest; for no matter what religious fact is being studied by a researcher in one discipline, he will have to call on the approaches, concepts and methods of the other disciplines, and consequently cannot do without a minimal familiarity with them.[1] As a result of this, just as the plural does crop out of the singular proclaimed by Christian theology, there is, conversely, a certain underlying unity in the apparent multiplicity of sciences of religion.

b) When one considers this diptych of Christian theology (or theologies) and the sciences (or science) of religion, it is evident that the subject can be treated from two different points of view. How Christian theology looks at the sciences of religions is one point of view; how the sciences of religion look at theology is another, and this other point of view is the one which interests us here. I see no objection to a possible third point of view which would be a synthesis putting the first two points of view in reciprocal relation and acting as a keystone to support the vault. One is free to predict its arrival on the scene, affirm that it is needed, or fear the consequences of its intervention. But if, after a century, we are still waiting for what Burnouf predicted would come in a few decades, should not we be even more cautious than he was, given the complexity which has intervened since his time? We are still struggling in the dark. Would that the destiny of sciences of religion and the providence of theology not permit this present century to end without announcing the break of day, even if the angel we are wrestling with must disappear, leaving us with a limp.

c) Finally, this means that the reader should not be surprised by the choice we have made and will be discussing on the pages to follow. It is a choice between two systems of gravitation. In one system the sciences of religion gravitate around a single theology and are subordinate to it; in the other system one or many theologies gravitate around the sciences of religions. As our preamble has already indicated, it is this second system of gravitation which concerns us here. This perspective may not suffice. But it is nevertheless a necessary one, even if it leads us to relativize both the content and the methods of theological absolutes.

Our first step is to determine the trajectory running from *theology* as a religious science of religion to the *non-religious sciences* of this religion or religions. Our second step is to examine a sample of this trajectory, and for this we have selected one which holds the record for longevity: Christian theology and history of religions. In our third step we shall take up three other examples which are more specifically sociological and note what seems to be their most significant points of tension: *Ethnology and missiology. Ecclesiology and sociology. Ecumenism and ecumenology.* We shall conclude the discussion with a few questions on the links between Christianity, religion and the sacred.

In accordance with the choice we have made, the material in our commentaries will be drawn from contemporary literature and will be non-theological. These commentaries may recapitulate analyses already made earlier in this book.

I. The Trajectory Running from Christian Theology to the Sciences of Religions

In his commentary on the history of relations between theology and the non-theological sciences of religion, Jean Séguy breaks the story into three phases:

The phase of *harsh mothers*. "To a great extent the history of relations between theology and the non-theological sciences of re-

ligions resembles a quarrel between generations within a family.
Mother theology has, for centuries, tried to prevent her daughters,
the "lay sciences," from leaving home. . . ."[2]

The phase of *foolish virgins.* This is the period of emancipation
for the lay sciences: history of religion, anthropology, ethnology,
psychology, sociology, etc. Not only do they rebel against their
theological matrix, they also boldly set up camp outside the
theological citadel. They act like foreigners and become natural-
ized citizens of another city.

Finally, the period of *repentant mothers* and *prodigal daughters.*
Theologies are converted to some of the methods and approaches
of the non-theological sciences. There is a decrease in anti-theologi-
cal polemics (already outmoded) in the non-theological sciences;
the doors are opened to believers and non-believers alike, on the
simple principle that neither belief nor non-belief can qualify or
disqualify research, since research has its own laws of procedure.

The only remaining problem is that of ultimate values in this community of researchers; but this problem, although it is now with us
as a fact of life, has never really been successfully conceptualized.[3]
These three phases suffice to introduce a look at the trajectory
running from theology to the sciences of religion.

Henri Charles Puech and Paul Vignaux have given a detailed account of the itinerary followed by "this novice, which is the Science
of Religions."[4] "We still argue about the date at which, sometime
during the nineteenth century, the name of this youngest daughter
was pronounced for the first time." However, aside from the label
and its appearance on the scene, we can trace her origins back to
Christian theologies since "in a sense the science of religions is no
more than a continued evolution of theological theses and meta-
physical views inherited from antiquity and the Middle Ages."[5]

According to Puech and Vignaux the factors responsible for setting
this in motion must have been:

A scholarly interest in Greek and Roman mythologies, stimulated
by Renaissance humanism.

Ethnographic data brought back from the New World by travelers
and missionaries, permitting a widening of the field of research and
reflexion which now "stretched from the religions of classic times
to Judaism and Christianity."

The controversy between Catholics and Protestants which not

only pluralized the interpretation of Christianity but also forced men to go beyond existing theology and seek their answers in the history of Christian origins and an objective study of dogmas.[6] At this stage "Biblical criticism was already questioning the authenticity of dates and sources of certain parts of the Scriptures, thus opening the way for future hypotheses and confrontations. . . ."[7]

The appearance of the great religious books of the East in the predominantly Christian European market. They were progressively translated and published.[8] We acquired a text of the Veda; in 1771 Anquetil Duperron produced a copy of the Zend-Avesta; in 1732 a first objective "life" of Mohammed was published. In 1760, under a pseudonym, Charles de Brosses published his *Culte des dieux fétiches ou parallèle de l'ancienne religion de l'Egypte avec la religion actuelle de Négritie.* It was not long before Champollion furnished the key to Egyptology. Comparative studies multiplied, and in their wake came a general burgeoning of rationalizations in which scientific intentions were amalgamated into impenitent philosophies ranging from Charles François Dupuis to Benjamin Constant.[9]

Directly and indirectly influenced by these studies, the sciences of religions spread rapidly and before long there were even university chairs devoted to research and teaching in fields like Egyptology, Assyriology, Indianology, Sinology, Iranology, Islamology, prehistory and ethnology. Initially, since Western sciences dealt with religions other than the dominant religion of the West, Christianity was little effected, removed as it was in space and in time—when Renan popularized "the idea of a scientific, non-confessional study of religions, particularly Christianity," he wrote about the Christianity of two thousand years ago. Almost a hundred years more would have to pass before the science of religion, through sociology, began its study of Christianity, first as a contemporary phenomenon and then as a tradition with origins in the past. The problem of its historical origins was cautiously approached and presented many difficulties.[10]

Poulat has ascertained in minute detail how the non-theological science of religions emerged in French institutions.[11] And France may be considered in all respects a pilot country for a study like this, since in other lands most teaching and research of religious

matters has either been confined to confessional or interconfessional
faculties of theology or, as in socialist countries, has been dominated
by the authoritarian ideology which until recently was the official
teaching of the Diamat (dialectical materialism) in the departments
of humane sciences.

In 1885 the faculties of theology, which had been an integral part
of Napoleon's university system, were almost completely done away
with. After violent and sometimes amusing debate, they were replaced
by a Fifth Section (called the Section des Sciences Religieuses) in the
Ecole Pratique des Hautes Etudes. At the time, Baron de Ravignan
deplored the event, saying: "Isn't it strange that the State, which
does not wish to maintain the study of theology in its universities,
has introduced into the Ecole des Hautes Etudes something as indeterminant as 'Sciences of religions.' "[12]

Yet this "indeterminant something" soon clearly defined its field
of study. As honorary president of this Fifth Section, Le Bras
praised the inventiveness of this French achievement which had
established forty professorships specializing in the sciences of religions and made their lectures available to the general public.
About one third of these chairs were specifically devoted to a scientific study of Christianity. Adjoining these was the Fourth Section
of the same school (History and Philology) with sixty chairs for
"exegesis of religious texts and study of the religious history of
civilizations as a regular program."[13] Finally, to these was added
the Sixth Section (Economics and Social Studies) with a dozen or
so chairs which recently "because of their general interest and the
needs of their annual program, have been treating religious material
and offering complementary courses and lectures on the subject."[14]
We will not mention the Collège de France and the many other institutes which have opened their doors to these studies.

If we have treated the case of France with a certain self-satisfac-
tion that is because ever since the revolution of 1789 it offers a remarkable example of the trajectory we have been studying: first
the Revolution, then the neo-Christianity of French socialism,[15]
the radicalism of its laicism, the experience in depth of modernism
at the beginning of this century, the dynamic energy of "social
Christianity" in its Protestant sector,[16] the belated but spectacular
social awakening in its Catholic sector, movements such as Christian

democracy and social Catholicism,[17] the organization of *l'Action Catholique* and *l'Action Missionnaire*.[18] All of these phenomena have attracted the attention of Christian theologians as well as those concerned with scientific research in the field of religion. . . . The interest was probably mutual.

Naturally, it is not possible here to give a detailed account, even for a single country, of all points on the trajectory which leads from Christian theologies to the nontheological sciences of religion. This appears even less possible when we consider that at the end points of the curve it is now sometimes difficult to distinguish between the two approaches. But, using some of Séguy's propositions, we can at least make a first sketch and break down the trajectory into four phases.

1. *The phase of confusion.* This could also be called the phase of non-differentiation, corresponding roughly to what Maritain called "sacral Christianity" or to what Lucien Febvre in a few pages of his *Rabelais* called the phase of tutelage, referring to the control exercised by theology over the sciences of man, even for many years after the natural sciences had escaped from theological domination. During this phase, epistemological tutelage and control was closely tied to the politico-theological system of Christianity, either as the official State religion or as the majority religion dominating public opinion. To deny the *cujus regio ejus religio* was, after all, a new idea in Europe, and it was not until the radical reforms of Christian Protestantism that the real challenge would come. It is generally recognized that the Anabaptists were foremost in championing the cause. For years the sociology of religion was wrapped in the swaddling clothes of social theology. And many of the sciences of religion during that time merited the boutade attributed (inaccurately) to Marx: "Bacon said that theology of physics was a virgin consecrated to the service of God and, therefore, sterile; when Bacon liberated physics from theology it became fecund."[19]

2. *The phase of collision.* Whether it be history, hermeneutics, textual criticism, anthropology or sociology, sooner or later the collision occurs: it is the crossing of the desert on the way to the promised land. During the French dispute of 1885, the collision came between the minister Armand Fallières and Mgr. Freppel. Fallières' position:

In the theological material taught in the schools of our country there is one part which must never totally disappear. It is evident that religions, no matter how one looks at them, are an integral part of human history and that there is every reason to examine them critically, compare them and show where they came from and what has influenced them, just as we would do with history itself.

Mgr. Freppel's rebuttal:

Either this examination, comparison and criticism will conform to Catholic teachings (and in this case why did you eliminate the study of theology from the State universities?) or else this examination, comparison and criticism will contradict Catholic teachings (and in this case you are betraying the principle of neutrality which led you to eliminate the faculty of theology in the first place). There is no middle ground.[20]

3. *The phase of collusion.* This *sic et non* is not as absolute as it seems and the garish verbiage has already disappeared from the scene. There have always been souls like Ghandi to whom "the love of truth has taught the art of compromise." Fusion and accommodation were soon to become the order of the day. A careful proselytizing would soon attempt to Christianize what was un-Christianizable. This is the phase in which geologies were adjusted to conform to Genesis,[21] Biblical criticism was more or less salvaged from the unbelievers,[22] modernism was channeled,[23] socialisms were re-Christianized and Christianities were neo-socialized,[24] sociologies were pastorized or theologized, and the bloodstream of ethnologies was drained off into apologetics.

We have seen how Feuerbach waxed ironic over the pseudo-sciences engendered by theologians in their efforts to sublimate their doctrines into "astro-theology," "litho-theology," "insecto-theology," "arido-theology" and "pyro-theology."

If the accommodations and collusions were like this in the natural sciences, one could expect them to be no less widespread in the even more propitious domain of human sciences.

4. *The phase of a coherence?* This is the phase that we seem to be entering now, although at an unequal pace, depending on what religion or what confession or even what school within the non-theo-

logical science of religion we are dealing with. As soon as one ceases to consider these various points of departure as anti-theologies, they tend to relax and cease to consider themselves theology's adversary. Nevertheless, we are left with a dual interpretation: on the one hand there is the auto-interpretation which Christianity makes of itself (this is theology); on the other hand there is the hetero-interpretation which the sciences of religion make of Christianity. But this hetero-interpretation is no longer based on the fact (which has become secondary) that the interpreter is of a different belief or has negative convictions about a belief other than the one being examined. It is now based on the fact that the interpreter speaks a different language.

Optimistic view: When the various sciences of religion, each in its own language, describe and rationalize the arguments which theology has expressed in its own language, they are really doing no more than repeating a process of translation already completed by theology, since the language of theology is quite different from the language of the kerygma and the catechism. If theology's translation and transcription of the original message are considered plausible, even necessary, for the life of religion, why is not this relationship between faith and rationalization equally practicable between theology and the sciences of religion? Shades of Saint-Simon!

Pessimistic and, perhaps, realistic view: Theology and the sciences of religion always have and always will speak different languages with no possibility of making an adequate translation from one to the other; here, more than ever, *traduttore tradittore.* They can coexist, but without ever becoming a single enterprise. There is no *Aufhebung* to effect a synthesis of thesis and antithesis. And the persistence of this contradiction is even a healthy sign. This tension, in the tradition of Proudhon, is basic to the only probable system of coherence. In this respect some of us still adhere more or less to the ideas of Proudhon.

II. Theology and the History of Religions

In the *corpus* of sciences dealing with religion, the history of religions has had a head start and has opened up new areas for exploration; this is why there is a tendency to identify the new fields of investigation with the parent form of inquiry. It is true that the profession of historian can induce a desire to become so comprehensive and so extensive that the field begins to look like the locus of all the social sciences.[25] If history in general is indeed the "science of man in time,"[26] then the history of religions includes not only all religions (since there has never been a religion which was not the religion of men living in time), but also almost all of the ways of studying these religions. This would include sociology, since the line of demarcation between social history and the sociology of history has proved to be very thin. It would also include theology, since every theological system is produced by a man or group of men working at a specific time, and since any detailed account of theological content would include the conditions under which it was produced, transmitted and accepted. This is why our reflections on the relation between theology and history also apply to the relation of these companion sciences to sociology.

From this point of view, one of the most interesting approaches to sociology is the route followed by Wach, the high church theologian and scholarly historian of religions. We have already pointed out elsewhere that Wach has two approaches and that he alternates between them; first he is the historian, concerned with being consistent with the facts as he extracts something like a sociology out of theology; then he acts like an impenitent theologian and uses his historical data to support a phenomenology, letting sociology and phenomenology coalesce into typologies which have been polarized by a latent ecumenism.[27] Indeed, ecumenism seems to be Wach's final goal: "It is difficult to see how a Christian theologian, especially if he be a sociologist and an historian to boot, could find rest in any but an ecumenically oriented theology."[28] There are many ways of combining these three terms (theology, history and sociology). The passage quoted indicates the way in which Wach combined them. Perhaps there are other ways to do this. They will be related to the way proposed by Wach, but at the same time quite distinct from it.

1. SPECULATIVE THEOLOGY AND POSITIVE THEOLOGY

The first effect of history of religions (as a non-theological science) on the inner structure of a theology will probably be an increased intensity and extension of positive theology. As has often been pointed out, the great temptation for speculative theology is to exploit positive theology's weakness for argumentation and end up using it as a simple storehouse of examples. *Probatur ex scriptura. Probatur ex traditione.* . . . In the heat of dispute apologists risk over-extending themselves by drawing their arguments from agreements and disagreements which, on examination, turn out to be merely extrapolations. In the end of the argument we get a triumphant demonstration of the true religion which is then identified with Christianity; this, in turn is identified with one or another of the Christian confessions which is then surreptitiously identified with one or another of its auto-interpretations; this self-interpretation turns out to be regulated, audited and defined by a set of requirements imposed by a previous historical event (whose history has been adjusted to conform to the needs of subsequent rationalizations; these requirements then turn out to be not only definite and defining, but also definitive. At least this is the "ideal type" (in Weber's sense of that phrase) of a speculative and apologetic theology which would domesticate all of history for its own purposes.

To understand the need for a counter-position opposing this ideal type of apologetic theology, one has only to reread the debate of two decades ago over the return to historical methods in face of the totalitarian arguments advanced by a certain scholastic theology (a restoration that was ultimately much indebted to the work of Chenu.[29])

What effect did this activation (or reactivation) of history of religions have on positive theology? First, it liberated the historian by giving autonomous status to his dossiers, each one of which could now be examined for itself, *en situation,* quite independent of any Church interpretation. Scrutinizing the data *en situation* meant that it was correlated to its own place in time, space and socio-cultural environment, with its own roots and manner of being; the data became, in the words of Paul Claudel, *genitum non factum,* engendered, not fabricated, and above all not fabricated, and above all not fabricated *post facto.*

And then this reactivation of historical method affected theology by relativizing the dossiers with a two-way point of view: the Christianizing of Constantine is also seen as the Constantinization of Christianity, to use an example more than a thousand years old. And, likewise, taking up another age-old theme, the Christianizing of a philosophy into a theology does not occur without a certain theologizing of Christianity. Or else, as in the diagnostic made by Troeltsch: perhaps the sect is only a latent protest which evangelical and apocalyptic religion makes against the established Church, and the religious Order is perhaps the ecclesiastication of a sect. Or, as others will maintain, the canonization of saints and the names given to them is in some respects an auto-canonization of rank and prestige such as may reign in any given society. If this is not true, then how is one to explain the rare presence of plebeians on those lists? Etc. Generally speaking, history tends to see a natural and social process where theology discerns natural and divine intervention. Perhaps one does not exclude the other. But the simple fact that the force of social processes is not excluded by the theory of divine intervention suffices to open up a wealth of texts, data and facts which positive theology can explore without constraint.

And lastly, the reactivation of historical method affected theology in what might be called its furthest reaches by de-normalizing these dossiers, which is to say, by dispossessing them of their value as norms. How many centuries did it take for a dossier labeled "heresy" to be recaptioned "a brotherhood which has left the fold"! And how many decades more will it take to pass from the dossier labelled "sect" to one called "religions of protest," from the dossier labelled "pagans" to one called "traditional religions"[30] or "unspoiled religions that testify to the human spirit,"[31] etc. And, more, generally, how long will it take to pass from the crypto-manicheism of a certain speculative theology to the peace-loving ideal of a positive theology which, as we have already said, would be both intensive and extensive. In its first stages, the history of religions is, like all early history, untouched by this manicheism:

> The lesson to be learned from the intellectual development of mankind is quite clear: the sciences have always become more

productive and ultimately more useful when they have deliberately shed the old anthropocentrism of good and evil. Today we would laugh at the chemist who distinguished between bad gases like chlorine and good gases like oxygen; but this was once a serious question, and if the early chemists had adopted this manichean classification they would have sunk into its mire of verbiage, much to the detriment of their knowledge of matter.[32]

This postulate implies that for any scientific study of religions the domain is not *a priori* divided into two, one side for the true or good religions and the other side for the false or bad ones. As Isambert once wrote in a critique of the phenomenological approach, a true knowledge of Christianity is not the same as a knowledge of true Christianity. More precisely, the problem of truth and error lies elsewhere: it depends on the degree to which recorded religious data conforms to the idea we have of it, whether we be believers, doubters or indifferent observers. It is in this sense that religions which theology holds to be false have a kind of truth for the sciences of religion and that a science of religion may point out errors in religions which theology holds to be true. Errors in this case would be illusions, the quality of imagination generating emotional response, memories which have been repressed or sublimated, etc. As Marx said: "One should not judge an era by the image it has of itself any more than one judges a man by the idea he has of himself. . . ." This does not imply that this process of self-presentation to self, which a good part of the time is unconsciously fictive or deliberately false, has not been fruitful for religions present and past.[33] But the question of value is quite different from the question of truth. Christopher Columbus' knowledge of geography had no value; it was partially imaginary and partially apocalyptic. Nevertheless it is true that he discovered the New World, even if he did think that it was Asia and that he had found the river flowing through Eden. Fictitious saints have not performed any fewer miracles than the real ones. In some cases one is tempted to say that they have performed more.

The fact is, as we have already pointed out, that the various sciences of religion started out by examining the truth of religions which are, so to speak, without value: dead religions, religions of other eras, marginal religions located in faraway corners of the globe. Even when they examined Christianity, they approached their subject by withdrawing from it. Before writing his *Life of Jesus,* Ernest Renan was a professor of Hebrew and Chaldean languages. And we all know that, even so, he did not seem sufficiently distanced from his subject.[34] Indeed, as Poulat points out, whenever the non-theological (so-called "positive") sciences have given up this objectifying distance of time and space they appear to be "irreligious" despite their claim to be "religious" sciences. This is still true today, and these non-theological sciences will probably continue to be thought irreligious, just as islamology is probably condemned in certain parts of Islam or the sociology of Marxism in countries under a Jdanovism or its equivalent.

And this will continue until positive theology integrates this stubborn resistance of the "positive" sciences, as it has indeed been doing for the past hundred years, before, during and after European modernism. The Old Testament, the New Testament, the patristic tradition and theological schools have all passed before the analytical eye of historians who would verify their documents and monuments. Then came the history of the other Christian confessions, bringing advantages to all three branches of Christianity as, unencumbered by teratological descriptions, they increased their knowledge of each other. The effect of historical studies on the smaller Christian sects has been slower to take hold, despite the campaign *spes contra spem* led by Emile Léonard.[35] Historical studies of the great living non-Christian religions are beginning to have an effect, but only in a way once described by Heiler as: what happens when a religious history is polarized by an inter-religion cooperation.[36] As for the last stage, the one which Heiler associates with the seventh candelabra in the Soufi rite symbolizing "those Seekers after God who belong to no religion,"[37] it presents a vast open field for nonbelievers and those who serve no god, and may constitute what Le Bras called "one of the principle chapters, certainly one of the most moving, in all of sociology of religion." One could point out that this last phase is still inchoative and that the field is as yet barely defined.[38] And, since this is largely a contemporary phenomenon, historians have handed it over to sociology and the theologies for whom it is now a meeting ground.[39]

2. THEOLOGY AND PHENOMENOLOGY

Whereas, in matters historical, theology must check its concrete data with a science of religion, in phenomenology it confronts yet another science of religion with which its abstract data must be checked. In one sense, a phenomenology is an ally, since it is something like a meta-theology; in another sense phenomenology is a competitor, at least insofar as any hetero-interpretation competes with auto-interpretations. But, in light of the often very close ties between them, it is evident that this alliance (or rivalry) between a phenomenology and theology can effect the form of sociology itself.

Relying exclusively on a comparative approach, phenomenology does indeed discern recurring types and essenses, forms and categories that are *a priori* to religious experience;[40] and because of this it tends to speak in terms of universals which apply to individual religions or to the group in which they belong. This means that it is heading down the road toward the archetypal structure in which a supertheology will finally gobble up history. The same could be said for structural analysis (which is phenomenology's adversary, but nevertheless related to its approach, at least on this point).

This gives rise to a new confrontation. Whereas a theology thinks of itself as a whole to which the various sciences of religion belong, phenomenology, particularly in the study of religion, willingly considers itself to be that "whole," a kind of theology of theologies in which any particular theology constitutes only one of the parts. Whereas history tends to consider theology as a moment in time, phenomenology tends to consider it as one example of a kind.

In the phenomenology-oriented grid set up by Wach, religious *experience* as such is considered to have three forms of *expression:*

1. Theoretical expression: doctrine.
2. Practical expression: cult.
3. Sociological expression: religious community.

Therefore theology is only one of the theoretical forms of religious expression after the phase of primitive mythologizing.[41] Wach describes the process in the following manner:

What is expressed by the primitive mind as myth is conceived of in terms of doctrine at a more advanced level of civilization. . . . With the situation permitting and the necessary sociological conditions being given, the way is now prepared for the establishment of an over-all *authority* to decide and define doctrine. A more or less unified system of a normative character ("doctrine") is thus substituted for a variety of independent mythological traditions, associated only by chance. This marks the origin of "theology" proper. The work of collection, redaction, and codification continues. The written tradition now replaces the oral tradition in the form of sacred writings. In order to rationalize the fundamental conceptions which are the expressions of particular religious experiences, theologians develop normative systems of faith bolstered with appropriate apologetic defenses. Concise summaries are embodied in creeds, while more elaborate reflections and meditations regarding the contents of the faith are left to the theologians. Theology eventually produces philosophy.[42]

By applying his method to theology, he has given a beautiful example of a phenomenological "genesis." As the rest of Wach's text shows, this genesis is induced step by step from observations made on a variety of religions, both ancient and modern, dead and living (at least seventeen different religions are cited in support of his constructed model). Thus the origins he refers to are *a priori* and of an ideal type which can be used for all particular religions. According to this view Christian theology is not only just one of the phases in the doctrinal expression of Christian experience; it is also just one of many theologies, all of which represent a similar phase in the development of their respective religious experiences. Another way of saying this would be: not only does theology speak a different language than phenomenology; it is also blind to the double sense that phenomenology sees in it.

This being the case, it is not easy to imagine what would be the structural basis of a mutual appreciation. Could they make an alliance? An ecumenically oriented theology such as the one sought by Wach could then find in phenomenology a way of arriving at "a comprehension of the various religions deeper and more adequate than their own understanding of themselves."[43] But to theology this

is bound to seem ambiguous. It would also seem ambiguous to sociology. As for Wach, although he was certainly tempted by this desire to comprehend (fully presented in his *Verstehen*), at least he
continued to heed sociological explanations, even the functional ones
which had been duly localized, characterized, dated and detailed. But
Wach's open mind is not always the case. For example, in Mircéa
Eliade's *Traité d'Histoire des religions* there seems to be an alliance
between the phenomenology doing the research and the theologies
being researched; this involves an implicitly uneasy alliance with
history as such and is explicitly recalcitrant to all detailed sociological documentation.[44]

A structural organization like this can also set up a tension, and
this tension can be two-pronged. For the phenomenology of religion
also moves in two directions.

On the one hand, phenomenology hangs its conceptualizing on the
idea of Providence in history, something like a harmony preestablished
by God. An existential theology (as are most Christian theologies)
would be uneasy about the way this overlooks God's intervention in
history. After all, Christians are etymologically messianic; they believe that it is in the nature of human history to be upset by interventions of divine history (and vice versa); this explains those who
resist the idea of gratuitous grace, blind faith and the *a priori*
necessities of a whole program for world history. Kierkegaard resists Hegel. Dostoievsky resists the Grand Inquisitor; and, from
Dostoievsky come the essential ideas of Nikolai Berdiaeff's person-
alism.[45] Kierkegaard, Dostoievsky and Berdiaeff are not highly regarded
in the annals of sociology of religion. This may be regrettable. At any
rate, it does not mean that these men have nothing to tell us in
this field.

On the other hand, although phenomenology does not tie its conceptions to the structure of some divine Spirit, it does tie them to
the structure of the human mind in the manner of structural analysis; and it does tie them to the impersonal structure of "myths"
and "logics" which, without being a part of any one human mind,
does function in all of them. And this theology will have to explain the nature of this self-consciousness in respect to which it
appears to be a simple consciousness with no means of self-appraisal.
In like manner, in days past, theology had to explain itself by in-

voking the idea of *natura naturans* and *natura naturata*. And, just as Spinoza once yearned for *natura sive Deus,* theology could certainly evoke a *conscientia sive Deus*! But would not this be a confession of failure and lead to its own demise? As for the sociology of religion, it is not likely to renounce a conceptualizing procedure and should not do so; but it would make a grave error to lock itself into a single sociological structure, whether this be considered absolute or just one of the possibilites.[46]

3. THE THEOLOGY OF HISTORY AND THE HISTORY OF THEOLOGIES

"You have lost the game because your conception of History remains the same as Bossuet's in his discourse on universal history." This was the boutade that a well-known man-of-letters once made to a young theologian. The young man would be less disconcerted today since the theology of history now includes a theology of terrestrial realities (an unexpected progeny of Saint-Simon's "terrestrial morality"); it also includes the theology of "the Temporal" or theologies treating the temporal annex of the Church-spiritual; indeed, it now also includes theologies treating what a generous but equivocal slogan calls "all religion in all of life," as well as the theologies of "prolonged incarnations" (*incarnations continuées*) which have been theologically protested by other theologies. A whole vocabulary, both conciliatory and ironic, has grown out of these endeavors.[47]

This effort to re-theologize history has its own *raison d'être*. It represents a protest against a previous theology which either reduced human history to an offshoot of Eternity or else (and also) sublimated failures in human history by interpreting them as successes for Eternity. It may well be that the manifestations of this protest in Catholic theology came about as the third phase of a process and implies two antecedents. First there was the religious reform of Protestantism with its economic ethics analyzed in detail by Weber, its substitution of worldly virtues for other-worldly virtues, its redistribution of elements in the tripartite community of clergy, laymen and monastics, its association of religious virtues with atti-

tudes favorable to capitalism, its belief that economic success in
this world is a sign that salvation is assured in the next one.[48]
The second phase in this protest was the phase of "social reform,"
since that was the term which these neo-Christianities used for
early forms of socialism: in his *Nouveau Christianisme* Saint-
Simon had already proposed an ecumenical and Promethean
"theology of history" and the fumbling young socialisms hardly
did more than copy it.[49]

From the point of view of the social history of modern religions,
contemporary theologies of historical realities such as work, lay
life, earthly happiness and man's mastery of nature, represent
no more than a reissue *ad intra* of old messages which had already
been sent *ad extra* but were neither heard nor heeded. Nevertheless, despite its late arrival on the scene, this theology of history
and historical actions is very welcome, especially at a moment
when, because of technical progress and the revolutionary developments in sanitation which accompany it, because of the unequal
development in agricultural production and demographic reproduc-
tion, the history of mankind is in danger, and only worldwide
concerted human action can ward off the threat.[50]

But the intervention of this theology is one thing; delimiting
the field of this intervention is quite a different problem. Sometimes it looks as if, according to these new points of view, everything which had not yet been "theologized" was now considered
indefinitely and interminably theologizable. However, these more
or less explicit claims run into three limiting factors which are all
sociological as well as theological.

a) *Limitations which the de-theologized imposes on the theologizable:* Doubtlessly it is a healthy sign that theologies of history, although they may have been formulated in the terms of Christian
theology, very soon learned to distinguish between two Christianities: the sacral Christianity of the Middle Ages and the profane
Christianity which a later age has been called upon to establish.
It is also a sign of lucidity that at this point Church theologies soon
began to evolve into theologies of lay life. But the very idea of
desacralization and declericalization implies that in this process
a whole order of factual questions must escape from the control
of theology and theologians.[51] If this did not happen, theologians

would be forced to improvise theology's *raisons d'être* in episte-
mologies or other disciplines for which they are not prepared. Moreover, there is every reason to believe that theologians have been
quite willing to submit to the rigors of these new disciplines which
offer something like a vocation, yet dispense them from exercising
their former profession. Whether or not this professional intervention in "the Realm of the Temporal" is tied to one of the natural
sciences or to a human science, or to both of these at once, each
of these intervening disciplines does carry its own weight; and although theology of history was welcome to officiate at their baptism, it would not be welcome as their master.[52]

b) *Limitations imposed on the theologizable by the non-theologizable:* When we cited the well-meaning slogan "All religion in all of
life" we saw how this attitude only led to a dilemma.

On the one hand this slogan calls for a Christianized society moving toward a Christian state, or at least a state controlled by Christian politics; or sometimes, on a more modest scale, it calls for the
establishment of some Christian social institution such as a labor
union or a youth movement. All of this would be produced *for
and by* Christians; and, even when it is also *for* non-Christians, it
would be a Christian show. But this process leads to the opposite
of theologization: theocracy, presbyterianocracy and Christian-
ocracy.

On the other hand this calls for a Christian society or institution
to be encysted in an over-all non-Christian society. But these cysts
are ghettos, and this is the "pillarization" described by Dutch
sociology. It is as if they thought that their program to confession-
alize a society or an institution would be justified by its intensity
but disqualified by its extension—since intensive and extensive
qualities exist in inverse proportion to each other. Because of this
dialectic and a program of de-confessionalization, such experiments
sooner or later subscribe to some form of de-theologization, even
when this process is firmly held in check by Church authorities.

Obviously, the "profanization" of "Christendom" seems to imply
a progressive diminishing of theological control,[53] and this calls
for a counter-weight lest the theological enterprise be so watered
down that it becomes vulnerable to Feuerbach's attack.

c) *The limitations imposed by the history of theologies:* The wave

of "theologies of history" is a social fact, an historical event that
has been dated and documented. It is also a phenomenon that has
not been seen before; and it is probably this aspect which makes
theology of history of special interest to sociology of religion for
which the content of the message is less important than the attitude
taken toward it—or the fact that the message exists, is transmitted
and received, competes with a parallel message, and will someday
be replaced by another message. The subsequent message, for
example, might be one already received and recorded in the literature concerning theology of history:

> Making not only individuals, but also society, submit to the
> laws of the Gospels, this is then the task of *l'Action Catholique*.
> . . . It is a magnificent task and is indeed identical with the
> task of establishing the Kingdom of God on earth. . . . The
> organization of social Christianity is a complex reality. . . .
> Its body is the State, its soul is the Church. . . . May we all
> contribute to the ultimate victory of the most beautiful and
> noble of causes: the system of a Christian social order, which
> is to say, the Kingdom of God on earth. . . .[54]

It is not the task of scientific analysis to confirm or deny a theological message like this. But it can and should examine it in the
light of other theological messages which are different or contradictory; the analysis should ask itself questions about its own approach and about the implications of the message it is approaching
(for example: what is meant by submitting societies to the laws of
the Gospel?[55] The analysis should ask for definitions (for example:
what precisely is meant by "the Kingdom of God" whose body
is the State and soul is the Church?[56]). Analysis should ask for
identifications of entities such as "the Kingdom of God on earth"
and "the system of Christian social order." And after this analysis
of content, the message should be compared with other past and
present messages, noting their isomorphisms and discordances. To
situate the message one asks: who sent it? in whose name did he
send it? who received it? how did he use it? etc. After asking questions like these, a theology of religion cannot fail to enter a field
of history and even of sociology of theologies. Once again, the theology's apparent absolute will have been relativized. This, of course,

is why on the preceding pages we suggested that for the sciences of religion *amica theologia, magis amica veritas.* One cannot help remembering the controversies which arose when Thomism, the queen of theologies, was examined from an historical point of view, or when the "historical method" lagged in setting up a theory of *genres* for classifying the absolute nature of canonic literature. This never-ending conflict can itself, in turn, be viewed from the perspective of theology: "The God who withstands us is the same as the God who gives us the strength to stand up against Him," said Ernest Hello about a century ago in a commentary on Jacob's night of struggle with the Angel. It is likely to be through this formula or some similar parable that the believer doing research in the sciences of religion will come to realize that a confrontation of his belief and his science is probably both inevitable and salutary. One might expect this route to lead him to regard all of history itself (including the history of theologies) as a theological proposition, despite the fact that in doing so he would, at the same time, be making a sociological statement.

III. Christian Theology and the Sociology of "Homo Religiosus"

By borrowing Marc Bloch's comprehensive definition of history we have already introduced into our reflexions on the history of religions a part of what we have to say not only about the non-theological sciences but also about those which are not specifically historical, such as sociology. The field is immense and, since we cannot do justice to it here, we refer the reader to the brief which we have already mentioned.[57]

A few reflections come to mind, if only to serve as an introduction to that brief or as a conclusion to the remarks being made here. These reflections are comments on three scientific approaches and three matching theological approaches: ethnology and missiology, sociology and ecclesiology, ecumenism and ecumenology.

1.ETHNOLOGY AND MISSIOLOGIES

It would be simplistic and even foolhardy to maintain that Christian missiologies benignly claim to have been no more than the pure and simple forebearers of Truth to a world living in darkness. There are many examples of missionary movements which think of those whom they have evangelized as a first step in the evangelizing or re-evangelizing of the evangelizers themselves.[58] But, whenever this simplistic formula has been used (and it has been used), a makeshift missiology has been exposed to (or, in the case of a lucid missiology, has confronted) several principles which, more and more, are being considered as postulates by the active ethnologies.

1) When faced with Christian religions (especially Catholicism and Protestantism), non-Christian religions (both universalist and ethnicized) have assumed the configuration of a dominated religion faced with a dominating religion; or, more precisely, the configuration of a religion in a dominated culture facing the religion of a ruling culture. An extreme example of this would be the religion of a colonized people facing the religion of the colonizers.[59] This is why the loyalty of a religion to a population (or, the population's loyalty to a religion) depends on the way in which this religion permits its people to resist the submission demanded of them; or even, more simply, it depends on the manner in which this religion makes it possible for the alienated population to identify itself.

2) In the wrenching asunder of loyalties so characteristic of people in the Third World, one of the middle terms for this identification has been (and often still is) to accept and simultaneously refuse Christianity by espousing new versions of the Christian religion, making it paramessianic, messianic and millenarian.[60] Examples of this can be seen in the messianic peasant revolts in South America, the outbreak of nativism in North America, the black Christs in the South Sahara region of Africa, the Cargo cults in Oceania, etc. Sometimes these movements are limited to the establishment of new religious cults, sometimes they spread into the field of social action and revolt. In any case, missiology is now considered to include this "messialogy."

3) In today's movements for national independence the tradition-

al or majority religion often tends to become a people's cultural means of national identification, and (when Christianity is the religion imported by the occupying power) it serves as their means of resistance and protest to the occupation: this is what Von der Mehden shows in his comparative study of three countries in Southeast Asia. The local religion becomes the "emblem" (to use Durkheim's word) of independence, of identity and national unity.[61] This is why missiology and its messages, with an acuity hitherto unknown, faces the problem of its "ethnicization," "nationalization" and "acculturation."[62]

4) Finally, in this worldwide movement toward political, sociocultural and socio-economic independence and therefore also in the planning and programming of the development which this independence implies, Christian theories will, rightly or wrongly, be judged by their non-proselytizing contribution to what is generally known as Cooperative Development.[63] From this come the cultural (economic, ecumenical and meta-ecumenical) problems of missionary activity.[64] The new order of problems which this raises for missiology are not dissimilar to those already imposed on theology insofar as the latter has been progressively led to treat traditionally Christian countries as "fields of mission."[65] This is why the ties binding ethnologies to missiologies can be considered similar to those binding sociologies to ecclesiologies.

2. ECCLESIOLOGIES AND SOCIOLOGIES

Sociology's impact on ecclesiology is more recent than the one made by history or even ethnology, although, as Raymond Aron has pointed out, in the form of a sociology of history it goes back as far as Marx and even Montesquieu.[66] As a sociology of religion, its godfather was probably Saint-Simon; Marx and Engels were certainly its precursors;[67] Comte held the baby at the baptismal fount;[68] Durkheim and the French school early in this century guided it into maturity;[69] and, as everyone knows, since the 1930's Le Bras has been bringing it to the attention of theologians.[70] Finally, there are three men responsible for the groundwork of all contemporary reflexion on the subject: Weber, Troeltsch and Wach.[71]

Sociology's ties to ecclesiology can be seen in four phases:

1. *From classical ecclesiology to a social theology.* In this phase social life is no longer considered to be a product of individual moral virtues: no longer does "the patience of the poor and the generosity of the rich assure each of them an equal chance for eternal salvation." Social life becomes subject to a detailed list of normative precepts, all derived from theology. The social doctrine of the Church (or churches) is supposed to be matched in practice by Christian institutions of the society and in the society. The name of "Christian sociology" was even given to one such ecclesiology when it was applied to the sphere of social action. This name has many times been derided for its ambiguity. But, in fact, it has persisted as an intra-theological development of theology: social philosophy and social theology as distinct from sociology; Christian theologies of society as distinct from sociologies of Christianity and the sociology of these theologies.

2. *From a social theology to a pastorate sociology.* To the extent that theology runs into what we have called "the already de-theologized" or the "forever non-theologizable" its specific efforts are deflected from the problems of applying Christianity *to society* and diverted into the methodological problem of applying sociology *to ecclesiastic life:* the morphology and demography of "Christian peoples"; the typology of their Church membership; the topology of cults and their locations; analysis of vocations and calls to the priesthood; evaluations of increase and decrease in fidelity to the Church; estimations and correlations of these factors . . . etc. This sector has generally been known as the field of pastorate sociology or socio-ecclesiastic research, but not without controversy over the precise relation between this sociologizing theology (which some, like Leclerc, still call "socio-theology") and the non-theological sociologies sometimes referred to as "scientific" or "independent."[72] In order to distinguish between the two approaches some people have proposed that two terms be used: "religious sociology" and "sociology of religion."[73]

3. *From a sociologizing theology to a sociologized theology.* In this phase we meet up with the locus of history and, consequently, with the conjunction of theological subject matter (see above) and the methods of a sociology which has pushed beyond empiri-

cism and moved toward an operative or even cooperative sociology: this new sociology, by suppressing the distinction between the sociologizing subject and the sociologized object, soon affirms the need for self-inquiry, self-consciousness and self-development. There is a hypothesis that this sociologized theology should perform what Newman called a "consultation with the faithful."[74] This is obviously impossible or at least not advisable unless it is matched in practice by some corresponding institutional development like a congregationalism (i.e., a Church which both participates and is participated in).

4. *From a theological sociology to a non-theological sociology.* This trajectory really embraces the three phases which preceded it by moving from a previous *terminus a quo* to a future *terminus ad quem*. Its point of departure is indeed similar to Comte's, in which the theology, according to Arbousse-Bastide, is so ultra-religious that it can be self-consistent only by ending up in a religion and its cults. Its point of arrival is the one proposed by Wach: a sociology that is no more Christian than it is Moslem, Buddhist or Jewish: a non-theological sociology of all theology and all religion. This is independent sociology of religion; it is equally distant from apologetics and polemics, and it is ruled solely by its own epistemology, methodology and deontology.[75] It is not utilitarian and therefore its hands are clean. But we do not really know what to do with it: this is probably what Péguy meant when he said it has no hands at all. There is little corresponding praxis for this basic research.[76] Its praxis will come only with the emergence of religious phenomena out of a mass media and/or a generalized ecumenism.

5. *Ecumenism and ecumenology.* We have reserved the term "ecumenology" to translate the word *Œkumenik* proposed by a German theoretician, and we are using it here to differentiate between the scientific approach to interreligious and interconfessional relations and the historical ecumenisms which advocate one or another of these interrelations.

The various stages of ecumenism have often been described as stages in the development of a theological science for the Christian church.[77] The movement is from polemics to apologetics, from apologetics to symbolics, from symbolics to *Konfessionskunde,* and from this to ecumenism properly speaking (inter-denominational within a confession, then interconfessional within the one or many Christian religions).[78]

Just as often, the various entries to the ecumenical world have been tabulated in order of accessibility: after inter-denominational relations (within Protestantism) and interconfessional relations (within Christianity) come interreligion relations (among the great religions on a worldwide religious front) and then relations between convinced believers and convinced non-believers.[79] All, including atheism, are included in the Universal Declaration of Human Rights as formulated by a commission for the United Nations.[80]

Making a projection from the outline of these two evolutions, we see ecumenology as the point of intersection between a more and more intensive desire for peaceful coexistence and a more and more extensive desire for a universal belief. Thus ecumenology confronts every ecumenism with the same double question about its intensity and its extension, and, in any case, offers these points as a frame of reference. It is not unwarranted to suppose that in this formula we are touching the keystone for the whole architecture of relations between the sciences of religion and the Christian and non-Christian theologies. And it is strange to note that this ultimate problem has taken so long (and will certainly take longer) to come to the foreground: the problem of an ecumenology which views with scientific objectivity the various Christian and non-Christian ecumenisms and is the sole Telstar permitting efficient and rapid transmission and reception of messages sent and received by the various religions. Perhaps this is, after all, only the final example of a dialectic which appears everywhere as soon as theologies are referred to the sciences of religion. But in saying this we are simply formulating (or reformulating) a position which, as we pointed out at the beginning of this chapter, may seem arbitrary.

As a brief conclusion, let me point out how the sciences of religion ("religiologies" as they are called in Poland) are probably no more than one sector of a vaster science; this is the science of the sacred, something which might be called "hierology." For, as Otto demonstrated, as Durkheim once proposed and, all things being equal, as Bergson affirmed, any particular religion is never more than one Path to the Sacred, leading us to it, bringing us back from it, enabling us to live with it without dying of it; for, as Durkheim said: "This exaltation itself cannot last! It is too exhausting."

From this comes a series of observations on the relation of Christian theology to sociology of religions.

1. Christianity may well be beyond the reach of theology, and some writers have called for a de-theologizing of Christianity which would bring about a passionate re-mythologizing of that religion.[81] Theology may be one of the "scientific" ways of dealing with Christianity and it would be improper to deny it this role, for there are many sciences in the house of the sciences of religion; and although the fact that one is a theologian does not suffice to qualify as a scientist, this fact does not prevent a man from being one. And, conversely, the fact that one is a scientist does oblige one, in a certain field, to be or become more or less a theologian. But there are also other non-theological, scientific ways of dealing with Christianity, and it does not seem probable that a premature *Aufhebung* can effect a syncretic accolade coalescing theology's auto-interpretation with the hetero-interpretation of these sciences.

2. There are religions outside of Christianity, and among them are religions without any god, such as the ones noted by Durkheim and the ones so stubbornly dreamed of by Comte who wrote: "Whereas the Protestants and the deists have always attacked religion in the name of God, we would like to do away with God in the name of religion."[82]

3. There may be a Christianity outside of religion, such as the Christianity sought by Bonhöffer, a Christianity for a world that has "grown up."[83] This hypothesis has produced a complete interpretation of the Judeo-Christian role in world history.[84]

And Christianity itself cannot be seen in perspective until it is co-related with other religions outside of Christianity or with a Christianity outside of any religion.

4. Finally, even if every religion were a religion of the sacred, this would not mean that the sacred is monopolized by any one religion or even by religion in general. There is a nonreligious sacred, a sacred outside of religion, just as there are religions outside of Christianity. And even if all religions were religions of the sacred, they would be embracing a sacred which in itself might or might not be religious, producing a combination of a religion

and a non-religion, a religion of "yes" and a religion of "no."

5. Perhaps there is even a denial of religion which ultimately feeds on a denial of any sacred whatsoever, something like a refusal to be alienated when one suspects that the price of alienation is too high. If Proudhon had a religion (Proudhon, who smelled an aberration in every messianism), it was probably something of this sort. This would also apply to the young Engels who fled from the cathedral lest he succumb to the intoxication induced by the organ music.

There are then, scattered here and there, many modes of being not only outside the Church, but also outside of Christianity and even outside of all religion and, ultimately, outside of the sacred. However, none of these escape the problem raised by "irreligion," a problem about which Le Bras said: "Its sociology will probably turn out to be the most moving of all sociologies of religion."

Moreover, this is why theology and sociology move in different gravitation fields. Their differences are rooted in their fundamental precepts. Theology is at the stage of diagnosis: *Extra Ecclesiam nulla salus*;[85] sociology is still (and will long remain) at the stage of auscultation: *Ne impedias Musicam*. . . .

Conclusion

Throughout the preceding pages one question has been with us all along the way: does sociology of religion belong to religion or to non-religion?[1] A variety of answers have been given and they have navigated between Charybdis and Scylla, a dangerous voyage against which we have recently been warned by William Montgomery Watt.[2]

There is the answer of the faithful believer: only he who practices a religion can know a religion; there is the variant of the apologist who says that knowledge of the true religion is the same as true knowledge of religion; there is the sub-variant of the fundamentalist who says that he who knows the true religion knows the falsity of all others; there is the sub-variant of the ecumenist who says that he who knows the truth of the true religion knows the value of all other religions, etc.[3]

Then there are the answers of the critic and the polemicist. We have already quoted Henri Lévy-Bruhl: "To understand mysticism it is not necessary to be a mystic. *Au contraire.*" Renan added a few nuances by suggesting that to understand a religion one must enter it, live it . . . and then leave it. As for the great Weber, did not he describe himself as "insensitive to the music of religions?"

Harnack specified that to understand religions it is necessary to know at least one of them, and he who knows one knows them all. Wach who quotes Harnack in order to dissociate himself from that position produces other texts in which his view nevertheless seems quite close to it: "Only someone who knows religion because he practices some form of it can be expected to say something meaningful about it."[4] But Yinger answers Wach by saying: "This is an invitation to obscurantism and is similar to the insistance of psychoanalysts that only those who have been psychoanalyzed have any right to make valid comments on classical Freudian theory."

Yet this same Yinger wisely adds: "There are things to be said about a religion that can be said only by those who participate in it; there are other sorts of observations which can be made by someone who follows another belief; and, going further, there is a study which can be made by someone who denies all belief. The scholar, as such, need not share any of the prejudices implicit in these observations, for each approach can offer him an appreciable amount of data for the development of his own theory of religion. . . ."[5]

We have already cited Lévi-Strauss who, from a similar but more developed point of view, made this comment on Marcel Mauss and his dialectic of within and without:

> In order to have a total understanding of a social fact one must comprehend it in its totality; which is to say that, although one comprehends it from without as a thing, *an integral part of this thing-observed is the subjective (conscious or unconscious) comprehension of the observer when he lives this social fact as if he were a native rather than observe it as an ethnologist.* The problem is to know how one can realize this ambition which is not only to comprehend an object simultaneously from without and from within, but also much more: for *the subjective understanding* (of the native or the observer who is re-living the experience of the native) *must be transposed into the terms of an objective understanding,* bringing into play certain elements of an ensemble whose validity depends on a systematic and coordinated presentation. . . .[6]

This methodological complexity makes it impossible for any sociology of religion to be watered down into the facile vocabulary of a sociomancy based on "the death of the gods and religions" such as we find in Nietzsche and Engels[7] or based on the survival and even resurrection of the gods as outlined by Durkheim[8] —even though the aura of these implied predictions (in the vague form of Prometheus or Sisyphus) clings to research as significant as theirs.

When applied to our examination of the present state of sociologies of religion, this complexity may not lead us to a logical axiom, but it does lead us to a mythical symbol borrowed from the story in Genesis.[9]

> So Jacob was left alone, and a man wrestled with him there till daybreak.[10]

When the man saw that he could not throw Jacob, he struck him in the hollow of his thigh, so that Jacob's hip was dislocated as they wrestled.[11]

The man said: "Let me go, for day is breaking," but Jacob replied, "I will not let you go unless you bless me."[12]

He said to Jacob, "What is your name?" and he answered, "Jacob." The man said, "Your name shall no longer be Jacob, but Israel,[13] because you strove with God and with men, and prevailed."[14]

Jacob said, "Tell me, I pray, your name." He replied, "Why do you ask my name?" but he gave him his blessing there.

Jacob called the place Penuel, "because," he said, "I have seen God face to face and my life is spared."

The sun rose as Jacob passed through Penuel, limping because of his hip.[15]

I was once talking with Mircéa Eliade about the subjective presuppositions in a science like sociology of religion. When I raised the question of the minimum of subjective religious experience required for an objective knowledge of religion or religions, he gave me a spritely answer: "After all, it probably is enough to have had . . . dreams."

Even if Jacob had only been dreaming during that night described in Genesis, and even if the compilers and commenters have only been dreaming about what the narrators had dreamed that Jacob dreamed, do not these dreams, like the dreams about Prometheus, Sisyphus and so many other archetypes, suffice (at least provisionally) to sustain the aura around a frame of reference?

Notes

Foreword

1. See Henri Desroche, *Socialismes et sociologie religieuse* (Paris: Cujas, 1965), p. 4.
2. Gen. 32:25-33. See Conclusion, below.

Chapter One

1. Emile Louis Burnouf, *La Science des religions*, 3rd ed. (1870), p. 2.
2. Henri Charles Puech and Paul Vignaux, "Les Sciences religieuses" in *Les Sciences sociales en France, Enseignement et Recherche* (Paris: Hartmann, 1937).
3. Mircéa Eliade, "Crisis and Renewal in History of Religions," in *History of Religions*, vol. 5, 1 (1965), pp. 1-7.
4. As far as we know, the recent work by Roger Mehl is the only one formally entitled a "treatise." This is his *Traité de sociologie du protestantisme* (Neuchâtel: Delachaux et Niestlé, 1965).
5. Roger Bastide, *Eléments de sociologie religieuse* (Paris, 1935).
6. Gustav Mensching, *Sociologie religieuse* (Paris: Payot, 1951; Ger. ed., 1947).
7. Joachim Wach, *Sociology of Religion* (London: Kegan Paul, 1947). Fren. ed. (Paris: Payot, 1955) unfortunately does not include all the critical material found in the English edition.
8. Gabriel Le Bras, *Etudes de sociologie religieuse*, 2 vols.: 1, *Sociologie de la pratique religieuse dans les campagnes françaises* (Paris:

Presses Universitaires de France, 1955); 2, *De la morphologie à la typologie* (Paris, 1956).
9. John Milton Yinger, *Religion, Society and Individual. An Introduction to the Sociology of Religion* (New York: Macmillan, 1957). Fr. trans., *Religion, Sociéte, Personne* (Paris: Editions Universitaires, 1964).
10. Thomas Ford Hoult, *The Sociology of Religion* (New York: Dryden Press, 1958).
11. Max Weber, *The Sociology of Religion* (Boston: Beacon Press, 1964). Review in *A.S.R.*, vol. 18, no. 217. Add to this the recent publication of J.E. Prades, *La Sociologie de la religion chez Max Weber* (Paris-Louvain: Nauwelaerts, 1966); Raymond Aron, *Les Étapes de la pensée sociologique* (Paris: Gallimard, 1964), "Max Weber et la sociologie de la religion," pp. 529-550; Julien Freund, *La Sociologie de Max Weber* (Paris: Presses Universitaires, "Collection SUP-le Sociologue"), "La Sociologie religieuse," pp. 153-190.
12. Roger Bastide, *Religions africaines au Brésil. Vers une Sociologie des interprétations des civilisations* (Paris: Presses Universitaires, 1960).
13. Joachim Wach, *Types of Religious Experience. Christian and non-Christian* (Chicago: Chicago University Press, 1951). See also the valuable résumé "La Sociologie de la religion" in Gustav Gurvitch, ed., *La Sociologie au XXe siècle* (Paris: Presses Universitaires, 1947), 417-447.
14. Gabriel Le Bras, *Histoire du droit et des institutions de l'Eglise en occident. Prolégomènes* (Paris, 1955). Vol. 7, *L'Age classique* (Paris, 1965). See also *Institutions*

ecclésiastiques de la chrétienté mé-diévale (Paris, 1959), Book 1, Pre-liminary remarks and Part 1; also Books 2 and 6 (Paris, 1964).

15. Max Weber, *The Protestant Ethic* (New York: Scribner). Available in French under the title *L'Ethique protestante et l'esprit du capitalisme* (Paris: Plon, 1964).

16. We have recently tried to evaluate this contribution. See Henri Desroche, *Marxisme et religions* (Paris: Presses Universitaires, 1962), and *Socialismes et sociologie religieuse.*

17. Ernst Bloch, *Thomas Münzer, théologien de la révolution,* trans. Maurice de Gandillac (Paris: Julliard, 1964; Ger. ed., 1921; 2nd. ed., 1962). See also O. Furter, "Utopie et marxisme selon Ernst Bloch," *Archives de sociologie des religions, A.S.R.* 21, (Jan.-June 1966), pp. 3-22.

18. Ernst Troeltsch, *The Social Teaching of the Christian Churches* (London: G. Allen; New York: Macmillan). Several editions but none in French.

19. In *A.S.R.,* 20-21, 1965-1966.

20. See Paul Arbousse-Bastide, "Auguste Comte et la sociologie religieuse," *A.S.R.,* 22, pp. 3-58.

21. See J. Sumpf, "Durkheim et le problème de l'étude sociologique de la religion," *A.S.R.,* 20, pp. 63-74. Also Aron, pp. 345-362.

22. Marcel Mauss, *Sociologie et anthropologie,* Introduction by Claude Lévi-Strauss (Paris, Presses Universitaires, 1968). See also J. Cazeneuve, *Sociologie de Marcel Mauss,* in "Collection SUP-le Sociologue."

23. *Sociology of Religion. A Trend-report and Bibliography* (Paris, UNESCO, 1956). Contains 891 selected titles, classified and documented. See also the thirty-five hundred titles in Hervé Carrier and Emile Pin, *Sociologie du christianisme. Bibliographie internationale* (Rome, 1964); A. Luchini, *Enquête sur la production, la distribution et la consommation du livre religieux en France* (Paris, 1964).

24. By No. 22, after eleven years of service, more than six thousand titles of articles and books had been analyzed in these bulletins.

25. For a systematic bibliography of the sociology of religion, regarding the presentation of a trend-report, see article by F. Isambert in *A.S.R.,* 1, pp. 141 ff.

26. In classifying the cards we asked ourselves how it was that each title led us toward or away from another title. We hoped, by this system of "spontaneous" attractions-and-repulsions to arrive at an idea of the number and relative size of the piles.

27. Some idea of this extended approach can be found in another bibliographic tool: Henri Charles Puech, "La Bibliographie générale," in J. Vandier, *La Religion égyptienne,* Collection "Mana," and in his *Introduction à l'histoire des religions.* Also see Carrier and Pin, *Sociologie du christianisme,* reviewed in *A.S.R.* 20, no. 76.

28. Although this development is quantitatively measured by the great number of titles, the qualitative development in pioneer research, such as the work done by Jacques Berque and his Department of Islam and the Sociology of Mohammedanism, should not be underestimated. On Islam, see also: Reuben Lévy, *Introduction to the Sociology of Islam* (1933); Joseph Chelhod, *Introduction à la sociologie de l'Islam* (1958); Henri Laoust, *Le Schisme dans l'Islam. Introduction à une étude de la religion musulmane* (Paris, 1965), reviewed in *A.S.R.* 21, no. 191; Montgomery Watt, *Islam and the Integration of Society* (London,

1961); idem, *Mahomet* (Paris, 1962), reviewed in *A.S.R.* 15, nos. 180 and 181; Vincent Monteil, *L'Islam noir* (Paris: Seuil, 1964), reviewed in *A.S.R.* 18, no. 181; Jean Claude Froelich, *Musulmans d'Afrique Noire* (Paris, 1962); Maxime Rodinson, *Islam et capitalisme* (Paris, 1966). See also the Colloquium on the Sociology of Mohammedanism (Brussels, 1967) at which Rodinson presented his paper "Problematique de l'étude des rapports entre Islam et Communisme."

On the religions of India, see: Louis Dumont, *Homo hierarchicus. Essai sur le système des castes* (Paris: Gallimard, 1967). On Southeast Asia, see: reports of Willem Frederik Wertheim and his book *East-West Parallels. Sociological Approaches to Modern Asia* (La Haye, 1964), reviewed in *A.S.R.* 212.

29. On Protestantism, see the European Colloquia on the Sociology of Protestantism. The first colloquium met in Strasbourg, May 1959. See: "Actes" in *A.S.R.* 8, pp. 3-158. On Catholicism, see International Conferences on the Sociology of Religion, inaugurated in Louvain, 1948. The second of these conferences was also held in Louvain, 1949; the third, in Breda, 1950, proceedings published in *Lumen Vitae*, vol. 6, nos. 1-2 (Jan.-June, 1951), pp. 7-387. The Eighth Congress was held in Montreal, 1967.

There is also an association which is methodologically and organizationally distinct from the preceding colloquia: Le Comité Internationale de Recherches sur la Sociologie des Religions, sponsored by the Association Sociologique Internationale.

30. See Henri Desroche, "Dissidences religieuses et socialisme utopiques," in *Année sociologique, 1952* (Paris, 1955), pp. 393-429. Since 1952, investigation in this field has been continued by Jean Séguy. See "Bulletin bibliographique" in *A.S.R.*, passim.

31. This distance does not yet exist in cases when a religion is co-extensive with its society. Nor does it exist when a sociology is co-extensive with its religion, and the result in each case is the same impossibility of defining the sociology of religion. This is precisely what Paul Arbousse-Bastide observed in Auguste Comte: "Comte's sociology is so closely tied to religion that one cannot fit a sociology of religion into the over-all framework of his thought . . . as one could do with a sociology of economics, of domestic life or esthetics. . . . It is not sufficiently distant from its subject matter . . . to permit the elaboration of a 'sociology of religion'." Arbousse-Bastide, *A.S.R.* 22, p. 42.

32. Durkheim has commented on this distancing. "The religious ideas held by the faithful are not just figments of the imagination, yet they are not to be considered as a set of privileged intuitions . . . and we must therefore submit them to an examination similar to the one which substituted scientific and conceptual representation for our sense experience of the objective world. . . ."

33. This taboo was also pointed out by Durkheim: "The world of religious and moral life still remains forbidden territory. This explains the sharp resistance one encounters every time one tries to submit religious and moral phenomena to scientific examination. . . ." Emile Durkheim, *Formes*, p. 614.

34. Jean Paul Sartre, *Critique de la raison dialectique* (Paris, 1960), p. 51 and p. 55: "We see the relationship between the sociologist and his subject matter as a reciprocal one: the inquirer can never be 'outside' one group without at the same time being 'inside' another one."

35. Joachim Wach, "La Sociologie de la religion," pp. 427-428.

36. Christopher Dawson, *Dynamics of World History* (London, 1957), p. 86.

37. The extreme of this view, as presented by Ludwig Feuerbach, is paraphrased by A. Lévy: "No matter how much you read and write on the religious cults of antiquity, unless you can personally feel why it is that to-day man is still drawn to a belief in the divinity of the moon, the plants and the animals, the historical fact will remain, for you, a dead letter. . . ." A. Lévy, *La Philosophie de Feuerbach* (Paris: Alcan, 1904), p. 139.

38. Durkheim emphasizes the tension attending this second step: "From the fact of religious experience and the fact that it is based on something, it does not follow that the reality which gave birth to the experience conforms to the idea which believers have of it," *Formes,* p. 530. Durkheim openly expresses this reticence in explaining "origins" in *Vocation de la sociologie religieuse* (Paris: Casterman, 1958), p. 31.

39. Once more, Durkheim should be cited: "The collective consciousness is not just an epiphenomenon on a morphological base. . . . In order for it to appear there must have occurred (*sui generis*) a synthesis of individual consciousnesses. Now this synthesis releases a whole world of feelings, ideas and images which, once they are born, obey laws of their own," *Formes,* p. 605. On "reductivism" see below, Chapter Three.

40. For notes on this, see Jean Labbens, *La Sociologie religieuse* (Paris: Fayard, 1959), p. 12.

41. Wach, "Sociologie de la religion," p. 427.

42. Ludwig Feuerbach, *La Religion,* translated by Roy (Paris, 1884), pp. 72-73.

43. Examples of this can be found in certain pontifical declarations: "The relation between the rich and the poor, a problem which concerns so many economists, will be perfectly resolved as soon as it is admitted that poverty is not without dignity, that the rich man should be merciful and generous, that the poor man should be content with his lot and his work, since neither the one nor the other was born for those perishable worldly goods and the poor man will go to heaven by virtue of his patience, the rich man by virtue of his generosity." Leo XIII, Encyclical Letter on the Origin of Civil Authority (29 July 1881).

44. Sample of these successive changes of position in H. Mathieu, *L'Objectif de l'A.C.—l'ordre social et chrétien* (Paris: Spes, 1937), pp. 8-9.

45. Jacques Leclerc, "Sociologie religieuse et théologie" in *Sociologie religieuse et sciences sociales,* Actes du 4ᵉ Congrès de Sociologie Religieuse (Paris: Ouvrières, 1955), pp. 159-167.

46. This has been analyzed and situated by Gabriel Le Bras in his reflexions on the differences between scientific and pastoral sociology. See: *A.S.R.* 8 (July-Dec. 1959), pp. 5-14.

47. Marie Dominique Chenu, *Introduction aux sciences des religions* (Paris: Cujas). See chapter on position of theology and historical methods. He makes this position clear in numerous other articles. On the theology of the sociology of religion, see *Paroisse et mission* 5 (1950), pp. 5-9; On the sociology of knowledge and theology of faith, see *Recherches et débats* 25 (1958), pp. 71-77. These two studies are reprinted in *La Foi dans l'intelligence* (Paris: Cerf, 1964), pp. 59-68. Elsewhere, a discussion of tradition

and sociology of faith in *Eglise et tradition* (Paris, 1963).

48. Durkheim, *Formes*, p. 605.

49. In a sense which includes but goes beyond recorded religious practices, since it includes both the practices and the refusal to practice, the variations in religious regression as well as progression.

50. Some people deplore the absence or the tardy appearance of such affirmations in the sociology of Catholicism. A. Z. Serrand, *Evolution technique et théologie* (Paris: Cerf, 1958), pp. 147-148.

51. Ibid., pp. 150-151. Italics mine.

52. See L. G. Adam, *La C.F.T.C., 1940-1958.*

53. "Secularization" is the term proposed by Yves Congar.

54. J. P. Kruyt, "The Influence of Denominationalism on Social Life and Organizational Patterns," *A.S.R.* 8 (July-Dec. 1959), pp. 105-112.

55. Such as the ghetto parish as conceived by the missionary movement.

56. See A. Dumas, "Dietrich Bonhöffer et l'interprétation du christianisme comme non-religion," *A.S.R.* 19, pp. 5-30; also on Bonhöffer, Henri Desroche, "Sociologie et irreligion," ibid., pp. 3-4.

57. Wach, *Sociology of Religion,* pp. 7-8.

58. In light of the work by F. Boulard (*Premiers itinéraires en sociologie religieuse*) this is likely to result in a checkerboard presentation of French society. See the vocabulary set up by Jacques Maître, "Catholicisme français contemporain. Variété et limite de ses dénombrements," *A.S.R.* 2, pp. 27 ff.; also "Les Dénombrements de catholiques pratiquants en France," *A.S.R.* 3, pp. 72 ff. For works on Protestantism, see Mehl,

Traité de sociologie du Protestantisme, Chapter Six, "La Pratique religieuse."

59. Moreno, for example, proposes a sociology which will serve as an instrument for a self-guided society, something like a government of the people, for the people and by the people.

60. That is, ideals of the sort one pursues but never attains.

61. The alternative of what we call "sociologizing theology" has been named, variously: "pastoral sociology," "missionary sociology," and "socio-ecclesiastic research." In any case it is essentially a sociography that has been "promoted to the rank of sociology." This is the expression used, typically. See Bernhard Haering, *Forces et faiblesse de la religion,* Fr. trans. of Ger., 3rd ed. (Paris, 1964). Also, more recently, J. Laloux, *Manuel d'initiation à la sociologie religieuse* (Paris, 1967) in which can be found useful retrospective bibliographies on the subject; Sabino S. Acquaviva, *L'Eclipse du sacré dans la civilisation industrielle* (Paris: Mame, 1967) which offers a more objectified presentation.

62. This is the vast sector common to pastoral sociology and independent sociology, emphasized by Le Bras who comments on the subdivisions of this sociography as a descriptive science. *A.S.R.* 8, pp. 6 ff.

63. Thomas Luckmann, *Das Problem der Religion in der moderne Gesellschaft* (Freiburg: Rombach, 1963). Reviewed in *A.S.R.* 17, no. 179.

64. See below, Chapter Three.

65. See below, Chapter Four.

66. Jean Piaget, "Le Problème des mécanismes communs dans les sciences de l'homme," in *L'Homme et la société* 2 (Oct.-Dec. 1966), p. 6.

67. See below, Chapter Six.

68. Roger Bastide, *Sociologie des maladies mentales* (Paris: Flammarion,

1965). In his dedication the author says: "This is a book about maladies which are, more often than not, sacred." See also the interesting study by Y. Bertherat on the work of Albert Béguin and the relations between madness, secularization and the sacred: Y. Bertherat, "La Folie porte de l'oeuvre," in *Esprit* (July 1967), pp. 1013-1026.

Chapter Two

1. Gabriel Le Bras, *Etudes de sociologie religieuse* (Paris: Presses Universitaires, 1956), vol. 2

2. Ibid., pp. 765-766.

3. We have tried to analyze this development elsewhere. See Henri Desroche, "Domaines et méthodes de la sociologie religieuse dans l'oeuvre de Gabriel Le Bras," in *Revue d'histoire et philosophie religieuse* No. 2 (Strasbourg, 1954) (hereafter cited as Desroche, "Domaines et méthodes.")

4. Marc Bloch, *Apologie pour l'histoire ou métier d'historien* (Paris: Colin, 1961), p. 15.

5. Gabriel Le Bras, "Notes de statistique et d'histoire religieuse," in *R.H.E.F.* 22 (1936), p. 485.

6. Le Bras, "De l'Etat présent de la pratique religieuse en France," *Revue du folklore français*, 4 (1933), p. 193.

7. Le Bras, *Etudes*, vol. 2, p. 801.

8. Le Bras in Desroche, "Domaines et méthodes."

9. Ibid.

10. See Pie Duployé, *La Religion de Péguy* (Paris: Klincksieck, 1965); also our review of this book in *A.S.R.* 20.

11. "A true science of history does not yet exist. . . . The billions of obscure people without whom none of the great abstract accomplishments in history would have been realized and who, mark my words, have never profited from any of these accomplishments, do not have any place in our annals. They have lived, they have been sacrificed for the good of abstract humanity, and that is all we know." M. Bakounine, *Dieu et l'état*, pp. 60-61.

12. F. Boulard, *Premiers Itinéraires en sociologie religieuse* (Paris: Ouvrières, 1954, 1966), p. 49. This is a restatement of Gabriel Le Bras: "All the explanations that I have been able to suggest are, in a sense, historical, even those which seem to have no connection with history." G. Le Bras, "Statistique et histoire religieuse," *R.H.E.F.* 17 (1951), p. 439.

13. Limiting ourselves to work done by the "Groupe de Sociologie des religions," see studies by Jean Séguy on the sociology of religious sects, by Isambert on the relation between Christianity and the working classes, by Émile Poulat on doctrinal disputes (modernism) and pastoral disputes (worker priests), and by Jacques Maître on "popular religions."

14. See a summary table of this in our study of Le Bras in Desroche, "Domaines et méthodes," p. 139.

15. "In fact, ever since the first surveys, it has been clear that the immense majority of Christians fall into one of three categories for accepting (either on their own or on family authority) the solemn acts of religious practice, whether they be periodical or limited to special occasions: as conformists, they are either seasonal, observing or devout." *Cahiers Internationaux de Sociologie* 1 (1946), p. 43.

16. This was an early slogan of the *Action catholique*.

17. This is the title of a work by J. Lebret. The point of view is integrated in his *Diagrammes de sociologie re-*

ligieuse, Collection Sagma.

18. See Roger Martin du Gard evoking the attitude of Jacques Copeau on his novel *Jean Barois*: "For Copeau's biographers let me add this trait: at that time, unbelievable as it may seem to us today, Copeau was absolutely incapable of interest in any discussion on religious faith. A propos of *Jean Barois,* I noted that one day Jacques Rivière said to him in my presence: 'I don't know anyone as indifferent as you are to religious problems! Why you don't even have any idea of what they could be!' To this, Copeau replied, laughing: 'That is quite true! And I'm glad of it!'"

19. "The more that religious practices are generalized in a group, the less deep-rooted they will be in any one individual member" (Le Bras).

20. Even though, according to Hegel, as Sartre has pointed out (*Critique,* p. 99), "appearance, as such, has a reality."

21. See statements by Hubert and Mauss: "The state of religious attitudes in France could be analyzed accurately in the same way that statisticians evaluate the state of national morality through statistics on morals and criminal behavior," (1902-1903). Mauss has said: "We do not make sufficient use of quantitative methods; we certainly could measure the frequency of church attendance. . . . The history of religions is not used to numerical calculations. . . ." (1924-1925). On the same subject Gabriel Le Bras has said: "We count the number of steers and horses, but who ever thought of compiling statistics on the number of people who practice religion" (1932). This is echoed by L. Febvre: "Isn't it incredible that on the subject of prayers, pious practices, the most important and wide-spread devotions,

even on many of the big pilgrimages, we are always reduced to getting our information from brief notes dispersed in articles and out-of-the-way periodicals, and that these notes are, all too often, dictated by interests quite foreign to those of history. . . ." (1932).

22. They can be found by going through the *Trend-report,* and the bibliographical bulletins of the *A.S.R.* for the past ten years.

23. See: F. Boulard, *Premiers Itinéraires.* Also pertinent are small articles on methodology in *Cahiers du clergé rural.*

24. It has become customary to refer to the prototype survey by Jacques Petit in *A.S.R.* 1.

25. See the inventory and classifications used in 1957 by Jacques Maître in *A.S.R.* 3, pp. 72-95.

26. See the manuscript copy of a collection of surveys made in Spain by M. Abellan, Diplôme E.P.H.E. Also, on Italian surveys: Silvano Burgalassi, *La Sociologia del cattolicismo in Italia* (1965).

27. See the remarkable review by Jean Danielou of Mircéa Eliade, "Traité d'histoire des religions" in *La Maison de Dieu* 22 (April-June 1950). "Liturgy is the meeting place for the revelation of God through recurring cosmic cycles and the revelation of God through particular historical events. . . ."

28. Anita Brenner, *Idols Behind Altars* (New York, 1928). In the same sense, Friedrich Heiler, evoking what he calls "primitive religious realism," or the "basic spontaneous religion of the peasantry," underlying and working against the main currents of historical Christianity, is not far from sharing this point of view when he poses the question "Have our people ever really been converted to Christianity?"

29. Taken from a discrepancy in the

rate of religious practice, either between two moments in the same
place, or between two different places
at the same moment.

30. Yves Congar *Jalons pour une
théologie du laïcat* (Paris: Cerf); also
H. Kraemer, *Théologie du laïcat,*
Feb., 1966.

31. Charles Fauvety, *La Religion
laïque. Organe de la régénération so-
ciale, 1876-1879.* Influenced by the
ideas of Fourier.

32. Colette Moreux, "Vie religeuse
d'une paroisse canadienne en voie
d'organisation et, plus particulière-
ment, de 90 de ses habitants,"
(thesis, 1967), p. 267.

33. R. Sévigny, "L'Expérience
religieuse et l'actualisation de soi,"
(thesis, Montreal, 1966).

34. Ibid., p. 173.

35. For the same approach, see
Henri Desroche, "Approches du
non-conformisme français," *A.S.R.*
2, pp. 45-54. In this article we tried
to show that beyond the so-called
"sectarian" nonconformism (minimal in France), there exists throughout the country a competing "cultural" nonconformism of those people
who adhere only selectively to the
practices of the Church. We suggested
that this nonconformism might well be
the religion of the majority in France:
"of ten to fifteen million Frenchmen." In his introductory remarks
to this article Le Bras stated that he
"favored the second of these figures,
providing that they apply only to
adults."

36. The proceedings of this colloquium have not been published. To
date, Kruyt's remarks have not appeared in print.

37. Most of the surveys deal with
variables within religious practice
and are not concerned with a correlation between external variables
and religious belief. On the variables

of belief combined with the variables
of practice, see R. Goldstein's attempt
to "analyze questions about belief
held within the types of religious practices previously presented," in his
article "Les Jeunes travailleurs af-
frontés à leur vie de foi," in *Economie
et humanisme* (Nov.-Dec. 1966), pp.
62-69. For a discussion of religious
practice without belief, using the example of Mendelssohn, see Hegel,
Philosophie de la religion, translated
by Vera, vol. 1, p. 359.

38. Durkheim also notes this in
Formes, p. 63.

39. "The supreme mystification of
positivism is its claim to approach social
experience with no ideas *a priori,*
whereas in the very beginning it decided to deny one of the fundamental
structures of this experience and to
replace it with its opposite." Jean Paul
Sartre, *Critique de la raison dialectique*
(Paris, 1960), p. 98.

40. "The plurality of meanings in
History cannot be revealed to others
or to themselves except in the form
of some future total view, at the same
time depending on it and in contradiction to it. . . ." Ibid., p. 63.

41. Joachim Wach, *The Types of Religious Experience. Christian and non-
Christian* (Chicago: University of Chicago Press, 1951), p. 208.

42. See Henri Desroche, "Sociologie
et théologie dans la typologie religieuse
de J. Wach," *A.S.R.* 1, pp. 41-63.

43. Joachim Wach, *Sociology of Religion* (University of Chicago Press,
1944). All page references are to this
edition.

Chapter Three

1. Even though alien to this sociology, it will have in some way assured
its success. Likewise, there is a certain
basic economic fatalism, quite alien to

Marxist thought, which has nevertheless been responsible for the success
of a certain brand of Marxism. See
the analyses of Antonio Gramsci in
his *Œuvres choisies*, p. 440.

2. This *a priori* is of an allusive
or illusory epiphenomenal religion.
It is strange that this *a priori* is not
mentioned by any of the pioneers in
sociology of religion. It is not to be
found in Durkheim: "One must be
careful not to see this theory of religion as merely a rejuvenated form
of historical materialism: this would
be to misunderstand our thought. . . .
Collective consciousness is more than
a simple epiphenomenon of its morphological base, etc." *Formes*, p.
605. Nor is it to be found in the
writings of Marx, for the historical
materialism of the type to which
Durkheim refers does not at all resemble Marxist theory, as has once
more been demonstrated, quite
arbitrarily, by Louis Althusser in
his *Pour Marx* (Paris: Maspero, 1966).

3. See our review of Louis Althusser's *Pour Marx* in "Dernière
Instance et premier rôle," *A.S.R.*
23, pp. 153-157. Also the first of the
Thèses by Palmiro Togliatti cited in
Roger Garaudy, *De l'anathème au
dialogue* (Paris: Plon, 1965), p. 118.

4. On this see T. Parson's introduction to Max Weber: "Weber early
became acutely aware, as many par-
ticipants in the discussion still are not,
that the problem of causation involved
an analytical problem, one of the iso-
lation of variables and the testing
of their significance in situations
where they could be shown to vary
independently of each other." Max
Weber, *The Sociology of Religion*
(Boston: Beacon Press, 1964), p. xxi.
This is why there is a "sharp con-
trast between his methodology and
the positivistic reductionism." Ibid.,
p. xxiii.

5. Underlining is ours. See Claude
Lévi-Strauss, *Anthropologie structurale*,
p. 17.

6. ". . . which exists only by virtue
of the group's refusal to give up a
habit." Ibid.

7. The one which is already anticipated in the group's desire to innovate
a behavior pattern.

8. Karl Mannheim, *Ideology and
Utopia*. See Chapter 4, "The Utopian
Mentality," pp. 173 ff.

9. See the weighty and significant
induction made by F. Boulard,
*Premiers Itinéraires en sociologie re-
ligieuse*, Paris: Ouvrières, 1954),
pp. 35, 46.

10. As one says "geomancy" and
"chiromancy." Just because this
"sociomancy" (this state of knowing
what the future holds for a society)
is not a science does not mean that
it cannot be an object of scientific
study. After all, there have been recent developments in the sociology of
utopias, messianic religions and imaginary societies.

11. "Religious motives may work
positively and negatively. They 'build
up' and they 'pull down.'" It is our
thesis that the constructive force of religion surpasses its destructive influ-
ences. Fundamentally and ultimately,
religion makes for social integration
though it should definitely not be
identified with its effect. We have
tried to show that social integration
is not the 'aim' or 'purpose' of religion. . . ." J. Wach, *Sociology of
Religion* (University of Chicago Press,
1944), p. 381.

12. Hugo F. Lamennais, *Œuvres
posthumes* (Paris, 1856), pp. 180-183.

13. *Mémorial de Sainte-Hélène*, vol.
1, passim.

14. Durkheim, *Formes*, pp. 13, 305,
327, 495, 553, 597, 599, and 602
respectively.

15. Ibid., pp. 299-234.

16. Ibid., p. 313.

17. Joachim Wach proposed a similar dialectical relation between *experience* and *expression*, the latter being either theoretical (doctrine) or practical (cult). See Henri Desroche, "Sociologie et théologie dans la typologie de Joachim Wach," *A.S.R.* 1, pp. 41-63. Hubert defines religion as "the administration of the sacred."

18. From the Greek ιερός. I owe this neologism to a conversation with Michel Meslin. I might also have taken it from "hierophagy," a neologism previously proposed by R. A. Isambert. See *A.S.R.* 21, Bull. bib., no. 184. The Saint-Simonians called their detractors "hierophobes."

19. There is an arbitrary element in the vocabulary used here: "attest," "contend," "protest." The term "contention" is used here to designate what Wach called "protest within," by which he meant a protest occurring within the bounds of what is being protested. The opposite of this is Wach's "protest without" which designates a protest leading to secession. The word "contention" in this sense can be found in a recent Church leaflet, *La Contestation signe de santé de l'Eglise*, "Lettre No. 100," Dec. 1966-Jan. 1967.

20. "The science of religion should have as a principle that religion expresses nothing but what is found in nature, since there is no science except of natural phenomena." Durkheim, *Formes*, p. 98. This should be compared to Bergson's analysis: "Speaking generally, we hesitate to consider as primitive, meaning natural, a notion which we should not today form naturally." Henri Bergson, *The Two Sources of Morality and Religion* (New York: Henry Holt, 1935), p. 124. See Durkheim, *Formes*, pp. 100 ff.

21. On the distinction between "leading role" (*premier rôle*) and "decisive influence" (*dernière instance*), see Althusser, *Pour Marx*, and the review of this in *A.S.R.* 23, pp. 153-57.

22. This confusion is not the fault of Durkheim who said: "What constitutes a society is not only the mass of people it contains, the ground they occupy, the things they use and the movements they make, but also the idea that the society has of itself." *Formes*, p. 604.

23. Henri Lefebvre, *Somme et reste*, p. 83.

24. For an attempt to outline such a history, see: Henri Desroche, *Marxisme et religion* (Paris: Presses Universitaires, Coll. "Mythes et Religions").

25. For a geographical breakdown of religious classifications in France, see the *Symposium des A.S.R.* For figures on membership in various religious groups, see *A.S.R.* 2, 1956, pp. 17 ff.

26. As, for example, the *Duo sunt genera christianorum* in Gratian's *Decreta*. See also Yves Congar, *Jalons pour une théologie du laïcat*, 3rd ed. (Paris: Cerf, 1904). Also H. J. Fichter, *Priest and People* (New York, 1965), reviewed in *A.S.R.* 21, no. 207; H. Kraemer, *Théologie du laïcat* (Genève, 1966), reviewed in *A.S.R.* 22, no. 183.

27. Including the three-sided interacting operations of the terms: "clericalization of monasticism," "monasticizing of the clergy," "laicizing or laicalization of the individual clergyman," "monasticizing of the layman," etc. On this triangle see the study by Gabriel Le Bras, "L'Image du clerc," *A.S.R.* 23; also his seminar, *Relations historiques entre les trois 'états' (clercs, religieux, laïcs) dans l'Eglise de France*.

28. Example of this: protests in the public press over the dismissal of a worker-priest, a dismissal followed by a strike. See the pamphlet *Licencié parce que prêtre?* (1957).

29. Joachim Wach, *Sociology of Religion*, pp. 156 ff.

30. Emile Poulat, *Histoire, dogme et critique dans la crise moderniste* (Paris, Casterman, 1962), reviewed in *A.S.R.* 15, no. 199.

31. Such as the opposition of "old time religion" to a new program proposed by the established orthodoxy.

32. See Max Weber's analysis of early Christianity: "Jesus held in general that what is most decisive for salvation is an absolute indifference to the world and its concerns. . . ." *Sociology of Religion*, p. 273. Weber's analysis should be situated in its matrix of four coordinates: asceticism, mysticism, within-the-world, out-of-the-world; and the four types produced:

	asceticism	mysticism
within-the-world	1	2
out-of-the-world	3	4

See introduction by Parsons, pp. *li* ff.

33. Burnouf has pointed out this evolution leading from a priesthood (Brahmanic) as a caste in society to a monasticism (Buddhistic) as a casteless community (yet within an over-all society organized into castes). Emile Burnouf, *Introduction à l'histoire du bouddhisme indien*, p. 191. Also touched on in Louis Dumont, *Homo hierarchicus. Essai sur le système des castes* (Paris: Gallimard, 1967), p. 238.

34. With its own economic structure (aid, joint action, common ownership of goods), system of law (locally administrated), and social order (often based on the family) which are legally set up as regimes to be tolerated or permitted as exceptions to the rule.

35. This problem of over-all change

is increasingly being recognized as the fundamental problem in developmental strategies and procedures for activating them. Underestimating its importance leads to obstructions and distortions. See: J. Kavadias, "L'assimilation du 'message' scientifique et technologique" in *Rev. Int. Sc. Soc.* 18. 1966, no. 3, pp. 394-407.

36. See: Paul Arbousse-Bastide, "Auguste Comte et la sociologie des religions," *A.S.R.* 22, pp. 3-58 (especially pp. 41-43, 51 and 53).

37. The early Quakers considered it their religious duty to demonstrate their opposition to meetings taking place in church buildings.

38. See: L. Olofsson, *The Conception of the Inner Light in Robert Barclay's Theology.*

39. A. Laurentin claims that this type of refusal can be seen in early Christianity and in Christ: "He objected to the law he came to accomplish, the Sabbath that he took unto himself, the temple that he restored in his own flesh, etc."

40. The dialectical relation of the Old and New Testaments in Christianity; references to Buddha, Zoroaster and Jesus in Manichaeism. Integration of Jesus and the patriarchs into the Koran. On Mani, see the following much cited passage in H. C. Puech, *Le Manichéisme*: "Wisdom and good works have been brought to man in successive periods by the Messengers of God. At one time they were brought by the prophet Buddha in the region of India, at another time by Zoroaster in the region of Persia, in another by Jesus in the West. After these, Revelation and the gift of Prophecy have come to our age through me, Mani, the Messenger of the God of Truth, in Babylonia."

41. Hypothesis discussed by Congar who nevertheless admits: "There is something very interesting and true

in the views of this protestant historian." Yves Congar, *Vraie et fausse réforme dans l'Eglise* (1950), pp. 188-189.

42. Sartana Kartodirjo, *The Peasant Revolt of Benten in 1888, a Case Study of Social Movements in Indonesia* (1966).

43. See research reports of Balandier, Lanternari, M.I.P. De Queiroz, Guiart, Worsley, etc.

44. See Norman Cohn, *The Pursuit of the Millenium* (1951); W. D. Morris, *The Christian Origins of Social Revolt* (1949).

45. See Ernst Bloch, *Thomas Münzer, théologien de la révolution*, French translation by Maurice de Gandillac (1964); Karl Mannheim, *Ideology and Utopia*, pp. 190 ff. On Bloch as a typical sociologist of "incongruence," see P. Furter, "Utopie et marxisme selon E. Bloch," *A.S.R.* 21, 1966, pp. 3-22.

46. Jean Piaget, "Le Problème des mecanismes communs dans les sciences de l'homme," paper presented at the World Congress of Sociology at Evian, September 1966. Published in *L'Homme et la Société* 2, Oct.-Dec. 1966, pp. 3 ff.

47. Or *praxiologics*. This subject was too briefly and too summarily introduced in my note "De la sociographie de la pratique religieuse à une pratique de la sociologie des religions," *A.S.R.* 20, juillet-déc. 1966, pp. 3-6.

48. See Paul Arbousse-Bastide, "Auguste Comte et la sociologie des religions," *A.S.R.* 22, p. 52.

49. See Jean Séguy, "Suggestions pour une sociologie des liturgies chrétiennes," *A.S.R.* 22, pp. 145-151.

50. For examples of this, see A. F. Festugière, *Traité sur la contemplation platonicienne* (Paris: Vrin, 1950) in which he treats it as an exoteric form

of the "Theoria." The theme is also admirably pointed up by Alfred Métraux in his studies of Voodoo cults.

51. "The question before us now is whether or not . . . there is a small group of men capable of imposing this higher notion of theater which will give us all a natural and magical equivalent of the dogmas we no longer believe in." Also: "Everything in this actively poetic manner of theatrical representation leads us away from our present attitude towards theater as a psychological experience and enables us to accept its religious and mystical meanings which theater in its contemporary form has completely lost." Antonin Artaud, *Le Théâtre et son double* (1964), pp. 45 and 67-68.

52. Only a few of these will be treated in the pages that follow. The subject is touched on, although with a different vocabulary, in the ideas of John Milton Yinger, *Religion, Society and the Individual* (New York, 1957), pp. 52 ff. See particularly "The Functional Approach to Religion and Difficulties in the Functional Approach," pp. 56 ff. which utilizes and discusses the classic work of Talcott Parsons and Robert Merton.

Chapter Four

1. On this approach see Paul Mercier, *Histoire de l'anthropologie* (Paris: Presses Universitaires de France, 1966), Coll. SUP-le-Sociologue, pp. 106 ff.

2. Durkheim, *Formes*, p. 132.

3. Ibid., p. 133.

4. "Certainly we, too, consider that the main object of the science of religions is to successfully define what it is that constitutes the religious nature of man." Ibid., p. 132, note 5.

5. "We must first define what we mean by religion." Ibid.

6. "Forgetting any conception of religion in general, let us consider religions as concrete realities and try to draw from this what it is that they can have in common: for religion can only be defined in terms of those traits which are found wherever religion is found." Ibid., p. 32. How can one say that a social phenomenon is or is not a religious phenomenon unless one recognizes in it, realized or unrealized, "some conception of religion in general?"

7. Ibid., p. 65. For the discussion on the implications of "Church," see below.

8. "The notion of social structure is not related to empirical reality but to models constructed after observing it." Lévi-Strauss, *Anthropologie structurale*, p. 305.

9. See, for example, Friedrich Heiler, "The History of Religions as a Preparation for the Cooperation of Religions" in *Essays in Methodology*, edited by Mircéa Eliade and Joseph Mitzuo Kitagawa, a memorial to Joachim Wach (Chicago, 1951), pp. 132-160.

10. See the distinction made by Fortes and approved by Lévi-Strauss: "Structure cannot be apprehended in 'concrete reality.' In defining structure, we place ourselves, as it were, on the level of grammar and syntax, and not on the level of the spoken language." Lévi-Strauss, *Anthropologic structurale*, p. 325. These religious languages correspond to the level of "an *a priori* study of all the conceivable types of structure." Ibid., p. 345.

11. It is from this concept of "system" that Dumont reaches his concept of "structure." Louis Dumont, *Homo hierarchicus, Essai sur le système des castes* (Paris: Gallimard, 1967), pp. 60-65.

12. Robert Harry Lowie, "Le

Messianisme primitif, contribution à un problème d'éthnologie," in *Diogène* 19 (1957), pp. 80 ff.

13. "The recurrence of similar customs and institutions cannot be considered as proof of contact unless there is a continuous chain of facts of the same type permitting one to relate the extremities of the chain to each other through a series of intermediaries." Lévi-Strauss, p. 10.

14. Lowie, "Le Messianisme primitif."

15. Lévi-Strauss, p. 75.

16. "If the content of the myth is completely contingent, how can we explain that from one end of the earth to the other the myths are so much alike?" Lévi-Strauss, p. 229.

17. In Lévi-Strauss, p. 333.

18. Lévi-Strauss, p. 95.

19. As in ethnology of religion, in which as Lévi-Strauss points out there has been practically no research, and although "myths, rites and religious beliefs are promising material for structural studies." Lévi-Strauss, p. 348. This cautiousness may be explained by the fact that, especially during recent decades, the sociology of religion has been a sociology of Christianity, and that the structural sociology of Christianity has been admittedly antitheological. "Someday, in the light of an all embracing perspective, we will have to face the myth with which we are presently most concerned: the Christian myth. There is no reason to treat it as a privileged subject, different from the rest, as does Paul Ricoeur." Luc de Heusch, "Situation et positions de l'anthropologie structurale" in *L'Arc* 26, p. 16.

20. Jean Guiart, *Les Religions de l'Océanie* (Paris: Presses Universitaires de France), p. 2.

21. See "Le Questionnaire universel: pour une enquête sociologique sur toutes les religions" in Gabriel Le Bras,

in *Rythmes du monde* (1953), 1, pp. 56-61.

22. Roger Mehl, *Traité de sociologie du protestantisme*, Chapter Six, "La Pratique religieuse," pp. 98 ff.

23. Ibid., pp. 100-101.

24. E. R. Wickham, F. G. Dreyfus, P. Bolle, F. Andrieux.

25. In the sense of Karl Barth's celebrated aphorism: *Religion ist Unglaube*. Religion is the absence of faith. Faith is foreign to religion because: *"Was der Mensh in der Religion will? Rechtfertigung und Heiligung als sein eigenes Werk." Dogmatik*, 12 para. 17. Barth's aphorism is held by some to be nonsensical, a product of the theological ivory tower. See Claus Janco Bleeker, *Christ in Modern Athens* (1965), p. 93. It has been vigorously commented by others. See Roger Mehl, "La Contestation protestante" in *A.S.R.*

26. Balzac imagined an extreme case of this in *La Messe de l'athée*.

27. F. Jeanson, *La Foi d'un inconnu* (Paris, 1963). For the opposite and complementary sense, see the special number of *Jeunesse de l'Eglise: L'Incroyance des croyants*.

28. Friedrich Heiler, *La Prière* (Paris, 1921); see the section "Les Types de prière," pp. 39 ff.

29. Henri Bergson, *The Two Sources of Morality and Religion* (New York: Henry Holt, 1935), p. 153.

30. See Henri Desroche, "Théologie et typologie dans la sociologie religieuse de Wach" in *A.S.R.* 1, pp. 41-63; also end of Chapter Two above.

31. Joachim Wach, *Types of Religious Experience. Christian and non-Christian* (Chicago: University of Chicago Press, 1951), p. 59.

32. Ibid., p. 55.

33. "The intrinsic value attributed to myths comes from the notion that these events which are supposed to have taken place at a given moment in time also have a permanent structure. This relates them simultaneously to the past, the present and the future." Lévi-Strauss, p. 231.

34. Joachim Wach, *Types*.

35. Theoretical expression is "doctrine"; practical expression is "cult."

36. Joachim Wach, *Sociology of Religion* (University of Chicago Press, 1944), pp. 45-50.

37. Ibid., pp. 55 ff.; Gustav Mensching, *Sociologie religieuse* (Paris: Payot, 1951), pp. 14-15.

38. Wach, *Sociology*, Chapters Seven and Eight.

39. Ibid., pp. 158 ff.

40. See "Church, Denomination and Sect" in Wach, *Types*, pp. 187-208.

41. For Troeltsch the Church type is by its own nature extensive, but at the expense of a loss in intensity due to acculturation. The sect type is, on the other hand, deliberately intensive, but with a loss of extensiveness due to the selectivity of its criteria. See "Sect-type and Church-type Contrasted" in *The Social Teaching of the Christian Churches* (London: G. Allen; New York: Macmillan), 1, p. 331.

42. Jean Séguy, "Bulletin bibliographique" in *A.S.R.*

43. Guglielmo Guariglia, Vittorio Lanternari, de Queiroz, Talmon-Garber.

44. See F. Isambert, "La Phénoménologie religieuse," in *Introduction aux sciences des religions* (Paris: Cujas).

45. "A god understood is no god at all" (Tersteegen). Without going this far, see Mauss's interpretation as presented by Lévi-Strauss in *Sociologie et anthropologie*, Introduction, p. xxviii.

46. Unifying what was given as plural: the unity of a phenomenon recurring in time and in space. See, for example, the analyses of the rope miracle, androgyny and the return of the dead

in Mircéa Eliade, *Méphistophélès et l'Androgyne* (1962). For discussion of these pluralizations of god, of masculine and feminine, singular and plural, dyad and triad, etc., and of the disappearance of a single sense for many religious terms, see Gerardus Van der Leeuw, *Phénoménologie religieuse.*

47. Beginning with the bibliographical information published twice a year in the "Bulletin bibliographique" of the *A.S.R.*

48. For a discussion of the convergences and contrasts, see J. C. Gardin, "Analyse documentaire et analyse structurale en archéologie," in *L'Arc* 26, pp. 64-68.

49. Typologies lived: those typologies through which religious phenomena reach a self-interpretation. Typologies conceptionally assumed: those typologies which include both the phenomenon and its self-interpretation, both the presence of the religious fact and the way it sees itself.

50. "The more clear a structure appears, the more difficult it is to grasp its real nature." Yet there are good reasons "for considering the first as a road leading to the second." See the discussion in Lévi-Strauss, p. 309.

51. By analogy with the morphemes and phonemes of linguistics and the "gustemes" of culinary art.

52. Recognized by historians as well as by phenomenologists.

53. See Raymond Aron, "Formes élémentaires," in *Etapes*, pp. 345 and 360-361. In this provocative analysis Aron studies these different relations and does not disguise his discomfort and reluctance when confronted with Durkheim's propositions about religion and the sacred.

54. We prefer the term "experimental" to the term "empirical."

We are mindful of Durkheim's principle. "One will object that a single religion, whatever may be its field of extension, constitutes a very narrow base for an induction like this. We know very well what a widely based verification adds to the authority of a theory. Yet it is no less true that when a law has been proved by a well-conceived experiment this proof is universally valid." *Formes*, p. 593.

55. It would be interesting to make a comparative study of Durkheim and Rudolf Otto. One would find in them a large measure of agreement on the primary importance of the sacred; but in Durkheim one would find a primary emphasis on the study of the social conditions of existence and, as it were, of its explosion; in Otto the primary emphasis would be on a study of the content of the sacred and its phenomenological variables.

56. See Durkheim, *Formes*, passim. For example: "All religious beliefs assume a classification into two classes which the words sacred and profane designate clearly enough. A division of the world into two realms, one including all that is sacred, the other including all that is profane, this is the distinctive trait of religious thought . . ." (pp. 50-51).

57. Perhaps more accurately, Otto characterizes religion as "a schematizing of the irrational by the rational" (p. 95). Thus religion, for him, would be composed of a certain dosage of irrational elements (noumenal or sacred) and rational elements ("the administration"). "The presence of these two elements in a healthy and perfect harmony constitutes a standard for measuring the superiority of a religion and is a properly religious criterium" (p. 192).

58. A trend observed in contemporary art. The more it is polarized toward the sacred, the less welcome it will be

to religion. C. Bourniquel and J. G. Meili, *Les Créateurs et le sacré* (Paris: Cerf, 1966), pp. 18, 21.

59. For a discussion of sacrilege as a contagious form of the profane, see Durkheim, *Formes*, p. 587. The concept of "profanization" is post-Durkheim. It designates a desacralization which is not a profanation.

60. "Morality without God and atheism without Nature" (Burnouf); "An absolutely atheist doctrine" (Barth); "Religion without God" (Oldenberg), cited in Durkheim, *Formes*, pp. 41-42. In this text Oldenberg adds: "Thus Buddhism is atheistic in the sense that it is not concerned with the question of knowing whether or not there are gods" (p. 43). On Jainism, see pp. 45-46.

61. Durkheim, *Formes*, p. 49. "Thus religion goes beyond the idea of gods and spirits and, consequently, cannot be exclusively defined in terms of these."

62. See J. P. Deconchy, *Structure génétique de l'idée de Dieu chez les catholiques français* (Bruxelles: Lumen Vitae, 1967). Reactivation of a theology of divine names, using the techniques of psychology and mathematics.

63. For a discussion of the structural treatment of the triangle, see the model already cited and presented by Lévi-Strauss: "Le Triangle culinaire" in *L'Arc* 26, pp. 13 ff.

64. In discussing this problem, the views of Durkheim and Otto have been reviewed in the stimulating work by Roger Caillois, *Le Sacré*.

65. Durkheim, *Formes*, pp. 61-62. "In history we do not find religion without a church" (p. 60).

66. Ibid., p. 63.

67. "Sometimes the church is headed by a body of priests, sometimes it is completely without any official directing body." Ibid., p. 61.

68. See Yves Congar, *Jalons pour une théologie du laïcat* (1953 ed.), pp. 27-28 in which the author emphasizes the two sources of this distinction and its relativity: although one cannot be both a layman and a cleric, one can be a monk and at the same time be either a cleric or a layman.

69. See above.

70. See Henri Desroche, *Socialismes et sociologie religieuse* (Paris: Cujas, 1965), pp. 19-20.

71. Max Weber, *The Protestant Ethic*, Fr. ed., pp. 160 ff.

72. "Participation by laymen in the activities of the Church hierarchy." This is the credo of the participationist movement in the Catholic Church. Some will deem it artificial; others will see it as the only possibility. The first will deem this congregationalizing an ideal; the second will see it as an impossibility.

73. Wach is wary of a too facile identification of the sect with a popular ecclesiastical body and, in this sense, with laymen (*laos*: the people). A sect can be aristocratic and a High Church can recruit widely among the lower classes. *Types*, p. 203.

74. Durkheim, *Formes*, pp. 428 ff.

75. R. Carneiro, "Scale Analysis as an Instrument for the Study of Cultural Evolution," *Southwestern Journal of Anthropology* no. 18 (1962). This article was reviewed by J. Cuisenier, "Le Structuralisme du mot, de l'idée et des outils," in *Esprit*, May 1967, pp. 825 ff.

76. R. Carneiro, "Scale Analysis," p. 832, chart no. 6.

77. Ibid., p. 832. Chart no. 5: the number of traits, by society; the number of societies, by trait.

78. For in its present state it is obviously elementary and unusable

except for establishing a crude profile.

Chapter Five

1. "We are a long way from the idea that historical and geographical considerations are of no value in structural studies. . . . The work of G. Dumézil and the personal example of A. L. Kroeber prove that the historical method is in no way incompatible with a structural attitude." Lévi-Strauss, *Anthropologie structurale*, p. 319.

2. See: Viet on "le structuro-fonctionnalisme," pp. 130 and *passim*; on "le structuralisme génétique," pp. 143 and *passim*. It is generally recognized that Lucien Goldman, the pioneer of this second tendency, made an important contribution to the field in *Le Dieu caché* (Paris, 1955).

3. These propositions and this question were presented in a thesis: A. Touraine, *Sociologie de l'action*, pp. 40, 89, 137, 453-454.

4. Although this view is not that of Touraine, it is not completely absent from his analysis. See ibid., pp. 43 and 464-465.

5. Durkheim, *Formes*, pp. 312-313.

6. Ibid., pp. 534, 543, 544. This hypothesis could well serve as a guiding principle for a whole research. The trances and inspired messages of the Cevenol prophets are recorded in the *Théâtre sacré des Cévennes*. At the height of the crisis between theatre and the Church, Lucien Goldman describes the substitution which was at the origin of Racinian tragedy. See *Le Dieu caché*, p. 449.

7. Moreover, this is what confirms the practices of any given religion once it has been reassembled in the play of seasonal or yearly cycles. It occurs when these practices act out the historical presence of the founder and his misfortunes in a dramatization of his coming, his birth, his life, his death and resurrection. To this is added the miming of the same role by great actors who appeared after the founder.

8. Sartre, *Critique de la raison dialectique* (Paris, 1960), p. 44.

9. The "need to violate those rules which are ordinarily the most respected." Durkheim, *Formes*, p. 547. This retroactive canonizing can come about very quickly; less than a century after his death the asocial Gauguin became an object of veneration in Tahiti where his name was given to a street, a lycée and a museum.

10. Ibid., p. 545. Raymond Aron says that this possibility can give rise to formidable primary effects: "The time will come when modern societies will once more be seized by sacred delirium and it is from this that new religiousness will be born." Aron, *Les Etapes de la pensée sociologique* (Paris, 1964), p. 356. (The memory of Hitlerite ceremonies in Nuremberg bears this out, alas.)

11. See the pertinent studies by Métraux on voodoo, and by Bastide on the Candomblay cult: Alfred Métraux, *Le Vodou haïtien* (Paris: 1958); Roger Bastide, *Le Candomblé de Bahia*. Also: Alfred Métraux, *Haïti, la terre, les hommes et les dieux* (Paris, 1957), pp. 84-88. Also: Michel Leiris, *La Possession et ses actes théâtraux chez les Ethiopiens de Gondar* (Paris, 1958).

12. This orgiastic nostalgia is seen in places where song and dance have induced trances. Descriptions and observations of this resemble the "rolling exercises, jerks and barks" that I located in Shaker archives of the British Museum. See Henri Desroche, *Les Shakers américains* (Paris, 1955), pp. 116-117.

13. See Nietzsche's *The Birth of Tragedy*. Also the detailed commentary in J. Duvignaud, *L'Acteur, esquisse d'une sociologie du comédien* (Paris: Gallimard, 1965).

14. Metraux, *Le Vodou haïtien*, p. 89.

15. Desroche, *Les Shakers américains*, p. 117.

16. On this distinction and on the people's holiday as an exoteric manifestation of contemplative esotericism, see: L. Festugière, *La Contemplation chez Platon* (Vrin).

17. Durkheim, *Formes*, p. 553. Rituals described as "the means whereby a group periodically reaffirms itself." See information on mimetic and dramatic rites, pp. 514 ff.

18. On Durkheim's identification of this collectivity with a "church" see the discussion above—the subject will not be taken up again here. On individual experiences of ecstasy, see: J. Bruno, "L'Extase et ses voies d'accès" in *Critique*, juin 1967, pp. 555-568. In this article the author comments on two pieces by M. Lasky: *Ecstasy, a Study of Some Secular and Religious Experiences* (London, 1961) and *Ecstasy or Religious Trance in the Experience of the Ecstatics and from the Psychological Point of View* (Stockholm, 1963).

19. Just as a dialectical materialism will keep open the controversy between a mythologizing interpretation and a historicizing interpretation of Christianity. Was Jesus a real person who was later transformed into a myth? Or was he created from a collective myth and later endowed with historical reality? For a dossier on this controversy see H. Desroche, *Socialismes et sociologie religieuse* (Paris: Cujas, 1965), pp. 383-404.

20. Friedrich Heiler, *La Prière* (Paris, 1921), pp. 13-14. He emphasizes the extent to which great religious leaders are insignificant people socially. This does not mean that the great religious personalities, once canonized, are not socially important, as Pitrim Sorokin pointed out in *Altruistic Love* (1950). But that is another problem and comes under the subject of sociology of canonization, not the sociology of sainthood. On the latter, see: P. Delooz, "Pour une étude sociologique de la sainteté canonisée dans l'Eglise catholique," *A.S.R.* 13, pp. 17-44—particularly pp. 23 ff. on the distinction between "real saint" and "fabricated saint."

21. Henri Bergson, *Les Deux Sources de la morale et de la religion* (Paris, 1932), p. 217. During the second part of the book one can follow the development of this definition. See pp. 123, 127, 137, 146, 209.

22. Ibid., p. 285.

23. See: Ernst Troeltsch, *The Social Teaching of the Christian Churches* (New York, Macmillan), vol. 2, pp. 745 ff. Also the commentaries of Jean Séguy, "Ernst Troeltsch et sa sociologie du christianisme," *Cahiers du Cercle E. Renan* 8, no. 32, 4th trimester, 1961.

24. Quoted in Jean Séguy, "Ernst Troeltsch." This part of Troeltsch is hailed as quite exceptional by Gershom Sholem, "Mysticisme et société, un paradoxe créateur," in *Diogène* 58, 1967, pp. 3-28.

25. Henri Bergson, *Les Deux Sources*, pp. 227-229.

26. This is not the only image. Fire imagery is also predominant.

27. The images used reveal that the writer has opted for a sociogogical tradition. Even if one retains his conclusion, the content remains relative. Bergson shares Durkheim's taste for the tradition of frenzy and ferment, even though he believes that this is

the domain of privileged personal experience rather than of collective experience. But taking the proposition as it stands and supposing it to have been written for or by a mystic in the ataraxic tradition (especially if it has been written in the stifling, energy-sapping heat of the tropics), could not one just as well apply to it a vocabulary in which the terms hot and cold have been reversed?

28. Bergson, *Les Deux Sources,* p. 269.

29. With a mistrust of rudimentary elements when they are suspected of being only embryonic. Ibid., p. 295.

30. Uncovering this phenomenon (the creation of religious creators) is a contribution made by Bergson's *sociology*; Bergson's *philosophy* gives it a special meaning: "The Creation in this context is seen as something undertaken by God in order to create creators and provide Him with creatures worthy of his love." But this philosophical interpretation is not implied in the sociological analysis mentioned above. And, although his sociology does not involve this philosophy, it would be unfortunate if a rejection of this philosophy carried with it a rejection of this sociology.

31. See Hegel's *Philosophy of Religion.* "Here we face the problem of knowing how a religion is founded, in other words of knowing in what manner the substantive spirit reveals itself in a people's consciousness. This involves an event that can be characterized as historical. Its beginnings are imperceptible. Those who become the interpreter of this spirit are prophets and poets. Herodotus said: Homer and Hesiod gave the Greeks their gods. At this point we must take the action of Homer

and Hesiod into account, but their action was recognized only because the words they used expressed the Greek spirit."

32. "When we criticize or defend a religion how often do we consider what there is in that religion that is specifically religious." Bergson, *Les Deux Sources,* p. 286.

33. Homology in a brilliant article by Sertillanges, quoted below in this text.

34. See the thesis by Pie Duployé which has already become a classic. Also, in the same sense: Maurice Blondel, *L'Action*; and J. Lacroix, *L'Echec.*

35. "An essential distinction: the one between primary functions answering a present need of the social organism and secondary functions which survive only because the group is reluctant to give up a habit." See above.

36. Roger Bastide, *Les Amériques noirs* (Paris: Payot, 1967), pp. 133-134. This is Chapter Six, "Reiigions en conserve et religions vivantes."

37. This sociology of religion can and should be included in a sociology of social-life-as-theatre. On this point see: J. Duvignaud, *Introduction à la sociologie* (Paris: Gallimard, 1966), pp. 75 ff. (especially the chapter on "le drame social"). On the other hand this sociology of innovation affirms, laterally, something like a "theology of hope" that has been sensitized to a Marxism of hope similar to the one proposed by E. Bloch. On this see the provocative analyses by H. Mottu on the work of J. Moltmann (*Theologie der Hoffnung*): Mottu, "L'Espérance chrétienne dans la pensée de Jurgen Moltmann," in *Revue théologique et de philosophie* (Lausanne, 1967) 4, pp. 242-258.

Chapter Six

1. On this "reciprocal articulation of theory and practice" in Saint-Simon, Buchez and their schools, see F. Isambert, *Buchez ou l'âge théologique de la sociologie* (Paris: Cujas, 1967), pp. 15 ff.

2. See Raymond Saint-Jean, *Genèse de "l'Action": Blondel, 1882-1893* (Paris: Desclée, 1955). Reviewed in *A.S.R.* 22, no. 227.

3. Sertillanges, "Le Libre Arbitre chez Bergson et saint Thomas d'Aquin," *Vie intellectuelle*, 25 avril 1937, pp. 252-267.

4. Alain Touraine, *Sociologie de l'action*, p. 43.

5. See above, Chapter Three, Section 1.

6. A few traits: "Among peoples with no writing there is something like an excess of the sacred. . . . In our society, on the other hand, psychosomatic illnesses . . . betray a diminishing of the sacred" (Otto, *Le Sacré*, p. 270). "Nietzsche said: 'In former days one could seek refuge in a monastery; today our only place of refuge is madness.' Thus the insane asylum becomes a secularized monastery with the new liturgies of a world which, after chasing away the great Pan, is determined to kill off God. To a large extent, madness is a disease of the sacred" (ibid., pp. 269-270).

7. "The reciprocal relation between Theatre and Religion," seminar prepared for the year 1968-1969. See the collection *Le Choeur des muses* in the series *Recherches sur le théâtre*.

8. Jean Duvignaud, *Sociologie du théâtre* (Paris: Presses Universitaires de France, 1965; *Sociologie de l'acteur* (Paris: N.R.F., 1965); also *Introduction à la sociologie* (Gallimard: Coll. *Idées*, 1966), particularly the chapter on "Le Drame social," pp. 75 ff.

9. Including the effect of "continuing" education on the teaching of children.

10. See Emile Durkheim, *Education et sociologie* (Paris: Presses Universitaires de France, 1966), section on "Définition de l'éducation," pp. 37 ff.

11. Paul Arbousse-Bastide, "Auguste Comte et la sociologie religieuse," *A.S.R.* 22, p. 52. Also his *La Doctrine de l'éducation universelle dans la philosophie d'Auguste Comte* (Paris: Presses Universitaires de France, 1957).

12. "This extension . . . does not mean that the sociologist is condemned to non-intervention. . . . His role is one of educator and critic, etc." Touraine, *Sociologie de l'action*, p. 465.

13. See Gabriel Le Bras, "Différences entre la sociologie scientifique et la sociologie pastorale," *A.S.R.* 8, pp. 5-14.

14. Jean Duvignaud, *Sociologie du théâtre*, Introduction: "In order to exist man must first play a part; he acts out his existence in order to become a reality. . . . Collective existence becomes real when it dramatizes itself."

15. See the bibliography already indicated above, Chapter One, Note 61; Chapter Two, notes 21-26.

16. Bernhard Haering, *Forces et faiblesse de la religion* (Paris, 1964), Fr. trans. of Ger. 3rd. ed.

17. The studies were by Emile Poulat in "La Sociologie religieuse et son objet" in *Critique* 118, jan. 1967, pp. 229-242; and Jacques Maître, "Les Sociologies du Catholicisme français" in *Cahiers Internationaux Sociologiques* 24, 1958, pp. 104-124.

18. For just one sample of this, filled with references, see John Arthur Thomas Robinson, *The New Reformation*, Fr. trans. *La Nouvelle Réforme* (Paris: Delachaux & Niestlé, 1967). Particularly Chapter Three, pp. 55 ff.

19. The most recent and best of these has been set up by the collection *Etudes de sociologie* which has just published Jacques Maître, *Les Prêtres*

ruraux devant la modernisation des campagnes (Paris: Centurion, 1967).

20. For a fine example of the hypotheses used in a treatment like this, see J. M. Serreau on the theatre of Genet, Beckett and Ionesco. Remarks edited by P. Laville in *Bref*, fév-mars, 1967, p. 20.

21. Emile Poulat, "Le Développement institutionnel des sciences religieuses en France," *A.S.R.* 21, pp. 23-26.

22. John Arthur Thomas Robinson, *The New Reformation*, pp. 70 ff. The author formulates a similar thesis, but bases it on ecclesiastical teaching of theology. Referring to J. Cope's *Theology for Adults*, he points out once more the importance of setting up an organization for a system of "continuing" education (*extra muros*).

23. Already published in an article: "D'une décennie à l'autre. De la sociographie de la pratique religieuse à une pratique de la sociologie des religions," *A.S.R.* 20, pp. 3-6.

24. "One would be wrong to conclude from this that the religious system should entirely disappear: it should adjust itself to progress being made by the sciences." Saint-Simon, *Dernières paroles*.

25. "Whereas the Protestants and the Deists have always attacked religion in the name of God, we would do away with God in the name of religion." Auguste Comte, quoted in *P.A.B.*, p. 24.

26. "There is then in religion something eternal which is destined to survive all particular symbols representing it. . . . The day will come when our societies will know again the creative ferment, and when this happens new ideas will be born. . . . Although the work of the French Revolution was aborted, it does enable us to imagine what could have occurred in other circum-

stances: and there is every reason to believe that sooner or later it will come again. None of the gospels are immortal, and there is no reason to believe that humanity has become incapable of inventing new ones." Durkheim, *Formes*, pp. 609-611 and passim.

Chapter Seven

1. Henri Desroche, "Religion et développement: le thème de leurs rapports réciproques et ses variations," in *Archives de Sociologie des Religions*, 1961, vol. 12. Article reprinted in Henri Desroche, *Socialismes et sociologie religieuse* (Paris: Cujas, 1965), pp. 338 ff.

2. Weber's ideas were recently discussed in J. Freund, *La Sociologie de Max Weber* (Paris, Presses Universitaires de France, coll. SUP-le Sociologue), pp. 153 ff.; also J. A. Prades, *La Sociologie de la religion chez Max Weber* (Paris-Louvain, 1966); R. Aron, *Les Etapes de la pensée sociologique* (Paris: Gallimard), pp. 259 ff., particularly his discussion (pp. 540-542) of Weber's affirmation; Max Weber, *Ethique* (Paris: Plon), pp. 248-249. See also, Niles M. Hanson, "The Protestant Ethic as a General Precondition for Economic Development," in *Canadian Journal of Economics and Political Science*, Nov. 29, 1963, vol. 4, p. 462 ff.

3. Hanson, p. 473.

4. Ibid.

5. For example, this is unaccounted for in theories (which are, nevertheless, theological) of secularization such as advanced by J. A. T. Johnson: "The God hypothesis is not to be taken any more seriously here as a guide for the economy or a way of facing the problem of over-population than in the system set up by Laplace."

6. On this system of transmitting and receiving, see this chapter, note 12.

7. A. Niehoff and J. Niehoff, "The Influence of Religion on Socio-Economic Development," *International Development Review*, 1966, vol. 2, pp. 6-11.

8. Ibid.

9. See above, this chapter, note 1.

10. Traumatic reactions which can give rise to paradoxical experiences. But it is impossible here to make any detailed analyses of what these short-lived messianisms produced. See R. Bastide, "Le Messianisme raté," in *Le Prochain et le lointaine: Essai sur les rencontres des civilisations* (Paris: Cujas); also, Henri Desroche, "Les Messianismes et la catégorie de l'échec," *Cahiers Internationaux de Sociologie* 10 (35), juillet-déc. 1963, pp. 61-84; Festinger et al., *When Prophecy Fails* (Minneapolis, 1955).

11. See Henri Desroche, *Marxisme et religions* (Paris: Presses Universitaires de France, 1961). In the same line and sometimes with the same words, is Roger Garaudy, "Les Marxistes et les Chrétiens," in *La Lettre*, avril 1965, pp. 20 ff.; likewise, *De l'anathème au dialogue* (Paris: Plon, 1965).

12. For a more micro-sociological but also more operational presentation of this grid, see the interesting proposals of A. H. Niehoff and J. C. Anderson, "Positive, Negative and Neutral Factors: The Process of Cross Cultural Innovation," *International Development Review*, 1964, vol. 2, pp. 5-12. These proposals coincide with the system of emission-reception described above, but in the article's terminology this system becomes:

Emission	*Reception*
Behavior of	Behavior of
innovator	receivers
ACTION	REACTION

13. See the symposium, "Religion et développement" in *A.S.R.* 15, pp. 5-11; also Jean Séguy, "Sectes chrétiennes et développement," in *A.S.R.* 13, pp. 5-15.

14. Hanson, "The Protestant Ethic."

15. See, for example, the special number of *Parti pris* ("Pour une laïcisation véritable"), 8 avril 1965, vol. 2; also "Les Classes sociales au Canada français," in *Recherches Sociographiques*, 1965, vol. 6, p. 1.

16. In effect: "religion necessarily results in efficiency of production and frugality of consumption, and causes like this cannot help but produce riches. . . . But as riches increase, so does a people's love for the world in all its manifestations. Thus, although the form of religion remains the same, its spirit is surreptitiously undermined. . . ."

17. See Will Herberg's classic work, *Protestant, catholique et juif*; also, Henri Desroche, "Amérique religieuse ou religion de l'américanité? in *R.H.Ph.R.* 4 (Strasbourg, 1960).

18. This concept of the nation-class was first proposed by Henri Lefebvre.

19. F. R. Von der Mehden, *Religion and Nationalism in South East Asia, Burma, Indonesia and the Philippines* (Madison: University of Wisconsin Press, 1963).

20. Ibid., p. 10.

21. Ibid., pp. 24-25.

22. According to the title of P. Moussa's book.

23. Von der Mehden's examples do not exhaust the ways of looking at the relation between nationalism and religion. There are other cases, such as India, in which two dominated religions simultaneously gave birth to two states (India and Pakistan) and in which the religious community produced a "communalism" which is really nothing more than a quasi or hybrid nationalism. The case of India is studied in detail by L. Dumont in his *Homo hierarchicus*

(Paris: Gallimard, 1966), Appendix D, pp. 376-395.

24. P. Stibbe pointed this out in December 1962 during the Dakar colloquium on African routes to socialism. See his *Développement et socialism* (Paris: Présence africaine, 1963), p. 408.

25. *L'A.B.C. du paysan* by Francisco Juliao presents a remarkable example of this. See a long extract in Henri Desroche, "Aléas d'un coopératism sud-américain," in *A.I.S.C.* 15, jan.-juin 1964, p. 30.

26. Several research projects are currently underway on this four-part typology. The types which it sets up can naturally occur in combinations. Thus we get the combination of 3 + 4 which is now being used in research on a "pastorate of development."

27. When Maurice Montuclard speaks about the "transference of forms of sociability" he applies the same analysis and reaches the same conclusion. See his "L'Episode démocratique chrétien" in *Consience religieuse et démocratie* (Paris: Seuil, 1965), p. 205.

28. The pattern for the North Sahara area of Africa would naturally be different. Study of this particular case seems to have been the result of an article "Politics or Religion" published in *Révolution africaine* 191, Oct. 1966, pp. 21-22, about a project attributed to King Feisal of Saudi Arabia. The study was undertaken by an Islamic committee similar to the one set up by Vatican II for Christianity. See the glosses by J. Teillac in "Dialogue: Politique ou religion?" published in *L'Afrique et l'Asie* 77, 1st trimester 1967, pp. 39-43. The survey mentioned deals with African agents working in the program of cooperative development. They were requested to limit their

remarks to the problem discussed here.

29. See report on the most recent Bouaké survey and an evaluation of his preceding papers: Henri Desroche, "Syncrétisme et messianisme en Afrique Noire," *Archives de Sociologie des Religions* 16, pp. 105-108. On the preceding papers see: *Tradition et modernisme en Afrique Noire* (Paris: Seuil, 1962); *Les Religions africaines traditionnelles* (Paris: Seuil, 1965).

30. He does not consider the two principle types of nonreligion which, unfortunately, are included in the single term "non-religion" as used here may mean either the presence of a nonreligious conviction or the absence of any conviction, whether it be religious or not. For remarks on this diversity, but in an American framework, see Martin E. Marty, *Varieties of Unbelief from Nihilism to Atheism, from Agnosticism to Apathy* (New York, 1964).

31. Cheikh Amidou Khane, *L'Aventure ambiguë*; also G. Balandier, *L'Afrique ambiguë*.

32. See the subtle analyses of Michel Souriau in his *L'Ombre de Dieu*.

33. The proverb is quoted and commented on in the conclusion of Henri Desroche, *Socialismes et sociologie religieuse.*

34. Transcript edited by R. N. Bellah, *Religion and Progress in Modern Asia* (New York Press, 1965).

35. Ibid., p. ix.

36. We intend to return to this problem in the introduction to a re-edition of Saint-Simon's *Nouveau Christianisme* now being prepared for Editions Seuil.

37. See, for example R. Colin, "L'Animation et le développement rural en Afrique francophone," *Archives Internationales de Sociologie Coopérative* 20, juillet-déc. 1966, pp. 137-217. For a study of a case in

Northeast Brazil, see Henri Desroche, "Aléas d'un coopératisme sud-américain," pp. 9-41. For the problems of coming to self-consciousness, pp. 56 ff.

38. Soedjatmoko, "Cultural Motivations to Progress: the 'Exterior' and the 'Interior' Views," pp. 1-14.

39. N. Rostov, *Les Etapes de la croissance économique* (Paris: Seuil, 1962), p. 69.

40. In a colloquium on African development, in Marseille, 16-18 April 1964.

41. Another similar analysis in Rostov, *Les Etapes*, p. 63. "It is evident that the repeated occurrence implied the existence and the reality of a social group prepared to accept these innovations."

42. See Henri Desroche, "Fifth World Congress of Sociology: Report of Committee on Religion and Development," *A.S.R.* 15, pp. 5-20; also the symposium which follows, pp. 21-112. Further, the group of reports "Religion et politique dans l'Asie du Sud-Est," *A.S.R.* 17, pp. 45-96; O. Gelinier, *Morale de l'entreprise et gestion de la Nation* (Paris: Plon, 1965).

43. "Never in History do we see these imperious superstructures respectfully step aside when they have done their job, nor do they dissipate into thin air because it is time for his Majesty Economics to advance down the royal road of dialectics. Neither at the beginning nor at the end do we hear the solitary hour of the last command striking." Louis Althusser, *Pour Marx* (Paris: Maspero, 1966), p. 113. See also Henri Desroche, "Dernière Instance," and "Premier Rôle," *A.S.R.* 23.

44. Including a sociology of the pastorate. See, for example Henri Maurier, *Religion et développement:* *Traditions africaines et catéchèses* (Paris: Mame, 1965).

45. Willem Frederik Wetheim, *East-West Parallels: Sociological Approaches to Modern Asia* (La Haye, 1964), particularly Chapter Six, "Religious Reform Movements," and Chapter Seven, "Religion, Bureaucracy and Economic Growth," pp. 133-163, previously published in *A.S.R.* 12 and 15.

46. Ibid., p. 276.

47. Not invented here just to support our argument.

48. See the interesting socio-theological introduction to the French translation, written by V. Cosmao. *Populorum progressio* (Paris: Editions du Centurion, 1967).

49. A recent UNESCO document bases a whole series of problems on the distinction between "transfer" and "implantation." "It is implantation and not transfer that is being sought by the project. . . ."

50. See Henri Desroche, "Proposition de quelques thèses sur les classes sociales," in *Cahiers Internationaux de Sociologie* 40, 1966, pp. 157-158, particularly the passage suggested by Jacques Berque.

51. During Bouaké's colloquium (see *A.S.R.* 16, pp. 105-108) there was a heated controversy between the two analytic series: the series of messianic phenomena and the series of cultic possession. The first series was steeped in history, the second knew nothing of history; they both represented a global solution to similar situations, but the solution of each one implied the exclusion of the other. On this dilemma, see: Mircéa Eliade, *Le Mythe de l'éternel retour: Archétypes et répétitions* (Paris: Gallimard, 1949).

52. The words "developmentism" and "developmentist" have come into common use and . . . they are

terms of opprobrium in certain Latin-American university circles.

53. Soedjatmoko, "Cultural Motivations to Progress," pp. 6 ff.

54. "This result would require the existence of a group of scholars and intellectuals willing to devote themselves continuously to this endeavor, who would take it upon themselves to bring the many often unconscious assumptions on which social action and decision-making in our transitional societies are predicated into the daylight of consciousness, to try to make them explicit and open them to rational examination. This function would clearly be of great importance for more effective communication and might facilitate fuller mobilization of human resources for the purpose of speeding up economic development." Ibid., p. 9.

Chapter Eight

1. See reports of the interdisciplinary seminars set up by teachers and researchers for experimental work on a section of some common problem. Each year these reports are published in the collection *Genèses* (Paris: Cujas). The first year report (1968) was called *Introduction aux sciences humaines des religions* and will be referred to here as *I.S.R.*

2. Jean Séguy, "Panorama des sciences des religions," in *I.S.R.*

3. Yet see discussion in Roger Mehl, *De l'Autorité des valeurs* (Paris: Presses Universitaires de France, 1957); also P. Maydieu, *Le Désaccord*.

4. H. C. Puech and P. Vignaux, "Les Sciences religieuses en France," in *Les Sciences sociales en France: Enseignement et recherche* (Paris:

Hartmann, 1937). A revised version of this text is incorporated as a preface in the Symposium, *I.S.R.* The two authors refer to H. Pinard de la Boullaye, *Etude comparée des religions*, vol. 1: *Son Histoire dans le monde occidental* (Paris: Beauchêne, 1929).

5. On this point, see the studies of Georges de Lagarde, *La Naissance de l'esprit laïc au déclin du Moyen Age*.

6. In 1735 came the surmises of Jean Astruc on "the early memoirs Moses is supposed to have consulted in composing the book of Genesis."

7. Curiously, a Soviet author indicates that there was a similar conjunction in the development of social sciences and sociology in Marxist countries. "At that time Marxist dogma, which dominated the life in those countries, split into various tendencies (U.S.S.R., China, Jugoslavia) and each one claimed to be orthodox. The only way to break out of the vicious circle of sterile arguments about dogma was to support one or another of these theses with precise scientific documentation. . . . This was a delicate procedure and risked appearing "revisionist,' but the first steps in this direction were actually taken." V. Poremsky, *La Sociologie soviétique vue par les savants occidentaux* (mimeo, 1966).

8. Vernière, for example, showed the impact of "Chinese atheism" on the diffusion of Spinozism in Europe. See R. Vernière, *Spinoza et la pensée française avant la révolution* (1954), pp. 345 ff. He credits Diderot with the idea that Spinozism was related to Chinese atheism (p. 589). Paul Hazard had already explored this relation. See his *Crise*, vol. 1, pp. 27 ff. Paul Demiéville developed it further in his "Premiers Contacts philosophiques Chine-Europe," in *Diogène* 58, 1967, pp. 80-110.

9. See C. F. Dupuis and his sytem

of the *Origine de tous les cultes à partir d'un symbolisme astronomique* (1781-1795). Also, Benjamin Constant, *De la religion considérée dans ses sources, ses formes et ses développements* (1824). Note that this phase is contemporary to the phase of Saint-Simon which borrowed from Dupuis and had skirmishes with Constant.

10. The sociographic results of this approach can and have been used both for prolonging the "pastorate" approach and for developing a "materialist" interpretation. See Gilbert Mury, *Essor ou déclin du catholicisme français* (Paris: Editions Sociales, 1960).

11. Emile Poulat, "Le Développement institutionnel des sciences religieuses en France," *A.S.R.* 21, 1966, pp. 23-36, hereafter cited as "Le Développement institutionnel."

12. Ibid., p. 28.

13. Ibid., pp. 13 and 29.

14. Ibid., p. 29. For a more detailed inventory of these emerging non-theological sciences of religion in France, see the collected studies which will be reprinted in the Symposium *I.S.R.*

15. See F. A. Isambert, *Christianisme et classe ouvrière: jalons pour une sociologie historique* (Paris: Casterman, 1961); also his *Buchez ou l'âge théologique de la sociologie* (Paris: Cujas, 1967).

16. See Emile Poulat, *Histoire, dogme et critique dans la crise moderniste* (Paris: Casterman, 1962). On "social Christianity" and Protestantism in France, despite some valorous efforts, there is no equivalent of the work done on Germany by W. Shanahan, *German Protestants Face to the Social Question.*

17. See Maurice Montuclard, *Conscience religieuse et démocratie* (Paris: Seuil, 1965) and a previous

work by J. B. Duroselle, *Les Débuts du catholicisme social en France.*

18. For an introduction to this, see: R. Raymond and F. Dreyfus, *Les Forces religieuses en France.* On Missionary Action see E. Poulat's exploratory study, *La Naissance des prêtres-ouvriers* (Paris: Casterman, 1965).

19. Saint-Simon did not commit this error, since throughout the work he affirmed the decisive importance of Arab science.

20. Quoted in Poulat, *"Le Développement institutionnel,"* pp. 27-28.

21. C. Gillipsie, *Genesis and geology. A Lively Account of the Impact of Scientific Discoveries upon Religious Beliefs in the Decades before Darwin* (Cambridge, Mass.: Harvard University Press, 1951), p. 323.

22. See Albert Houtin, *La Question biblique.*

23. Emile Poulat, "Le Développement institutionnel."

24. Duroselle, *Les Débuts du catholicisme social en France.*

25. See Marc Bloch, *Apologie pour l'histoire ou le métier d'historien,* 4th ed. (Paris, 1961).

26. "There is then only one measure for Man in time and it forever needs to join the study of the living to the study of the dead." Ibid.

27. Henri Desroche, "Théologie et sociologie dans la typologie de J. Wach," in *A.S.R.* where the Wach symposium also offers a bibliography. See above, Chapter Two.

28. Joachim Wach, *Types of Religious Experience. Christian and non-Christian* (Chicago, 1951), p. 208.

29. See Marie Dominique Chenu, "Méthodes historiques et position de la théologie," in *I.S.R.* This article includes fragments taken from *Une Ecole de théologie, Le Saulchoir,* a work which over the years has, unfortunately, been neglected. See also

Karl Rahner, "Les Tâches actuelles de la théologie," in *Recherches et Debats* 51; this author also has several articles in the review *Concilium*.

30. "It is not impossible that one day our century will be looked upon as the first period in history to rediscover the widespread religious experiences abolished by Christianity." Mircéa Eliade, *Méphistophélès et l'Androgyne*, p. 12. On the rehabilitation of traditional religions, see also Bouaké's series published by Editions Seuil, especially *Les Religions africaines traditionnelles* (1965) and the epistemological commentaries by Jacques Jérôme Pierre Maquet on pp. 57 ff.

31. "The day will come when the West will not only have to know and understand the cultural universes of non-Westerners, but will also be led to value these as an integral part in the history of the human spirit; the West will no longer consider them as childish or aberrant episodes in an exemplary history of mankind. . . ." Eliade, *Méphistophélès et l'Androgyne*, Foreword.

32. Marc Bloch, *Apologie pour l'histoire ou le métier d'historien*, p. 81.

33. On the distinction between living religions and religions that have lived, see Roger Bastide, *Religions en conserves et religions vivantes*.

34. Emile Poulat, "Le Développement institutionnel," p. 24, note 3.

35. Yet, right now, I am reading a remarkable study by C. Lalive d'Epinay, "Le Pentecôtisme dans la société chilienne" (Genève: C.O.E.E., 1966, mimeo), in which the author draws many of his views on this dissident tradition from Émile G. Léonard. See also the various works

by Jean Séguy and his thesis, soon to be published, on the Mennonites.

36. Friedrich Heiler, "The History of Religions as a Preparation for the Cooperation of Religions," in *The History of Religions, Essays in Methodology*, ed. by Mircéa Eliade and J. M. Kitagawa (Chicago, 1959), pp. 132-160.

37. Ibid., p. 159.

38. I tried to raise this question in my *Socialismes et sociologie religieuse*, pp. 405 ff.

39. Yet see the colloquia organized by the Paulus Kellner Society, *Christentum und Marxismus heute. Gespräche der Paulus Gesellschaft* (Vienna, 1966).

40. See the discussion by F. Isambert in *I.S.R.*

41. For a more detailed discussion of the mythical and logical stages, see A. Mallet, *Mythos et logos, la pensée de R. Bultman* (Geneva, 1962).

42. Wach, *Sociology*, pp. 20-22.

43. Wach, *Types*, p. 29. Wach's formula was taken up again by H. Kraemer in *The Christian Message in a non-Christian World*.

44. Except through "exemplary situations . . . by means of which the human spirit takes cognizance of levels of reality which would otherwise remain inaccessible." Mircéa Eliade, *Le Mythe de l'éternel retour* (Paris: Gallimard, 1949), pp. 235-236. On Eliade see Thomas J. J. Altizer, *Mircéa Eliade and the Dialectic of the Sacred* (Westminster Press, 1963).

45. See Juan Luis Segundo, *Berdiaeff: une réflexion chrétienne sur la personne* (Paris: Aubier, 1963), p. 14.

46. See the recent discussion in a special number of *Esprit* (mai 1967), *Structuralismes, idéologie et méthode*. See particularly the article by Paul Ricoeur, "La Structure, le mot et l'événement," pp. 801 ff.

47. See A. Z. Serrand, *Evolution technique et théologies* (Paris: Cerf, 1965) in which the author distinguishes between eight strains found in this theology of history or Promethean theology. See also complementary analyses in Bernard Besret, *Incarnation ou eschatologie: contribution à l'histoire du vocabulaire religieux contemporain, 1935-1955* (Paris: Cerf, 1964).

48. See article by Julien Freund in *A.S.R.* 25. On the same theme, see M. J. Warner, *The Wesleyan Movement in the Industrial Revolution* (London, 1930) and J. Neff, *Les Fondements culturels de la civilisation industrielle* (Paris: Payot, 1964). Also the basic work of Richard Henry Tawney, *La Religion et l'essor du capitalisme* (Paris: Rivière, 1951).

49. G. Gurvitch, in a conversation, once characterized Marxism as "Saint-Simon seen through the eyes of a Proudhon."

50. See F. Dumont and B. Rozier, *Nous allons à la famine* (Paris: Seuil, 1960).

51. It has also been proposed that "desacralization" be considered equivalent to "profanization," that "declericalization" be considered equivalent to "laicalization" and that both processes be grouped under the term "deconfessionalization." But until this proposal was made, despite some lively attempts, the process of "de-Christianization" had hardly ever been interpreted as "deconfessionalization."

52. We have not mentioned the distortions to which a theology of intervention is exposed when it deals with worldly realities. See Mgr. Ivan Illich of Cuernavaca, Mexico, "L'Envers de la charité" in *Esprit*, May 1967, pp. 952 ff. The article treats collusion between the Church in South America and the Alliance for Progress.

53. Or, what amounts to the same thing, a theology of diminishing control. See the symposium *La Liberté religieuse, exigence spirituelle et problème politique* (Paris: Centurion, 1965), especially the article "Sur l'Ambiguïte de l'état chrétien," pp. 172 ff.

54. Henri Mathieu, *L'Objectif de l'A.C., l'ordre social chrétien* (Paris: Spes, 1937), pp. 8-9.

55. Also note that according to Troeltsch this has regularly been a project of extra or anti-ecclesiastical dissidences.

56. Especially if one remembers the homage which Marx paid to the papacy: "Its refusal to enter into a quasi religious alliance (the *Holy Alliance*) with the states testifies to profundity and a sense of strict consistency," and also testifies to the fact that "the universal Christian bond between peoples is the Church and not diplomacy or temporal alliances among the states."

57. See *I.S.R.*

58. To cite just one of these, let me mention Jérôme de Mendieta and his efforts to found an Indian Church in Mexico and thus carry out the Franciscan program for a return of the Church to its evangelical origins. See John Leddy Phelan, *The Millenial Kingdom of the Franciscans in the New World, a Study of the Writings of J. de Mendieta, 1525-1604* (Los Angeles). Vasco de Quiroga, a disciple of Thomas More, had the same project in 1535—he wanted to establish in Mexico a "rebirth of the primitive church." As Marcel Bataillon says, "it is surprising that no one seems to have noticed this." Finally, do not Jesuit and Indian messianisms come together with the founding of the celebrated Guaranis Reductions?

59. For a strong argument supporting this, see K. M. Pannikar, *L'Asie et la domination occidentale du XVᵉ siècle à nos jours* (Paris: Seuil, 1953).

60. See Vittorio Lanternari, *Les Mouvements religieux des peuples opprimés* (Paris: Maspero, 1962). Also the dossiers and references published in *A.I.S.C.*, passim, and the specialized research of G. Balandier, J. Guiart, P. Worsley, M. de Queiroz, Roger Bastide, A. Métraux, etc.

61. Fred Robert Von der Mehden, *Religions and Nationalism in Southeast Asia, Burma, Indonesia, and the Philippines* (Madison: University of Wisconsin Press, 1963). See comments on this above, Chapter Seven.

62. On the problem of Africanization, see G. Deroy, "Présence africaine et christianismes africains" (thesis, Louvain, 1966). For more complex and subtle interpretations, see Roger Bastide, *Religions africaines au Brésil* (Paris, 1960), and *Les Amériques Noires* (Paris: Payot, 1967).

63. Which does not occur without a veritable laicizing of missiology. For first approximations, see Jacques Chiflet, *Les Laïcs chrétiens en coopération internationale* (Paris: Fleurus, 1964), bibliography on pp. 243-261). Other approximations in John Joseph Considine, *The Missionary Role in Socio-Economic Betterment* (New York: Newman Press, 1960).

64. This is the general line in the work of L. J. Lebret. See his *Dynamique concrète du développement* (Paris, 1961), bibliography on pp. 536-537. Also his posthumous book, *Développement-Révolution solidaire* (Paris: Ouvrières, 1967). For a discussion of missiology, see H. Van Straelen, *The Catholic Encounter with World Religions* (London, 1966). For problems of catechism, see H. Maurier, *Religion et développement, tradition africaine et catéchèse* (Paris, 1965).

65. Making an effort to reconsider and even to rehabilitate the specific character of paganism despite the value prejudice which continues to be attached to the word. See Jacques Dournes, *Dieu aime les païens* (Paris: Aubier, 1963); also H. Maurier, *Théologie du paganisme* (Paris, 1967).

66. Raymond Aron, *Les Etapes de la pensée sociologique* (Paris: Gallimard, 1964).

67. Desroche, *Socialismes et sociologie religieuse*.

68. Paul Arbousse-Bastide, "Auguste Comte et la sociologie religieuse" in *A.S.R.* 22, pp. 3-58.

69. See articles published in *A.S.R.* 20-21 on this and on Durkheim.

70. Gabriel Le Bras, *Etudes de sociologie religieuse* (Paris: Presses Universitaires de France), 2 vols.

71. On Max Weber, see *A.S.R.* 9 (1960) and 16 (1963); on Joachim Wach, see *A.S.R.* 1 (1956) and 14 (1962); on Ernst Troelstch, see *A.S.R.* 11 (1961).

72. On pastorate sociology see the many articles by B. Haering, F. Houtard, F. Boulard, N. Banning, R. Daille, A. Fisher, J. Labbens, A.P.M. Goddijn. See above, Chapters One and Two.

73. J. Labbens, *La Sociologie religieuse* (Paris: Payard, 1959).

74. Serrand, *Evolution, technique et théologie*, p. 151. See above, Chapter One.

75. An attempt to define and diffuse this discipline has been made by the *Groupe de Sociologie des Religions* who edit the *Archives de Sociologie des Religions* and represent the working arm of the *Comité de Recherches*

en *Sociologie des Religions* under the auspices of *l'Association International de Sociologie.*

76. See Henri Desroche, "De La Sociographie de la pratique religieuse à une pratique de la sociologie des religions," *A.S.R.* 20, pp. 3-6. Also see above, Chapter Six.

77. See Yves Congar, *passim*; also Jean Séguy, "Ecuménisme et Ecuménologie," in *I.S.R.*

78. For a detailed account, see Jean Séguy, "Ecuménisme et ecuménologie."

79. For a typology of non-belief, see M. E. Marty, *Varieties of Unbelief* (New York, 1964).

80. "Every person has the right to freedom of thought, conscience and religion; this right implies freedom to change his religion or conviction as well as the freedom to manifest his religion or conviction. . . ." Article 18 of the Declaration of Human Rights adopted by the United Nations.

81. For an intuitive understanding of this as one of the premises of Péguy's thought, see Pie Duployé, *La Religion de Péguy* (Paris: Klincksieck, 1965).

82. Quoted in *P.A.B.*, p. 24.

83. See A. Dumas, "Dietrich Bonhöffer et l'interprétation du christianisme comme non-religion," *A.S.R.* 19, 5, p. 30.

84. A. Van Leeuwen, *Christianity in World History. The Meeting of the Faiths of East and West* (Edinburgh House Press, 1964). H. Kraemer, in the preface, judges the book to be an important event.

85. Even when this diagnosis is paired off with the Augustinian commentary: *Multi videntur intus sunt foris . . . foris qui sunt intus.*

Conclusion

1. Similar to the question raised about the history of religion. See R. Aubert, "Historiens croyants et historiens incroyants devant l'histoire religieuse," in *L'Histoire et l'historien* (C.C.I.F.: Fayard, 1964), pp. 28-43.

2. "Pursuing this line of thought, I sometimes feel that I am sailing between Scylla and Charybdis. Scylla is that modern scientific or meta-scientific idea that all religions are false. . . . Charybdis is that theology (or at least certain of its most extreme forms) which maintains that only one religion is true. . . ." Montgomery Watt, *Truth in the Religions, a Sociological and Psychological Approach* (Edinburgh University Press, 1963). Quotation is *re*-translated from the French.

3. These variants are analyzed in C. J. Bleeker, *Christ in Modern Athens* (Leyde: Brill, 1965).

4. Wach, *Sociology*, p. 10.

5. Yinger, *Religion, Society and the Individual* (New York: Macmillan, 1957), p. 4.

6. Marcel Mauss, *Sociologie et anthropologie*, introduction by Claude Lévi-Strauss (Paris, 1950), p. xxviii. Our underlining. These categories of within and without are also found in Simone Weil: "In the Catholic religion there has never been a philosophical house-cleaning. To do this, one would have to be both within and without." *La Pesanteur et la grâce*, p. 134.

7. "All possibilities in religion have been exhausted: after Christianity, after abstract religion of the absolute, after these no other new form of religion can appear. If Carlyle really understood Christianity he would see that after it no other religion is possible. Pantheism is no more possible than any of the others." Friedrich Engels, *Lage Englands.*

8. "In sum, the old gods are withering away and dying, and new ones are not being born. . . . The day will come when our societies will experience a period of new creative ferment. . . ." Durkheim, *Formes*, pp. 609-611.

9. The French text was set up with the aid and advice of my friend Jean Bottéro. The English text is from the *New English Bible* (Oxford University Press, 1970).

10. A "man" or "someone" (*îsh = vir*). A French translation by Septante rendered this as "an angel," from which comes the traditional image of the struggle between Jacob and the Angel.

11. Who has hit whom in the thigh? (*Wer hat den andern auf die Hüfte geschlagen?*) asks Gunkel. The sequence of action probably goes like this: Jacob did not succeed in dominating his adversary. He grabbed him and struck him in the hollow the thigh and so gained the advantage. The ad-versary then admitted defeat ("he cried and asked for mercy" according to Osée, XII, 5). But it is the winner who loses; the tables are turned on Jacob, the hold is a hold on himself: it is his own hip that has been thrown out of joint in the struggle during which he struck at the hip of his adversary.

12. "The man" is an unusual person who can only appear at night; come dawn, he must disappear.

13. Common etymology which this anecdote was intended to support. Its sense may be "God's wrestler," with the ambiguous suggestion that God was the cause of this struggle against God. This would convey the idea that "You bear the name 'God's struggle' because you have struggled against God."

14. The Jerusalem Bible reads: *Tu a été fort contre Dieu et contre les hommes tu l'emporteras.* A milder translation would be ". . . you strove with God and with men and prevailed."

15. 'Penuel' = the face of God.